Trappers of the Far West

Also available from the University of Nebraska Press

Mountain Men and Fur Traders of the Far West, edited by LeRoy R. Hafen. Selected, with an introduction, by Harvey L. Carter.

The subjects and authors are: Manuel Lisa (*Richard E. Oglesby*); Pierre Chouteau, Jr. (*Janet Lecompte*); Wilson Price Hunt (*William Brandon*); William H. Ashley (*Harvey L. Carter*); Jedediah Smith (*Harvey L. Carter*); John McLoughlin (*Kenneth L. Holmes*); Peter Skene Ogden (*Ted J. Warner*); Ceran St. Vrain (*Harold H. Dunham*); Kit Carson (*Harvey L. Carter*); Old Bill Williams (*Frederic E. Voelker*); William Sublette (*John E. Sunder*); Thomas Fitzpatrick (*LeRoy R. and Ann W. Hafen*); James Bridger (*Cornelius M. Ismert*); Benjamin L. E. Bonneville (*Edgeley W. Todd*); Joseph R. Walker (*Ardis M. Walker*); Nathaniel Wyeth (*William R. Sampson*); Andrew Drips (*Harvey L. Carter*); and Joseph L. Meek (*Harvey E. Tobie*).

TRAPPERS
of the Far West

Sixteen Biographical Sketches

Edited by LeRoy R. Hafen
Selected, with an introduction, by
Harvey L. Carter

University of Nebraska Press
Lincoln and London

First Bison Book edition: October 1983
Most recent printing indicated by the first digit below:

4   5   6   7   8   9   10

Library of Congress Cataloging in Publication Data
Main entry under title:

Trappers of the Far West.

Reprinted from: The Mountain men and the fur trade
of the Far West. Glendale, Calif. : A.H. Clark, 1965–
1972.

Includes index.

1. West (U.S.)—History—To 1848—Biography—
Addresses, essays, lectures. 2. Trappers—West (U.S.)—
Biography—Addresses, essays, lectures. 3. Fur traders—
West (U.S.)—Biography—Addresses, essays, lectures.
4. West (U.S.)—Biography—Addresses, essays, lectures.
5. Fur trade—West (U.S.)—History—Addresses, essays,
lectures. I. Hafen, Le Roy Reuben, 1893–
II. Carter, Harvey Lewis, 1904–
F592.M742 1983   978'.02'0922   [B]   83-5824
ISBN 0-8032-7218-9

Published by arrangement with the Arthur H. Clark
Company.

Contents

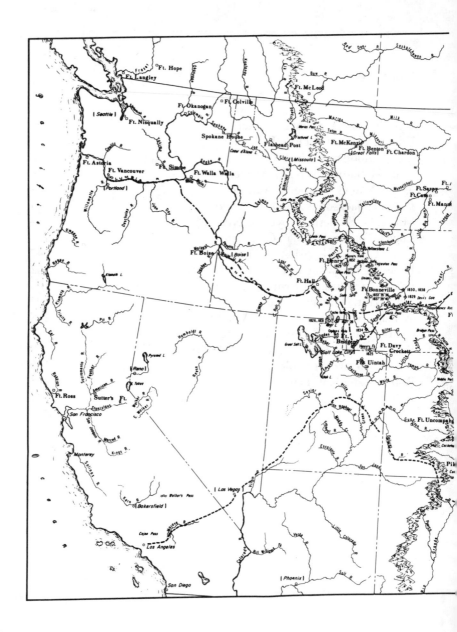

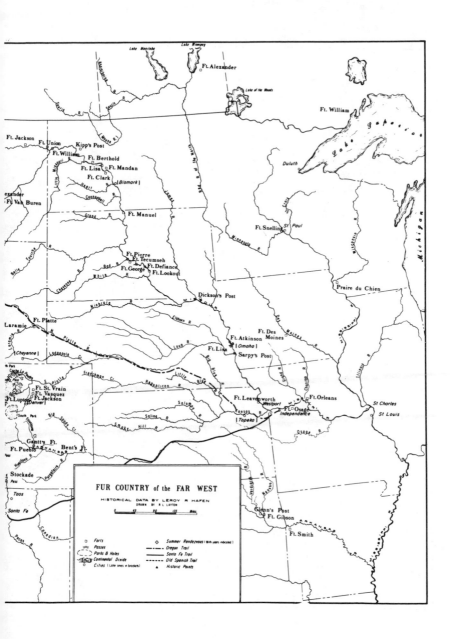

FUR COUNTRY of the FAR WEST

HISTORICAL DATA BY LEROY R HAFEN
DRAWN BY R L LAYTON

Introduction

A forerunner of the present volume was published as a Bison Book by the University of Nebraska Press in June 1982 under the title *Mountain Men and Fur Traders of the Far West*. The book was enthusiastically received, as well it might have been, since it made available eighteen sketches from a ten-volume set containing nearly three hundred sketches, *The Mountain Men and the Fur Trade of the Far West,* edited by LeRoy R. Hafen and published 1965 – 72 by the Arthur H. Clark Company. The present book contains sixteen short biographies of trappers and traders almost equal in renown to those of the previous book. Either volume, therefore, represents a dependable biographical approach to the western fur trade of the early nineteenth century. Taken together, the two books present a balanced and fairly comprehensive historical view of the subject.

Readers already familiar with the first book will recall that, in my introduction, a comparison was made between the Mountain Men of the early nineteenth century and the astronauts of the late twentieth century. No analogy should be pressed too far, but I believe it is fair to say that the men selected for the first book may be comparable to those astronauts who were chosen for the pioneer flights into space, culminating in lunar exploration, whereas the men selected for the present book are comparable to those astronauts who were chosen for less spectacular flights, after the public had become more accustomed to the idea of space exploration. All were genuine astronauts, by training and performance equally qualified, however, and any differences were those occasioned by personality, timing, and luck. In the same way, all are genuine mountain men by experience and capability in both my earlier and my present selection. I would readily concede that in most of the cases an interchange might be made between the men constituting my two lists without distorting the history of the western fur trade in any way. In both books, the average length of a biographical sketch is about twenty pages.

In comparing my two lists, however, there are a few differences that deserve to be mentioned. My first selection was composed of men who, on the whole, were more active in exploration than were those included in my second list. The present selection, on the other hand, consists of men of more varied ethnic origins than those in the previous volume. There is also a shift in geographical emphasis. Whereas the first book centered mainly on the area in which the rendezvous were held, the present book begins with the Southwest, shifts gradually to the rendezvous country, then veers back to the upper portion of the Southwest. Since the first volume began with St. Louis as the springboard from which the far western fur trade was launched, I have thought it appropriate to conclude the present volume with a return to that city as a continuing market for furs and as a source of supply for those who lingered in the trade during its declining years.

Although the thirty-four Mountain Men presented in the two volumes taken together cover very well the competitive years of the western fur trade from about 1822 to about 1846, there are, unavoidably, some regrets about necessary omissions. Of the British traders, David Thompson made notable geographic contributions and Thomas McKay, Michel Laframboise, and John Work were all deserving brigade leaders. Among the Americans, Andrew Henry, Kenneth McKenzie, and Joshua Pilcher have some claims to recognition. A case could be made for both Charles Bent and Antoine Robidoux just as easily as for their younger brothers, who have been included. Among those who are important for their literary and historical efforts, Osborne Russell and George Yount might well have been selected but were not. No attempt has been made to include those pioneering Frenchmen who were operating before the American acquisition of the Louisiana Territory or the very earliest American trappers who made the first Rocky Mountain incursions prior to 1820. But enough of what might have been.

A brief look at each of the individuals chosen for the present book will be of some aid to readers not only in explaining why each was selected but also in bringing readers to discern some logical order in what, at first glance, may appear to be a rather haphazard arrangement of the sketches.

Etienne Provost (1785–1850) typifies the majority of Frenchmen in the fur trade in that he was born in Quebec and migrated, at an early age, to St. Louis or its vicinity. His career is a good starting point, for our purposes, because he became a mountain man of the Southwest as early as 1815–17, which was before Mexico won its independence from Spain. He was probably the discoverer of the Great Salt Lake, but reverses at the hands of Indians in that area and his own lack of financial backing ended his career as an independent trapper. From 1828, for virtually the rest of his life, he was a brigade leader for the American Fur Company. Big and tough, he commanded the respect of his men, the awe of the Indians, and the highest wages from his employers.

James Ohio Pattie (1804–50) lived a life of high adventure and incredible misfortune for six years as a very young man. The rest of his life is obscure. The narrative of his veritable odyssey to Santa Fe and far beyond was published in 1831. It strikes the reader as basically true despite his exasperating handling of dates and his boastful exaggeration. Few have had more bad luck than Pattie, but since he accomplished all his wanderings as a "greenhorn," perhaps he was fortunate to survive and leave us the legacy of his recollections.

Louis Robidoux (1796–1868) turned up in Taos as early as 1823. His brothers François, Antoine, and Michel were all in Mexico at an early date and were all engaged in trapping beaver. Louis and Antoine became Mexican citizens, and although Antoine was better known and longer in the fur trade, Louis typifies the several Mountain Men who settled in southern California. Like many in that group, he became a large landowner but eventually lost his wealth. He is chosen to represent the six Robidoux brothers engaged in the fur trade, a family that outnumbered even the Bents and the Sublettes.

Ewing Young (1792–1841) was in Santa Fe and Taos contemporaneously with Pattie and the Robidoux brothers and their paths crossed or merged at times. He trapped more widely than any other American in the Southwest, going twice to California. He gave the youthful Kit Carson his start as a Mountain Man, and we would know far less of Young but for the memoirs of Carson and of Pattie. Young is nearly unique in that he did not remain in southern California but went to Oregon by land and settled there. In Oregon he locked horns with British authority as he had done in Santa Fe with Mexican authority. His was an independent life.

David Jackson (ca. 1785–1841), oldest but least known partner of the famous firm of Smith, Jackson, and Sublette, was one of the most successful and productive field captains of the trapping business. Much of the firm's success lay in his ability to compete with the British. After his firm sold out, he traveled to Santa Fe and engaged in a mule-buying speculation in association with Ewing Young. His most enduring monument is Jackson's Hole, Wyoming, just south of Yellowstone National Park.

Milton Sublette (1801–37), like Jackson, was associated with Ewing Young in Santa Fe, but at the beginning rather than at the close of his career. The second of the Sublette brothers, he was one of the five men who formed the Rocky Mountain Fur Company to buy out Smith, Jackson, and W. Sublette. It was a wounded leg, acquired in an Indian fight in the Southwest, that led eventually to his relatively early death. His reputation rivals that of his older brother, William, with whom he was, at times, engaged in business rivalry as well. He was a man of attractive personality, whose habit of impetuous action caused him to be called "the Thunderbolt of the Rockies."

Lucien Fontenelle (1800–1839), born on a Louisiana plantation, migrated upriver at an early age to St. Louis. An orphan, he nevertheless had received a fair education, as his well-written letters attest. Gradually he became, along with Andrew Drips and William H. Vanderburgh, one of the leaders of the American Fur Company in its successful effort to dominate the Rocky Mountains. Equally capable as field captain or in charge of a supply train, he was also a good businessman. Like his rival, Milton Sublette, he died before his fortieth year, but not as a drunken suicide as Joe Meek reported.

Although given a rather tepid endorsement in Sir George Simpson's well-known character book, Francis Ermatinger (1798–1858) served the Hudson's Bay Company well for many years. His trapping on the Snake River and his supervision of Fort Hall brought him in contact with American trappers, missionaries, and emigrants to Oregon, who invariably spoke of him in the highest terms. His brother Edward's inclusion here is incidental to the fact that both are treated in the same article. Of Swiss and Italian antecedents, the Ermatingers serve to remind us that not all Canadian fur traders were of Scottish origins.

James Pierson Beckwourth (1798–1866), usually called a mulatto, was one-quarter Negro, one-quarter Indian, and one-half white. One of the famous Ashley recruits, his first experience was in the rendezvous country, but he spent some time living among the Crow Indians. Later he went to the California gold mines, where he dictated his memoirs to T. D. Bonner. Still later he was in Colorado during the gold rush to that territory, and he returned to the Crow Indians to die. Like Pattie's, his was an important memoir, marred by considerable exaggeration and some outright lies.

James Clyman (1792–1881) had only a four-year career, 1823–27, as a Mountain Man but he kept a diary of great historical value in tracing the rise of the Rocky Mountain Fur Company and of such men as Jedediah Smith, William Sublette, Jim Bridger, and Tom Fitzpatrick during those eventful years. After some years on the Illinois and Wisconsin frontiers, he went to Oregon and California in 1844. Returning to Illinois, he then, in 1848, led a company of emigrants to California, where he became a pioneer settler of the Napa Valley. There he spent the rest of his long life. The diaries of his overland journeys are also of historical value, for he had a knack of discerning and recording matters of significance that otherwise would have remained unknown.

John Gantt (1790–1849), son of a minister and himself a former army captain, was the first to perceive the possibility of trade with the Southern Cheyennes and to erect an adobe fort on the Arkansas River. He lost out to his more aggressive and better-financed competitor, William Bent, and became for a time a guide for army explorations and emigrant trains. Like Nathaniel Wyeth and Benjamin Bonneville, he was an interloper who found the competition too rough. Yet he was in many ways a respected Mountain Man. Although he had a wife and son in Kentucky, he ended his days in California.

William Bent (1809–69) built Bent's Old Fort on the Arkansas river in 1834 and succeeded where Gantt had failed. Already experienced as a southwestern trapper, he dominated the region between Taos and Fort Laramie till his death thirty-five years later. He consolidated his position by marrying into the Cheyenne tribe and by building a business in buffalo robes when the beaver pelts declined in value. His fort was so well known to contemporary travelers that in 1976 the National Park Service could build an exact replica, which is annually visited by thousands of tourists and is a fitting monument to its original owner.

Charles Autobees (1812–82), an illiterate man of peculiar name, homely appearance, and rather uncertain heredity, exemplifies the common trapper who remained always in the West and "grew up with the country." He began trapping about the time that Ferris did, but unlike Ferris, Beckwourth, or Pattie, he left no writings to immortalize his deeds, real or fictional. Yet somehow a good bit came to be known and remembered about him, which is a tribute to his worth. The Fort Hall Account Books document his trapping years, and in the 1840s he worked for Simeon Turley at Arroyo Hondo, where the famous *aguardiente,* or Taos lightning, was distilled and whence it was distributed on both sides of the border. In the early 1850s he settled on the land at the confluence of the Huerfano and Arkansas rivers, where he became known as the oldest settler and the progenitor of numerous descendants, who gather to honor him annually to this day.

Warren Angus Ferris (1810–73) became a trapper for the American Fur Company in 1830. After six years, he went home to western New York and, in 1842, published *Life in the Rocky Mountains,* which was based on a journal he had kept. This book is an extremely valuable source for the years covered and has literary merit as well. An 1836 map made by Ferris shows a thorough knowledge of the Rocky Mountains. He spent his later years on land that he bought and farmed near Dallas, Texas. Ferris was an acute observer whose work accurately reflects the free spirit of the Mountain Men.

Manuel Alvarez (1794–1856) was a Spaniard by birth, who migrated to Mexico in 1818. Later he went to New York, thence to St. Louis, and engaged in the Santa Fe trade, becoming a Mexican citizen. About 1829, he decided to enter the fierce competition for the furs of the rendezvous country as an independent trader but ended by working for the American Fur Company. Returning to Santa Fe, he was associated with Charles Bent and became American consul at Santa Fe for some years and an important political figure after the American conquest of New Mexico. He had the businessman's ability to get along with whatever political regime is in control.

Robert Campbell (1804–79) came to the United States from northern Ireland in 1822. In 1825, he went to the Rocky Mountains with Jedediah Smith, on the advice of his doctor, who had diagnosed consumption. He became a great friend of William Sublette and together they challenged the American Fur Company for a time on the upper Missouri. Campbell emerged from the mountains with good health and ample funds. He spent his later years as a merchant and financier in St. Louis. To the end of his days he continued to buy furs and supply trappers. His reputation among the trappers was one of fairness and square dealing, and his credit with them was better than that of the United States government.

The life of the Mountain Man was a constant struggle with the forces of nature. There was an unremitting interaction between the Mountain Man and such practical advantages of civilization as he was able to bring with him, on the one hand, and the powerful forces of the physical environment which he had to contend with, on the other hand. He was able, by tremendous exertion, to exploit the great natural resource of fur-bearing animals in the mountain west with enough efficiency to render a profit to the companies and to make a living for himself. He had no thought of conserving this resource. The supply of beaver and mountain buffalo was greatly reduced, yet such were the difficulties under which he labored that it cannot be said that these species, or any other, were ever rendered in danger of extinction.

He was able to bring supplies to the mountains by pack animals and later by wagon trains in sufficient quantity to furnish not only himself but the Indians with superior weapons and traps to aid his quest for furs, but it was done at the cost of greatly reducing the profit to be gained. He was able to explore thoroughly the whole of the Far West and thus to render possible the future waves of economic development such as mining, stock raising, and agriculture, but at the cost of bringing to an end his own way of life.

It must be realized that the environmental forces were so powerful as to compel the Mountain Man to modify greatly his own way of life. He could have a family life only by marriage with an Indian woman. He had to adopt the Indian practice of moving with the seasons, and often with the food supply as well. He had to forget many of his own habits and learn from the Indians how best to cope with the environment. On balance, it must be concluded that both the Mountain Man and his environment forced temporary changes and adjustments from one another but that neither had a permanent advantage.

The Mountain Man was sometimes a conscious but perhaps more often an unconscious agent of Manifest Destiny. If he survived to old age he was apt to reflect on the course of his life with some satisfaction, for he could feel that he had been an active participant in the growth, expansion, and development of his country. He was conscious that he had seen much progress and had helped to bring it about. At the same time, he was very likely to view his years as a Mountain Man with a certain feeling of nostalgia. He was inclined to forget the physical hardships, the inflated prices, and the extreme dangers and remember with pleasure the high adventure, the freedom of choice, the closeness to nature, and the good comradeship of his early days. He had been to far places and seen and done remarkable things.

HARVEY L. CARTER

Trappers of the Far West

Etienne Provost

by LeRoy R. Hafen
Brigham Young University

Etienne Provost was so early and so persistently engaged
in the fur trade of the far West that in later years he was
called "The Man of the Mountains."[1] In the literature
referring to him, his name is given many spellings, the most
common being Provot, Proveau, and Provost. Since he did
not write, we are unaware of his preference; but the early
French spelling is Provost, and the pronunciation was
Provo. According to his birth certificate in Notre Dame,
Montreal, he was born in Chambly, Quebec, in 1785.[2] His
parents were Albert and Marianne (Menard) Provost.[3]

Of his early life we have no account. He first appears in
the records of the fur trade as a member of the Chouteau-
DeMun trading venture to the Rocky Mountains, 1815-17.
This was the initial large company to exploit the fur resources of the upper Arkansas and Platte rivers. After two
years of trade and two efforts to get favorable cooperation
from the Spaniards of New Mexico, the Americans were
captured and taken to Santa Fe. They suffered confiscation
of their furs and other property. After their release and
return to Missouri "Etienne Provott" and ten other men of
the party made a sworn statement about their treatment in
New Mexico, saying in part, "We remained in prison
(some of us in irons) forty-eight days."[4]

---

[1] Joseph Nicollet's report in *House Doc. 52,* 28 Cong., 2 sess.; reprinted as
"Nicollet's Account, 1839," in *South Dakota Historical Collections,* x (1920), 113.

[2] Roy M. Provost, Long Beach, California, in a letter to me of July 24, 1964, says
he saw the certificate at Montreal.

[3] Stella M. Drumm, "Etienne Provost," in the *Dictionary of American Biography,*
XIV, p. 250.

[4] "Statement and proof in case of Chouteau and DeMun of their loss and treat-

When Mexican independence from Spain was achieved in 1821, a number of Americans, including some previously imprisoned by the Spaniards, again turned their faces toward New Mexico. During the year 1822 four American parties of traders and trappers journeyed to Santa Fe and during the winter of 1822-23 several men pushed westward and northwestward across the continental divide to trap western waters.[5] Among these probably was Etienne Provost, who had formed a partnership with one Leclerc (Francois ?) and was in New Mexico in 1823 and perhaps earlier.[6]

By 1824 Provost was not only on Green River, but had pushed over the Wasatch Mountains into the Great Basin. There he suffered a tragedy that gave his name to the river near Utah Lake. Warren A. Ferris, a fur man in the mountains, gives some details of the affair in describing the Snake Indians and one of their chiefs:

> There is one evil genius among them, called the *"Bad Gocha,"* (mauvais gauche – bad left-handed one) who fell in with a party of trappers, led by a well-known mountaineer, Mr. E. Proveau, on a stream flowing into the Big Lake that now bears his name, several years since. He invited the whites to smoke the calumet of peace with him, but insisted that it was contrary to his medicine to have any metallic near while smoking. Proveau, knowing the superstitious whims of the Indians, did not hesitate to set aside his arms, and allow his men to follow his example; they then formed a circle by sitting indiscriminately in a ring, and commenced the ceremony; during which, at a preconcerted signal, the Indians fell upon them, and com-

ment by the Spaniards," in *Annals of Congress,* 15 Cong., 1 sess., II, pp. 1957-58. All of the eleven men signed with an x. Michael Carriere in a supplemental statement, said that he served the two years and was paid $200 as wages. Presumably, Provost received the same amount.

[5] "Answers of Augustus Storrs to Queries Addressed to Him by the Hon. Thomas H. Benton," etc., reprinted in A. B. Hulbert, *Southwest on the Turquoise Trail* (Denver, 1932), 93.

[6] See Benjamin O'Fallon's correspondence from Fort Atkinson August 1, 1823, to the Governor of New Mexico, *Bulletin of the Missouri Historical Society,* XVI (October 1959), 22-24. Provost had been out to New Mexico and had returned to the United States by August 1, 1823.

menced the work of slaughter with their knives, which they had concealed under their robes and blankets. Proveau, a very athletic man, with difficulty extricated himself from them, and with three or four others, alike fortunate, succeeded in making his escape; the remainder of the party of fifteen were all massacred.[7]

Ferris, on his map of the fur country, places Provost's name on present Jordan River, which runs from Utah Lake to Great Salt Lake. So one would assume that he means to report the misfortune as taking place on the Jordan River of today. Kit Carson told his biographer about the Provost tragedy and said that it occurred on the river named for Provost. But he does not indicate whether he meant the present Provo River that flows into Utah Lake, or the Jordan, which runs from it. In any case, the Utah Lake vicinity would be the locality of the massacre.

William Gordon, in his "Report to the Secretary of War relative to the Fur Trade," dated at St. Louis, October 3, 1831, said that in 1824 "8 men were killed at one time by the Snakes on the waters of the Colorado who were in the employ of Provost & Lubro [Le Clerc]." In the tabulation at the end of the document the party is given as "Provost & Le Clerc's Company," and the place of the tragedy as "Reta [Euta or Utah] Lake."[8]

What appears as a likely explanation of this tragedy is given by British traders. Peter Skene Ogden, in his letter of July 10, 1825, writes:

We were also informed by the Americans the cause of the Snakes

---

[7] W. A. Ferris, *Life in the Rocky Mountains,* ed. by P. C. Phillips (Denver, 1940), 308-09.

[8] Gordon's Report of October 3, 1831, in *Sen. Doc. 90, 22 Cong., 1 sess.,* p. 29. The numbers given as killed vary in the different accounts. Gordon, just cited, says eight. Ogden in his letter of July 10, 1825 (*Mississippi Valley Historical Review,* XXI, p. 68) says eight; and in another place says nine (Dale L. Morgan, *West of William H. Ashley,* Denver, 1964, p. 146). Ferris, previously quoted, says four or five escaped, of a party of fifteen. Kit Carson (D. C. Peters, *The Life and Adventures of Kit Carson,* New York, 1858, p. 246) says all were killed but four, but does not give the number in the party.

not being so friendly towards us as formerly, and which I regret to state the Americans too justly attribute to us, last Summer Mr. Ross consented most probably with such villains he had to deal with, he could not prevent them to go and steal the Snakes horses in which they succeeded, 12 of Mr. Ross's party were then absent in quest of Beaver and were with a large Camp of Snakes who were treating them most kindly, but on hearing this they pillaged them of all their horses and Furs, and in the scuffle they killed a Snake chief, shortly after a party of 7 Americans and one of our deserters fall on the Snakes Camp, and the Snakes lost no time in killing them all this also has greatly irritated the Americans against us, and they would most willingly shoot us if they dared.[9]

Etienne Provost has been credited with the discovery of Great Salt Lake.[10] If the attack on his party by the Snakes occurred on the Jordan River, as Ferris indicates, then Provost must certainly have seen the lake at least in the fall of 1824, if not before. James Bridger has often been given the honor of the discovery of the lake, but there is no contemporary record of this; and it is of doubtful authenticity. It is very likely that the Hudson's Bay Company trappers under Donald McKenzie and Michel Bourdon saw the lake while trapping the upper Snake River, Bear River, and as far east as Green River in the years 1818 to 1822.[11]

After the massacre of most of his men Provost led the remnant back over the Wasatch Mountains. On Green River, near the mouth of White River is a very large grove of sweet (round-leafed) cottonwoods, the twigs and bark of which provide excellent winter horse feed.[12] While Provost and some of his men wintered here, arrangements were made for his partner Leclerc to bring out supplies from New Mexico.[13]

[9] From Ogden's letter, edited by Frederick Merk, in the *Mississippi Valley Historical Review*, XXI (June 1934), 67-68.

[10] See the note written by W. M. Anderson in 1834 and published in J. H. Simpson, *Report of Explorations*, etc., 17.

[11] Alexander Ross, *Fur Hunters of the Far West,* edited by Kenneth A. Spaulding (Norman, 1956), 135-39, 152-53, 207-08.   [12] We visited this grove in 1962.

In the spring Provost led a trapping party northward, and on May 23rd came upon Peter Skene Ogden's company on the Weber River, some distance east of present Ogden, Utah. The Britisher records in his diary: "early in the day a party of 15 men Canadians & Spaniards headed by one Provost & Francois one of our deserters, arrived."[14] In the afternoon a party of Ashley's men, led by Johnson Gardner, also appeared, and confronted Ogden with a demand that he leave this territory, which Gardner said belonged to the United States. Being south of the 42nd degree of north latitude, they were all interlopers upon Mexican domain, except perhaps Provost, who was trading from a New Mexico base and presumably had a Mexican license.

Provost returned to the Uinta country, probably to receive expected supplies. On his way there with twelve men, he met W. H. Ashley on the Duchesne River, June 7th. Ashley, who had boated down the Green River and had cached supplies near the mouth of the Uinta, now employed Provost to return to Green River and bring back the cached goods. This accomplished, the two co-leaders pushed on, crossed the Wasatch Mountains and descended to the headwaters of Provo River.[15] Ashley crossed Kamas Prairie and descended Weber River, while Provost made a trip to the lake to trade with the Utes.[16] After rejoining Ashley on June 21st Provost appears to have continued with him to the gathering place on Henry's Fork of the Green.

Here was held the first rendezvous in the Rockies. Provost was present, and he and his men traded eighty-three beaver skins to Ashley for $207.50 and received in exchange

13 Pegleg Smith said that in February, 1825, some twenty-five of Provost's men returned from the Green River to Taos. – "Sketches from the Life of Peg-leg Smith," in *Hutchings' California Magazine*, v (1860-61), 319.

14 "Ogden's Journal," as edited by David E. Miller in *Utah Historical Quarterly*, XX, p. 181.   15 Morgan, *Ashley*, 117.

16 Ashley records on June 22nd: "Mr. Provo who went to the lake to trade with the Euteaw Indians returned last evening." *Ibid.*, 117.

coffee, tobacco, cloth, ribbons, etc.[17] Whether or not Provost
remained after the summer rendezvous of 1825 to continue
trade in the mountains or returned to New Mexico is not
definitely known. His partnership with Leclerc presumably
was terminated at this time. Jim Beckwourth says that
Provost was at the summer rendezvous of 1826, but of this
we are not certain.[18] In any event, he was back in St. Louis
in September 1826, and was doing business with B. Pratte
and Company. The account books of this organization give
details. "Etienne Provos" received cash payments, September 22 to 30, totaling $458.25; and for the same period
sundries of shoes, cloth, etc., amounting to $286.38. The cash
received October 2 to 14 totaled $483.55 (and the last item
was entered as "paid in full").[19]

The goods received in October indicated the stocking of
a trading venture, for it included 12 barrels of whiskey, 1 of
brandy, and 1 of rum; 4 dozen pipes, 186 pounds of tobacco,
blankets, muslin, flannel, and sundries at $1770.[20] Whether
these goods were for an independent venture or one for the
company is not clear.

B. Pratte & Company apparently were courting Provost.
B. Berthold, a member of the company, wrote to J. P.
Cabanné from Fort Lookout on the upper Missouri, December 9, 1826: "I dare not advise anything about the
project with Ashley. However, it seems to me that it would
be well for us to assure ourselves of Provost, who is the soul
of the hunters of the Mountains." [21]

In 1827 there were charges against Provost on the books

---

[17] *Ibid.*, 119.

[18] T. D. Bonner, ed., *Life and Adventures of James P. Beckwourth* (New York,
1931), 66. Beckwourth seems to mix events of the 1826 and 1828 rendezvous.

[19] B. Pratte & Company Journal M, 349, 353. I went through various Journals and
Ledgers of the American Fur Company in the library of the Missouri Historical
Society at St. Louis in the summer of 1967. They are each numbered by a capital
letter. Hereafter they will be cited by the letter and page.

[20] Journal M, 357; Ledger H, 207.

[21] Morgan, *Ashley*, 307-08. The original, in French, is in the Chouteau Collection, Missouri Historical Society.

in February, July, and August. Provost may have been in the regular employ of the American Fur Company in 1828, when this company was endeavoring to break into the trade of the Rocky Mountains, where Smith, Jackson, and Sublette were dominant. Provost would be an effective agent. It is said that in the fall of 1828 he was sent by Kenneth McKenzie to contact the trappers of the mountains and try to bring them with their trade to Fort Floyd, later Fort Union, at the mouth of the Yellowstone.[22]

Apparently Provost remained in the mountains during the winter working for himself, for in early July he was at Fort Tecumseh on the Missouri and was acting very independently. McKenzie wrote to Pierre Chouteau Jr. from the post on July 7, 1829:

> Provost is just arrived from his spring hunt, he is bound for St. Louis he will not give me five minutes to write you. . . Provost goes down to St. Louis in order to get equiped & come up immediately to trade with the Crows & trap at the same time. . . I forgot to say that Provost would not give me his spring hunt, but he owes me nothing.[23]

After arriving in St. Louis in the summer of 1829 Provost formed a trading agreement with the American Fur Company. In the company's account book it is entitled "Etienne Proveau's Advanture," and the sub-title is: "For the Following Sead [said] E. Proveau's advanture by him self (E. Proveau) in half with the American Fur Company." Then follows three pages of items listed and priced, including 9 horses ($47 to $110 each), 30 beaver traps, gunpowder, lead, pack saddles, rifles, tobacco, alcohol, etc. Provost provided $1450.17. Among the goods furnished by the American Fur Company were 3 dozen scalping knives,

---

22 H. M. Chittenden, *American Fur Trade of the Far West* (1935 edition), I, p. 330.

23 Quoted in D. L. Morgan and E. T. Harris, *Rocky Mountain Journals of William Marshall Anderson* (San Marino, Calif., 1967), 345. Hereafter cited as *Anderson Journals*.

3 doz. Wilson butcher knives, 18 bunches of blue glass beads, and 10 three-point blankets.[24]

At the time of this business transaction Provost married on August 14, 1829, Marie Rose Salle, *dit* Lajoie.[25] The accounts show expenditures on his wedding day for a razor, shaving box, brush, and a pair of three-point green blankets; and the next day the purchase of a "lot of ground, $100," and for "making plane and plotting for house, $5.00."[26]

Etienne soon left on his trading venture, leaving a credit with the company to be drawn upon by his wife as needed.[27] He reached the mouth of Kansas River in early October[28] and was in the Crow country during the succeeding winter.[29]

The "Proveau Advanture" appears not to have turned out well. Apparently Provost was induced to give up the partnership and accept employment with the American Fur Company's Upper Missouri Outfit, being given $605.59 for his share of the joint project.[30]

In January 1831, Provost carried dispatches from Kenneth McKenzie at Fort Union to Fort Tecumseh. The next month he set out with horses and goods to support Vanderburgh on Powder River.[31] His service was highly valued, for while the usual trader was given $200 per year, Provost's salary was $1,000 for the first and second years and $1400 for the third and fourth years.[32]

In the summer of 1832 Lucien Fontenelle and Provost

[24] American Fur Co. Account book P, 129, 542-44, under dates of August 13-15, 1829.

[25] Stella M. Drumm in the *Dictionary of American Biography*, XIV, p. 250.

[26] Book P, 544.

[27] The books show cash paid "to his lady " as follows: August 29, 1829, $50; Dec. 12, $25; Jan. 28, 1830, $22; April 6, $50; April 10, $47; June 8, $25; July 13, $25; Aug. 9, $50; and Aug. 23, $25. *Ibid.*, 544. Periodic amounts were given to her from Sept. 13, 1830, to July 30, 1831, totaling $175. Book R, 344.   [28] Book P, 542.

[29] McKenzie's letter of May 5, 1830, Chouteau-Papin Collection, Missouri Historical Society.

[30] This item is on the books under date of Oct. 10, 1830, Book T, 381.

[31] *South Dakota Historical Collections*, IX (1918), 147-49.

[32] Upper Missouri Outfit, Book T, 381; Book W, 244.

led a "Mountain Expedition" of some 50 men and 150 horses from Fort Union to supply the company's trappers under Vanderburgh. The train got a late start (June 19) and did not reach Vanderburgh, who was waiting at Pierre's Hole, so he moved over to Green River and there met the Fontenelle and Provost pack train on August 8th.[33] After delivering the goods Provost returned with the furs in September to the Missouri River and then continued with them down to St. Louis. Here, on June 5, 1833, he was advanced $465.46 from the Upper Missouri Outfit.[34] Then he went back up the river to Cabanné's post, north of Bellevue, where he was met and described by the famous steamboat captain Joseph LaBarge, who "found that veteran mountaineer, Etienne Provost, who at that time probably knew the western country better than any other living man. He had just come in for the purpose of guiding Fontenelle and Drips, partners in the American Fur Company mountain service, and owners of the trading post at Bellevue, to the Bayou Salade (South Park, Colorado), where they intended to spend the winter trapping beaver."[35]

The party did not go to South Park, but it did go to the mountains to the rendezvous on Green River. Fontenelle remained with the trappers, and Provost brought the furs back to the Missouri River, arriving at Fort Pierre on August 29, and then continuing on to St. Louis.[36] For his year's service ending in the fall of 1833, he was paid $1400.[37]

His accounts from October 10, 1833, to February 20, 1834, amounting to $1176.34.[38] From these it appears that he was converting his home into a lodging house.[39] He is listed as a tavern keeper in Account Book X, pages 56-58, with

---

[33] Ferris, *op. cit.,* 150, 156, 158.

[34] Book V, 142. His accounts during the preceding winter are also in Account Book V, 41, 48, 50.

[35] H. M. Chittenden, *History of Early Steamboat Navigation on the Missouri River* (Minneapolis, 1962), 38-39.   [36] *Anderson Journals,* 347.

[37] Book W, 244.   [38] Book U, 280.   [39] *Anderson Journals,* 347.

charges for such items as coffee, sugar, tobacco, a barrel of rice, one of rum, and 5 barrels of whiskey ($48.88). Then in March, 1834, there is a 4-page "Invoice of Mdze sent to Lucien Fontelle in charge of Etienne Proveau to be sold in the Rocky Mountains for the account and risk of the U.M.O., 1834." Among the items are blankets, coats, beads, rifles, shot, etc., to a total of $7,256.06.[40]

Provost took the route, new to the American Fur Company, by way of the Little Blue and Platte rivers. On the same trail, and ahead of Provost, went the companies of William Sublette and Nathaniel Wyeth. W. M. Anderson, accompanying Sublette, in his diary on May 6th mentioned passing Provost, and also Cerré (with supplies for Bonneville).[41] A report that Provost was attacked on the way out by Pawnees was denied; instead, he reached the rendezvous at Ham's Fork safely, and in mid-July set out on his return.[42] From Bellevue Lucien Fontenelle sent the furs (5,309 beaver and some other skins) down river to St. Louis and wrote on September 17, 1834: "I hardly think it necessary to have them [the furs] insured, although the river is very low, but the boat will be very strong, and will have a crew formed of the very best kind of voyageurs under the eyes of Mr. Cabanné, and the superintendence of Etienne Provost."[43]

The American Fur Company Accounts show the amount due Etienne Proveau on November 26, 1834, as $611.15. A subsequent entry shows $900 due him for services in 1835.[44] In 1835 Provost went out to Fort Lucien (Laramie) and returned to St. Louis in the winter. On January 31, 1836, W. L. Sublette wrote to Robert Campbell: "Since I came to St. Louis I have been informed that the two Prevoes has got in last evening and that they left Fontenell at St.

[40] Book Y, 6-9.   [41] *Anderson Journals,* 73.
[42] *Missouri Republican* (St. Louis), August 26, 1834.
[43] Printed in Chittenden, *American Fur Trade* (1935), I, p. 308.   [44] Book X, 58.

Charles. . . Report says Fontinell Intends quiting the Company and Joining Prevo and Some Others and gouing Out that he has purchases Some goods in Liberty."[45] On February 9, 1836, Sublette wrote again: "The two Prevoes left him [Fontenelle] at Liberty, sending whiskey up to the Black Snake hills."[46]

In the spring or summer of 1836 Provost, accompanied by Toussaint Racine, made a trip to "Fort Lucien." He was paid $225 for his service; Racine received $150.[47] They may have been escorting Joshua Pilcher, who went out for the American Fur Company to Fort Laramie and to the summer rendezvous and purchased the fort from Fitzpatrick and Fontenelle.[48] On July 20, 1836, Provost's account totaled $1265.81, less $228.97 charged for land he purchased.[49] During the winter of 1836-37 Provost made a 51-day trip to Council Bluffs, for which he was paid $100 on March 21, 1837. During his absence his wife had received $80 from the company.[50]

With the caravan taking trade goods to the summer rendezvous of 1837, Provost went as assistant to Captain Thomas Fitzpatrick. Also in the company was the famous Scotsman William D. Stewart and his personal party, including the capable artist Alfred Jacob Miller. No diary of the trip has come to light, but the numerous Miller paintings and accompanying written explanations by the artist give an important record of the journey. There were about thirty wagons and carts in the train. Two of the paintings are important to us here, for they give pictures of Provost in his fifty-second year. One shows the trapper train greeting a

---

45 Sublette's letter of Jan. 31, 1836, to Robert Campbell, Missouri Historical Society. The second Provost may have been Etienne's brother or nephew.

46 W. L. Sublette's letter of Feb. 9, 1836, to Robert Campbell, Missouri Historical Society. Photostat in my possession.   47 Book X, 210, 383.

48 Pilcher reports progress in letters written June 21st at Fort Lucien, Chouteau-Papin Collection, Missouri Historical Society. Also, see this *Series,* I, p. 155.

49 Book X, 257.   50 *Ibid.,* 58.

delegation of Indians. In the front line on his white horse proudly rode Stewart, and beside him are three other men, including on his mule, plump "Monsieur Proveau, a subleader, with a corpus round as a porpoise." In a second painting Provost is shown, fat and round, standing beside his tent and with hands cupped to his mouth is giving the loud call to gather in the horses.[51] In his fictionalized book *Edward Warren,* Stewart described "Old Provost the burly Bacchus" as "a large heavy man, with a ruddy face, bearing more the appearance of a mate of a French merchantman than the scourer of the dusty plains." [52]

Provost came back from the rendezvous in late summer and was paid $600 for his season's work. In December he left St. Louis for the posts in the Council Bluffs region.[53] When he returned to St. Louis on February 24, 1838, he brought news of the terrible smallpox plague that had wrought such havoc among the tribes on the upper Missouri.[54] Provost appears to have gone out to the rendezvous of 1838, for which service he was paid $450; and in December of that year was advanced $40 "for traveling expenses to Arkansas." [55]

Jean N. Nicollet, with young John C. Fremont as second in command, explored and mapped the country between the upper Mississippi and Missouri rivers in 1839. In their party, that set out from St. Louis on April 4th, went Etienne Provost. He was highly esteemed by the French scientist, who wrote in his report:

I had brought up [to Fort Pierre, present South Dakota] with me from St. Louis only five men who for my purposes were certainly worth ten. Four of them had proved themselves by numerous journeys

---

[51] M. C. Ross, *West of Alfred Jacob Miller* (Norman, 1951), plates 76 and 197, with accompanying written descriptions.

[52] Quoted in *Anderson Journals,* 348.   [53] *Ibid.,* 348.

[54] J. A. Hamilton's letter of Feb. 25, 1838, in the Chouteau papers, Missouri Historical Society.   [55] *Anderson Journals,* 349.

across the prairies, as well as voyages over the Rocky Mountains. One of they was Etienne Provost, known as "L'homme des montagnes," — man of the mountains. I may remark here that these western voyageurs are distinguished from the same set of men who do service in the northern lakes by their never singing; and although apparently sullen and discontented, are most faithful, cautious and courageous in the midst of all dangers.[56]

Fremont's appraisal was almost identical.[57] Provost was paid $750 for his service.

The business accounts show that Provost was in St. Louis, at least in February, August, and November, 1840. This year he formed a partnership with Clement Lambert. "Proveau and Lambert, Tavern Keepers" did business during the winter of 1840-41.[58] During 1841 and 1842 his name appears in many of the fur company business accounts, and from April to September of 1842 he worked for the Upper Missouri Outfit at $50 per month.[59]

Provost gave important assistance to James J. Audubon when the great naturalist ascended the Missouri River and gathered specimens for his collections and his famous drawings. Provost was paid $50 per month from June 13 to October 19, 1843.[60] Edward Harris, who accompanied Audubon and kept a good journal of the expedition, mentions Provost frequently. On June 24 he writes:

Bell went out with Provost before breakfast to try and shoot a Doe in the point of the woods above the Fort by imitating the cry of a Fawn on an instrument made by Provost yesterday, he did not succeed. After breakfast . . . I took Provost's call with me and tried it in a small island of timber . . . at the first call a Doe came within 30 feet of me.

June 29.   Went out with Provost and killed two does by using his call to bring the animals close. . .

July 8th   Squire killed a deer, using Provost's call.[61]

---

[56] Nicollet's Account in *South Dakota Historical Collections*, x (1920), 112-13, reprinted from *House Document 52*, 28 Cong., 2 sess.   [57] *Ibid.*, 77.

[58] *Anderson Journals*, 349.   [59] *Ibid.*

[60] P. Chouteau Jr. & Co., Ledger GG, 348, Mo. Hist. Soc.

The party left Fort Union August 16th and returned
down the river. At St. Charles, on the bend of the river a
little above St. Louis, Provost became "extremely drunk,"
left the party, and went by land to St. Louis.[62]

Provost went up the Missouri River again in 1844 and
was at Fort Union in October of that year. A year later his
arrival at Fort Pierre on November 2, 1845, was noted.[63]
His last voyage up river appears to have occurred in 1848,
on a steamboat commanded by Joseph LaBarge.[64] Even
though sixty-three years of age, old Provost still commanded
respect and exercised authority among both whites and Indians. Captain LaBarge tells that the Yankton Sioux were
preventing the men on the bank from loading wood on the
steamboat.

> [Provost] then went out himself onto the bank where the Indians
> were, and said, "Now, men, come out here and get this wood." They
> came and loaded up. "Now go on board," he said, and they went en-
> tirely unmolested. Provost went last, and before descending the bank,
> turned toward the Indians and asked them: "Why don't you stop
> them? Are you afraid of *me*?" The truth is they were afraid of him,
> . . . and understood that he would stand no foolishness.[65]

Chittenden tells of Provost's skill in managing recruits
being taken up the Missouri for service with the fur
company.

> It was a favorite pastime with that veteran mountaineer, Etienne
> Provost, who was often sent up in charge of recruits, to compel an
> early settlement which would determine all blustering and quarreling.
> He would form a ring on the forecastle and compel every braggart to
> make good his claims before the assembled passengers and crew. One
> after another would succumb, until one man would emerge from the

---

[61] J. F. McDermott, *Up the Missouri with Audubon: Journal of Edward Harris*
(Norman, 1951), 113-14, 119-20. For other incidents see pages 27, 98, 103, 124, 137,
140, 165, 169, 172-73, 176.   [62] *Ibid.,* 189.

[63] *South Dakota Historical Collections,* IX, p. 211.

[64] Morgan, in *Anderson Journals,* 350.

[65] Chittenden, *Steamboat Navigation,* 180.

contest victorious over all the others. He would then be awarded the championship, and receive a red belt in token thereof.[66]

Provost died in St. Louis on July 3, 1850.[67] His funeral service was held in the St. Louis Cathedral, still standing west of the new, impressive, 630-foot Gateway Arch in the Jefferson Memorial to Westward Expansion.

His wife and a grown daughter survived him. His estate papers are preserved in the Probate Court Records at St. Louis, where I examined them in July, 1967. A purported will of April 1, 1839, was denied by the widow and was not accepted by the Probate Judge, Peter Ferguson. "Mary Provot," the widow and her daughter Mary were the only heirs. An inventory of the estate and the final expenses are itemized. The real estate and personal property included the home at Second and Lombard Streets, St. Louis; some pieces of land in Lee County, Iowa; and lots in Keokuk, Iowa, and Nashville, Tennessee. Cash on hand was $102.70 and household furniture was appraised at $78.95.[68]

Etienne Provost was a legendary character in his own lifetime. When the Mormons founded a town beside Provo River in 1849 and named it Provo, they were unaware that the fabled character they honored was still alive in St. Louis.

---

[66] *Ibid.*, 128-29.

[67] The notice in the *Missouri Republican* of July 4th said: "Died. Yesterday afternoon, about 4 o'clock Mr. Etienne Provot, an old resident of this city.

"The friends and acquaintances of the family are invited to attend his funeral, This afternoon, at 4 o'clock, from his late residence on the corner of Lombard and Second streets, to the Cathedral burial ground."

[68] Among the furniture and household items listed were: 12 chairs, $12; 1 rocking chair, $2; 1 bureau, $8; 1 spitton, 10 cents; 1 setee, $1; 1 clock, $8; 1 glass globe, 50 cents; 1 picture of President of the U.S., 10 cents. The funeral expenses included: Extra fine finished velvet coffin with handles and overcase delivered, $25; for Hears [hearse] and 5 carriages, $17.50; 6 pairs gloves and 2 pieces of crepe, $7; 16 W Spurm Candles at 45 cents, $7.20; burial service St. Louis Cathedral, $6; attendant clergyman to cemetery, $3.

"Final Medicine" from the druggist: mustard, 10 cents; Flaxseed, 5 cents; Black tea, 5 cents; rice, 5 cents; pins, 5 cents; ginger, 10 cents; oil, 5 cents; Laudanem, 10 cents; whiskey, 10 cents; ginger, 10 cents; vinegar, 5 cents; Brandy, 10 cents; mustard, 10 cents; total $1.00.

James Ohio Pattie

by ANN W. HAFEN
Provo, Utah

It is strange that so few people have ever heard the name of this cultural hero of the Southwest – James Ohio Pattie. Yet as early as 1831 his exploits were published in a book, "one of the most stirring tales of frontier adventure ever recorded."[1] This odyssey of a youth's persistent search for a fortune in furs, covers six years of wandering "where wilds, immeasurably spread, seem lengthening as they go."

Unlike most Mountain Men, James Pattie had enough schooling to be able to write of his adventures. Two of his letters that have survived verify this.[2] But whether he himself wrote the major part of the published story, or whether he told it to editor Flint is still a moot question. This problem, after all, is one primarily for the literary critic. In any event, our main concern is with the recorded experiences of this western trapper.

"Mr. Pattie," writes editor Flint, "thinks more of action than literature, and is more competent to perform exploits, than blazon them in eloquent periods. . . The simple record of events as they transpired, painted by the hungry, toil-worn hunter, in the midst of the desert, surrounded by sterility, espying the foot print of the savage, . . . will naturally bear characteristics of stern disregard of embellishment. To alter it . . . would be to take from it its

---

[1] M. M. Quaife, in his edition of *The Personal Narrative of James O. Pattie of Kentucky* (Chicago, 1930), p. xiv.

[2] His letter written to J. C. Jones, American Consul at the Sandwich Islands, was published in the *St. Louis Times* of July 7, 1829, and elsewhere. A letter written by Pattie at Mexico City June 14, 1830, was sent to the former companions he had left in California. A photocopy of this is in the Bancroft Library, University of California, Berkeley.

keeping, the charm of its simplicity, and its internal marks of truth."[3]

Pattie's Narrative has appealed to historians as a valuable source on the history of the Southwest. It has been re-published in three selective historical series – by R. G. Thwaites in 1905; Milo M. Quaife in 1930; and W. H. Goetzman in 1962. In addition R. G. Cleland, in the fullest account of the fur trade of the Southwest, gives Pattie the most prominent place.[4] These distinguished editors and historians have given Pattie and his book high appraisals.

Thwaites writes: "The narrative impresses the reader with a sense of its verity, and has the charm of simplicity and vigor. . . A thrilling tale of pure adventure, ranging all the way from encounters with grizzly bears, and savages who had never before seen a white man, to a revolution in a Latin-American state, Pattie's narrative has long been a classic."[5] Quaife's volume says: "It contains an unconscious picture of the psychology of the frontiersman – brave, enterprising, resourceful, but despising the Indian, treating him heartlessly and often murdering him with a clear conscience. It is the forerunner of all those blood and thunder tales of Indians and the Wild West."[6] Goetzman calls Pattie "an authentic American hero."[7] Cleland sees the volume as "an authentic over-all picture of the early days of the fur trade in the extreme Southwest and a true account of some of the most dramatic incidents connected with it."

James Ohio Pattie was born in Kentucky about 1804, a few years before those other famous Kentuckians, Kit Carson and Abraham Lincoln. His grandfather was a Virginian

[3] *The Personal Narrative of James O. Pattie, edited by Timothy Flint.* Reprinted as volume XVIII in R. G. Thwaites, *Early Western Travels* (Cleveland, 1905).

[4] R. G. Cleland, *This Reckless Breed of Men* (New York, 1950).

[5] Thwaites, *op. cit.,* 18.   [6] Quaife, *op. cit.,* p. vi.

[7] *The Personal Narrative of James O. Pattie* (Philadelphia, 1962); Goetzman's Introduction, p. v.

who migrated to Kentucky during the tempestuous years
when the region was known as the dark and bloody ground.
James' father, Sylvester Pattie, was born in August, 1782,
in Kentucky, while the settlers were battling the Indians.
When James was about eight years old, the family moved
farther west, to Missouri, where Sylvester set up a grist mill
and a saw mill on the roaring Gasconade River.

James was one of nine children who tasted the joys and
the fears of a frontiersman's family. All went well till James
was twenty years old, when his mother died of tuberculosis.
Her youngest baby was buried beside her. The husband,
dejected at the loss of his wife and unhappy in his desolate
home, finally concluded to seek a change of scene by going
on a trading venture up the Missouri River. His son James
begged so earnestly to go along that his father consented.
After selling his home and putting the children with relatives, Sylvester purchased trade goods and supplies from
St. Louis and prepared to set forth. Says James O. Pattie:

> Our company consisted of five persons. We had ten horses packed
> with traps, trapping utensils, guns, ammunition, knives, tomahawks,
> provisions, blankets, and some surplus arms, . . .
>
> June 20, 1824, we crossed the Missouri at a small town called
> Newport [some 60 miles above St. Louis], and meandered the river as
> far as Pilcher's fort [at Bellevue, 9 miles above the mouth of the
> Platte], without any incident worthy of record, . . .[8]

From here they soon pushed on to Cabanné's Post, about
ten miles above present Omaha, where they met Sylvester
Pratte, who had a trading party some distance up the Platte
River, headed for New Mexico. The Patties continued to
Council Bluffs, where, says Pattie,

> the commanding officer demanded to see our license for trading with
> the Indians. We informed him that we neither had any, nor were
> aware that any was necessary. We were informed, that we could be

---

[8] This, and all following quotations not otherwise credited, are from the Thwaites
edition of Pattie's *Narrative*.

allowed to ascend the river no higher without one. This dilemma brought our onward progress to a dead stand. We were prompt, however, in making new arrangements. We concluded to sell our surplus arms in exchange for merchandize, and change our direction from the upper Missouri, to New Mexico. . . Our object and destination being the same as Mr. Pratte's, we concluded to join his company on the Platte.

They left the Bluffs July 30th, and pushed westward to the Pawnee villages. These friendly Indians were of special interest to Pattie and he made a careful report concerning their rituals and habits. The chief gave the Patties a stick painted with characters which would help the travelers through other Indian tribes, as the party made its way to the place on the Platte River where the Pratte party was assembled enroute to Santa Fe. When the Patties arrived, Sylvester Pattie was invited to take command of the company, because of his long experience of leadership. At the roll call, the company was found to number 116. They had over three hundred mules and horses.

Traveling west and southwest they encountered other bands of Indians and also had dramatic experiences with buffaloes and grizzly bears. The party finally reached Taos, and then continued to Santa Fe, arriving early in November. The town, Pattie said, had between four and five thousand inhabitants. They asked the governor for permission to trap beaver on the "Helay" (Gila) River, but permission was at first refused, it being illegal for foreigners to trap in Mexican territory.

Word came that the Comanches had made an attack on one of the towns and had carried off some of the women. Help of the trappers was solicited. James and his father joined the rescue party that finally caught up with the Indians and succeeded in putting the marauders to flight and rescuing the women. James' heroic part in rescuing a former governor's beautiful daughter, Jacova, made her and the governor his permanent friends.

After the victorious party returned to Santa Fe, the governor in gratitude for their help, gave the Americans a license to trap. The trappers were divided into small parties. The group to which James and his father were attached, went down the Rio Grande and then westward toward the Gila River by way of the Santa Rita copper mines. There they hired two Spanish servants to guide them to the Gila. On the headwaters of this stream they found good trapping. Upon exploring the country Pattie saw many bears. He and his companion had encounters with the animals but escaped serious injuries.

On the St. Francis River, an upper branch of the Gila, they found so many beaver that they soon had over 250 pelts. Returning to the main stream, they cached their furs. Upon descending the Gila, they met some destitute fur hunters who had been attacked by Indians. The Patties supplied them with horses and food to enable them to return to the copper mines. James Ohio had some remarkable experiences with the bears of this region. He shot one big bear in a cave, and the company stopped to dry the bear meat and render ten gallons of fat from the animal.

Upon continuing their journey down the river, they were shocked to come upon the remains of white men recently killed by the Indians; they had been dismembered and roasted for food as if they were wild animals. One of the heads, with a hat on, had been stuck on a stake and arrows shot into it.

Continuing their journey they reached a new stream, which produced so many pelts that they named it Beaver River. Here they had a brush with Indians, who stole all their horses and left them afoot. However, the Indians had accidentally left four of their own horses behind. Pattie killed some antelopes and noted that there were wild hogs in the region. They again cached furs and then turned back for supplies, reaching the copper mines April 29, 1825.

James traveled toward Santa Fe, stopping enroute to see Jacova and her father. At Santa Fe, he obtained fresh horses and new supplies, and returned to the mines, arriving June first. With despatch they set out with horses to secure the furs cached on their hunt. Arriving at their biggest cache, they found that Indians had carried off every pelt. Continuing to the little cache they found the pelts safe. With these they made their way back to the copper mines.

James Pattie took stock of the gains in this the first year of their expedition. There was little to show for the year of hard labor, fatigue, hunger, danger, and Indian peril. But being young, about twenty-one years old, he concluded that the West always gives a man another chance, provided he still has life and health.

The Spanish owner of the copper mines invited the party to stay and work at the camp, especially to guard the mines from the marauding Apache Indians. In addition to receiving one dollar a day, Pattie was to be taught the Spanish language – an advantage to a sojourner in the Southwest.

One of Pattie's early assignments was to go to Salt Hill for a load of salt. Sylvester Pattie was pleased with his employment at the copper mine. The Spanish owner, having had his fill of trouble with Indians, offered to lease the mines to the Patties for $1,000 a year, for five years. Sylvester agreed to try the arrangement for one year.

Soon after, a party of French trappers came along, enroute to western trapping fields. After winning his father's consent, James joined the company, eager to try again for a fortune in beaver streams. Although James does not identify this party, it was most probably a group of French-Americans from St. Louis led by Miguel Robidoux. Before long they met the Indians that formerly had robbed the Patties. James recognized his father's horse which was being ridden by one of the raiders. The Indians professing friendship to

Americans, gave back 150 skins and three horses. They then smoked the pipe of peace together. These Indians said they hated the Spaniards but not the Americans. Pattie gave them some red cloth. The Indians warned them of three hostile tribes that were ahead.

When the trapping party reached the junction of the Gila and Salt rivers, a little west of the site of modern Phoenix, the curious Frenchmen strolled around the Indian Village without caution. Pattie warned the leader that he suspected these Indians and suggested that the trappers leave before trouble developed. The Frenchman laughed and called Pattie a coward, saying Pattie could leave when he pleased, but declared that the party was not ready to go. Pattie spoke privately to one Frenchman, a close friend, and the two went out about four hundred yards, where they made a separate fire but did not unsaddle their horses.

The main party made camp, allowing several Indians to help. Pattie and his friend packed up their mules ready to move. At midnight they heard a loud whistle, the signal for the Indian attack on the Frenchmen. Soon came the sound of war clubs and the groans of dying men, along with the yells of the savages. Pattie and friend prepared to defend themselves, and when a party of Indians came racing toward their camp they met them with gun fire. The red men halted, then retreated. Pattie and his friend raced off toward a high mountain, south of the river. They traveled all night, until they found security in a nook of a creek, where they and their animals could rest.

From an eminence they saw far off a black speck coming toward them, and thought it was a bear. Upon closer approach it proved to be their own French captain, who had escaped the massacre. His head was battered by the clubs, and he was still bleeding. He explained that he personally had retained a pocket pistol, when their arms were stacked by the tree to please the Indians. By using his pistol he made his escape, but the rest of his men were massacred.

Toward evening they looked down from their eminence to see three fires in the distance with figures around them in an evening camp. They could see horses about. Upon going closer to observe, they heard voices in English. Pattie shouted, "Friend, Friend," and ran toward the camp. "Where in God's name did you spring from?" the white men asked. Explanations soon followed, and the first decision was to revenge the massacre of the French party.

Pattie and his companions had come upon the Ewing Young company of trappers. Pattie reports:

We were now thirty-two in all . . . we all formed under a genuine American leader, who could be entirely relied upon. His orders were, that twenty should march in front of the pack horses, and twelve behind. In the evening we encamped within five miles of the Indian village, and made no fires. In the morning of the 31st, we examined all our arms, and twenty-six of us started to attack the village. When we had arrived close to it, . . . two of our men were then ordered to show themselves on top of the bank. They were immediately discovered by the Indians, who . . . raised the yell, and ran towards the two persons, who instantly dropped down under the bank. There must have been at least 200 in pursuit. . . This brought the whole body abreast of us. We allowed them to approach within twenty yards, when we gave them our fire. They commenced a precipitate retreat, we loading and firing as fast as was in our power. They made no pause in their village, but ran off, men, women, and children. . .

We appropriated to our own use whatever we found in the village that we judged would be of any service to us. We then set fire to their wigwams, and returned to our camp. They were paid a bloody price for their treachery, for 110 of them were slain. At twelve we returned to the village in a body, and retook all the horses of the Frenchmen that they had killed. We then undertook the sad duty of burying the remains of the unfortunate Frenchmen. A sight more horrible to behold, I have never seen. They were literally cut in pieces, and fragments of their bodies scattered in every direction, round which the monsters had danced and yelled.

From near the junction of the Gila and the Salt River (which Pattie calls the Black River), the trappers moved up the Salt Fork and found it dotted with beaver dams. When they reached the junction of the Salt and Verde rivers, the party divided, part going up each stream. Pattie's early and accurate description is worthy of reproduction:

> The left fork heads due north, and the right fork north east. It was my lot to ascend the latter. It heads in mountains covered with snow, near the head of the left hand fork of the San Francisco [of western New Mexico]. On the 16th, we all met again at the junction of the forks. The other division found that their fork headed in snow covered mountains, as they supposed near the waters of Red [Colorado] river. They had also met a tribe of Indians, who called themselves *Mokee* [Hopis]. They found them no ways disposed to hostility.

After trapping their respective streams, the two parties again met at the forks of the Salt and Verde; then pushed down the Salt to the Gila, descending to the Colorado.

> The point of junction is inhabited by a tribe of Indians called Umene [Yumas]. Here we encamped for the night. On the morning of the 26th, a great many of these Indians crossed the river to our camp, and brought us dried beans, for which we paid them with red cloth, with which they were delighted beyond measure, tearing it into ribbands, and tieing it round their arms and legs; for if the truth must be told, they were as naked as Adam and Eve in their birth day suit. They were the stoutest men, with the finest forms I ever saw, well proportioned, and as straight as an arrow.

From the mouth of the Gila the trappers ascended the Colorado, "a deep, bold stream. The bottoms are a mile in general width. . . Near the river are many lakes, which abound in beaver."

Continuing up the river they came to some "Cocomare-copper" Indians; farther on, to the Mojaves. The chief was "dark and sulky"; he demanded a horse as tribute for the beaver being taken by the trappers from the river. Upon being refused, he speared one of the horses. He was soon cut down by bullets. War was on. It continued intermittently for several days, as the trappers continued up the river. In a final surprise assault at night, an Indian band killed two whites. Next morning eighteen trappers went in pursuit and finally reached and attacked the Indian camp. "We killed a greater part of them," said Pattie. "We suspended those that we killed upon the trees, and left their bodies to dangle in terror to the rest, as a proof how we retaliated agression."[9]

The route of their continuing journey up the Colorado River is difficult to determine. Pattie reports:

> We reached a point of the river where the mountains shut in so close upon its shores, that we were compelled to climb a mountain, and travel along the acclivity, the river still in sight, and at an immense depth beneath us. Through this whole distance, which we judged to be, as the river meanders, 100 leagues, we had snow from a foot to eighteen inches deep. . .
>
> [Finally] we arrived where the river emerges from these horrid mountains, which so cage it up, as to deprive all human beings of the ability to descend to its banks, and make use of its waters. No mortal has the power of describing the pleasure I felt, when I could once more reach the banks of the river. Our traps, by furnishing us beavers, soon enabled us to renew our stock of provisions. We likewise killed plenty of elk, and dressed their skins for clothing. On the 13th we reached another part [fork] of the river, emptying into the main river from the north. Up this we all trapped two days.

They appear to have ascended the San Juan River some distance and encountered friendly Navajoes, whom they asked about a route over the Rocky Mountains. Following the Indians' advice the trappers took "the left hand fork," probably at the site of Grand Junction, Colorado, and ascended the Colorado River.

[9] The date of this brush with the Mojaves is in doubt. Pattie places it early in March, 1826. It could well have been several months later. This would place it between Jedediah Smith's summer visits of 1826 and 1827, and would explain the unexpected hostility Smith experienced when returning to the Mojaves in 1827.

The crossing was a work, the difficulty of which may be imagined from the nature of the case and the character of the mountains. The passage occupied six days, during which we had to pass along compact drifts of snow, higher than a man on horseback. The narrow path through these drifts is made by the frequent passing of buffaloes, of which we found many dead bodies in the way. We had to pack cotton-wood bark on the horses for their own eating, and the wood necessary to make fires for our cooking. Nothing is to be seen among these mountains, but bare peaks and perpetual snow. Every one knows, that these mountains divide between the Atlantic and Pacific Oceans. At the point where we crossed them, they run in a direction a little north of west, and south of east, further than the eye can reach.

On the 7th, we struck the south fork of the Platte, near Long's Peak, and descended it five days. We then struck across the plain to the main Platte, on which we arrived on the 16th.

The further tour, as related by Pattie, is confusing. He says they reached the Big Horn, Yellowstone, and Clark's Fork of the Columbia. But this is not likely, as he says: "We ascended this river [Clark's Fork] to its head, which is in Long's Peak, near the head waters of the Platte. We thence struck our course for the head waters of the Arkansas, on which we arrived July 1st." [10]

From the upper Arkansas they crossed over to the Rio Grande and descended it. "On the first of August," Pattie says, "we arrived at Santa Fe, with a fine amount of furs. Here disaster awaited us. The governor, on the pretext that we had trapped without a license from him, robbed us of all our furs." James returned to his father at the copper mines.

After a few days of recuperation, he set out on a trading venture, deeper into Mexico. With pack-horses and a servant, he went south to Janos, on the Casas Grandes River,

---

[10] Pike's map shows the Yellowstone heading in South Park, Colorado, and Pattie says that "all these streams upon which we have been trapping, rise from sources which interlock with each other, and the same range of peaks at very short distances from each other. These form the heads of Red river of the east, and the Colorado of the west, Rio del Norte, Arkansas, Platte, Yellow Stone, Missouri and Columbia."

crossed the mountains to Sonora, and eventually reached "Ymus" [Guaymas] on the Gulf of California. Returning, he re-crossed the rough mountains and finally reached Chihuahua, "the largest and handsomest town I had ever seen." He then traveled northward to El Paso, and thence back to his father and the copper mines, which he reached November 11th. The trip, according to his figures, took about forty-six days. In his account, he gives specific, accurate, and intriguing descriptions of the country, the people, and their customs.

Pattie's next venture took him on a hunting trip with fifteen Americans to the Pecos River, east of the Rio Grande. Here his party was attacked by Mescaleros, and he was wounded by an arrow in the breast and one in the hip. Trapping northward they reached a Spanish town in time to spend New Year's Eve at a fandango there. He returned to the copper mines about two months later.

Next his father sent him to El Paso to buy wine and whiskey for his trade at the mines.

Sylvester Pattie's mining and trading venture at Santa Rita prospered. Then evil days came upon him. He entrusted $30,000 to his Spanish clerk, who was to go to Santa Fe, or if necessary to St. Louis, to purchase trade goods and supplies. The man disappeared. James went in search of the miscreant, going as far as Santa Fe and to Chihuahua, but no trace was ever found.

In desperation the two Patties finally decided to turn again to trapping. Sylvester got a type of passport, dated September 22, 1827. At Santa Fe a party was formed, of which Sylvester was chosen captain. They set out for the Gila and Colorado rivers. Despite all precautions, differences developed among the trappers, and on the lower Gila the company divided into two groups.[11] There remained in

---

[11] Of this company and their experiences we have another account that supplements and corroborates that of Pattie: "In the fall of 1827 a party of about 15 men,

the Pattie party only eight men: the two Patties, Richard Laughlin, Nathaniel M. Pryor, William Pope, Isaac Slover, Jesse Ferguson, and Edmund Russell. These men continued trapping down the Gila to its mouth. Here again they encountered the Yuma Indians, whose friendship appeared questionable.

Says Pattie: "In the midst of these multitudes of fierce, naked, swarthy savages, eight of us seemed no more than a little patch of snow on the side of one of the black mountains." Despite cautions, the whites lost every horse to the crafty Indians during a terrible storm of thunder and lightning. "We were one thousand miles from the point whence we started, and without a single beast to bear either our property or ourselves."

To meet their needs they fashioned canoes out of tree trunks, loaded furs and traps into them, and floated down stream on the Colorado River. Eight boats were required to carry their possessions. One night they caught thirty-six beavers and the next night sixty. They continued trapping with surprising success. On January 1, 1828, they met a new tribe of Indians – much smaller than the Yumas – who shot arrows at their boats. On the 18th of January, the trappers reached the backwater of the tide from the Gulf of California.

When the tide returned we got into our crafts, and descended with it, still expecting to find Spanish settlements. We continued in this way to descend, when the tide ran out, until the 28th, when the surf

under Pattie as their leader, was made up in Taos, to trap the Gila river from its sources down to the Colorado. . . [On the way they separated into two groups] The two parties continued on down the Gila until they reached the Colorado, trapping beaver upon it for some distance above the mouth of the Gila, and downstream to tide-water. The party commanded by Mr. Workman returned to New Mexico. . . [Pattie's band continued to California]." This account, probably by the notable southern California pioneer, J. J. Warner, was published in the *Alta California,* July 2, 1865, and reprinted in Cleland, *op. cit.,* 194-95. There is also a separate account of this party, of which George Yount was a member, in C. L. Camp, *George Yount and his Chronicles of the West* (Denver, 1966), 43-65.

came up the river so strong [the powerful tidal bore] that we saw in a moment, that our crafts could not live, if we floated them into this tumultuous commotion of the water. . .

The fierce billows shut us in from below, the river current from above, and murderous savages upon either side on the shore. We had a rich cargo of furs, a little independence for each one of us, could we have disposed of them, as we had hoped, among the Spanish people, whom we had expected to have found here. . .

There were no such settlements — Every side on which we looked, offered an array of danger, famine and death. In this predicament what were furs to us?

They finally concluded to abandon their canoes, bury their furs on shore, and make their way across the peninsula to the coast of California, which they thought could not be very distant. By February 16th, they had started off on foot with packs on their backs, each pack containing two blankets, a quantity of dried beaver meat, and a rifle with ammunition. Making their way through the marshy river bottom was slavish and fatiguing, but here they were able to find plenty of fresh water to drink. Throughout their further journey, the lack of drinking water caused their greatest suffering.

When they arrived at a salt lake, they fixed little rafts to carry their packs on, and swam forward, each pushing his own burden. On reaching the west shore of the lake, they found an Indian settlement, where one Indian could speak Spanish, being a fugitive from the "Mission of St. Catherine" — Santa Catarina in Baja California. The Indians, all stark naked, were friendly. The women admired the red shirts of the white men and were curious to see the white skin under them. So, with dried fish they bribed one of the men to strip before them. The red cloth was so prized by the Indians that the trappers tore some of their shirts into strips and traded these to the women. "They tied the strips round their legs, arms, and heads" and were overjoyed.

The bewildered travelers employed two Indian guides,

and headed westward to find Spanish settlements. The sand deserts, the mountains, and the glaring heat were ordeals, but their thirst was almost beyond endurance. Finally Sylvester Pattie and Isaac Slover slumped down to die. The others managed to push on until they reached a stream of water. Here James filled his powder horn and hurried back to save his father, while another companion returned to rescue Slover.

> We found them in the same position in which we had left them, that is, stretched on the sand at full length, under the unclouded blaze of the sun . . . Their lips were black, and their parched mouths wide open. Their unmoving posture and their sunken eyes so resembled death, that I ran in a fright to my father, thinking him, for a moment, really dead. But he easily awakened, and drank the refreshing water. My companion at the same time bestowed his horn of water upon Mr. Slover. In the course of an hour they were both able to climb the hill, and some time before dark we rejoined the remainder of our company.

After further travel, including a two-day climb over a sharp-rocked mountain, they found some Christian Indians from the Mission of Santa Catarina, who conducted them to the mission. From there they were taken by stages through other missions and finally to San Diego. Here they were so fatigued that they slept, despite hard ground and annoying fleas. "By morning my body was as spotted as though I had the measles, and my shirt specked with innumerable stains of blood, let by the ingenious lancets of these same Spanish fleas."

The next day the Americans were ushered into the general's office for endless questionings. He considered them spies, and when offered their passport from Santa Fe he tore it to pieces. He then ordered the men remanded to prison, each in a separate confinement.

Captain John Bradshaw of the American ship "Franklin," with Rufus Perkins as supercargo, visited James in his cell. They would purchase the furs from the men if these could be recovered from the cache by the Colorado River, but the Mexican leaders would not permit the trip.

During the confinement, a sergeant and his pretty sister eased the rigors of the comfortless cells. Once James managed to visit his father by talking to him through the grates of his door. Later, James received from his father a note written in blood in place of ink, saying he was very ill, and without hope of recovery. On the 24th of April, 1828, Sylvester Pattie died in his cell. The sergeant's sister brought a black suit for James to wear to the funeral. Six soldiers escorted him to the burial.

In the meantime, Bradshaw's vessel was seized on a charge of smuggling. Many letters written in English came to the general, who called out James to translate them. After several such services, James and the general arrived at a better understanding. Finally the Mexican authorities permitted six of the Americans to go with pack horses for the furs, but retained James in his prison cell as a hostage. The men made the difficult trip to the Colorado River, and returned on the 30th of September. Not a fur was recovered; all had been spoiled by the flooding of the river. Only the traps were rescued. Two of the men, Pope and Slover, did not come back, but continued east to New Mexico.

While the trappers were absent, Pattie wrote a letter to the American consul, John C. Jones at Hawaii, informing him of the imprisonment of the Americans, and asking help for release. When Captain Bradshaw slipped out of San Diego Harbor, he carried the letter with him. The news finally reached Boston and was published as follows:

FROM THE BOSTON COMMERCIAL [?]

A copy of a letter from a number of Americans, prisoners at San Diego, California, to Mr. John Coffin Jones, American Consul at the Sandwich Islands, asking the intercession of that gentleman in their behalf, has been received at the Merchants' Hall. This letter is signed by James O. Pattie, Richard Lochlyn and Nathaniel Prior of Kentucky, Isaac Strover [*sic*] of Santa Fe, William Pope of Indiana, Jesse Furguson of Missouri, and Edmund Russell of Pennsylvania, all of whom belonged to a party of Americans, twenty in number, which started from Santa Fe in New Mexico, on the 18th of August 1827, with the intention of trapping Beaver. This party, it is stated, was headed by Silvester Pattie of Lexington, Kentucky, who, after experiencing much severe and cruel treatment, died in prison at San Diego on the 24th May, 1828. It appears that the party separated soon after starting; and that the above individuals, after taking a quantity of furs were made prisoners on the 13th of March, 1828, at St. Catalina in lower California. From this place they were carried on to other settlements, and at length found themselves in the prison in San Diego, . . . Mr. Rufus Perkins, supercargo of the ship Franklin, of Boston, applied to the authorities of the place for the release of the prisoners, but his application was unsuccessful. . . the Governor came to the determination of allowing them (with the exception of one, who was detained as security) to proceed to the place where they had desposited [*sic*] their furs, for the purpose of bringing them in. . . Thus are seven poor defenceless Americans treated with more indignity and cruelty, than so many highway robbers.[12]

Pattie and his companions remained in prison until their release came about in a strange way. A smallpox epidemic spread through the province, carrying off scores of California's inhabitants. It was learned that Pattie had some vaccine, which his father had brought in his medicine kit, and that he was competent to vaccinate the people against the scourge.

The general promised Pattie his liberty and pay for his services if he would vaccinate all the people on the coast. On January 18, 1829, Pattie began his work. The Fathers at the missions were to fill out legal forms stating the number that were treated. Pattie proceeded up the coast, vaccinating the Indians at the missions and the citizens of the pueblos. He says he vaccinated 24,000 persons.

After reaching San Francisco in June, he was employed to cross San Francisco Bay to the Russian settlement at

---

[12] St. Louis *Times*, July 7, 1829.

Bodega and inoculate the people there, being given one hundred dollars for this service.

Back in San Francisco, Pattie sought out the priest who was to pay him. The priest handed him a note which said that Pattie was to be paid "one thousand head of cattle and land to pasture them." Then he found out that he was to receive this payment only "after he becomes a Catholic, and a subject of this government."

James Ohio Pattie was angry. He had been half promised one dollar for each vaccination – money to carry him back to his homeland. When Pattie expressed his disgust, he was ordered from the house. Pattie went; he obtained his rifle, and proceeded to a ranch, where he procured a horse. He mounted the animal and rode to Monterey. On arrival there, he found an American vessel in port, just ready to sail.

> Meeting the Captain on shore, I made the necessary arrangements with him for accompanying him, and we went on board together. The anchor was now weighed, and we set sail. . . We continued at sea for several months, sailing from one port to another [to conduct trade.]

Finally, on the 6th of January 1830, they returned to Monterey and learned that there was a revolution in the country. Pattie had no desire to become involved; instead he went otter hunting. He killed sixteen otters in ten days, and earned three hundred dollars.

John C. Jones, the American consul, to whom Pattie had written his complaints, sailed into Monterey. Jones advised Pattie to make a list of his grievances and carry the paper to the president of Mexico, in an effort to obtain reimbursement. While waiting the departure of a vessel for Mexico, Pattie and others attended the festivals at some of the missions. The contest between grizzly bears and bulls filled the Americans with astonishment.

On the 8th of May, 1830, with a fresh passport, Pattie departed on the "Volunteer," and arrived at San Blas on the 18th. From here Pattie and friends traveled overland to Mexico City. There he sought out the American consul, who introduced him to the president of Mexico. The president appeared sympathetic, but unable to redress the wrongs. Pattie was advised to carry his grievance to the president of the United States, when he returned to that country. This information, Pattie wrote in a letter to his former companions in San Diego.[13]

Impatiently, Pattie carefully packed his possessions in two strong suitcases, one with his precious keepsakes, the other with clothes for his journey, and on June 18th started in a stagecoach for Vera Cruz. Enroute a band of fifty bandits held up the coach and robbed the passengers, allowing Pattie to retain only his case of clothes. From Vera Cruz he sailed to New Orleans, arriving August 1st. The next day the *Louisiana Advertiser* noted the arrival of Pattie and gave some account of his adventures. Senator J. S. Johnston of Louisiana, interested himself in Pattie, and paid for the wanderer's passage up the Mississippi. He also gave Pattie a note of introduction to Timothy Flint of Cincinnati. This notable writer and editor was thrilled with Pattie's story, and hastened to prepare it for publication. It was issued in 1831.

Of the subsequent life of Pattie we have but scant knowledge. William Waldo, who throughout his long life had contact with many pioneers of the Southwest, gives two bits of information. First, he asserts that Pattie was for a time a student at Augusta College in Kentucky after his return from the West. He also states:

> This man Ohio Pattie, the last of that unfortunate expedition [to California], left my camp in the Sierra Nevada Mountains, amidst

---

[13] A photostat of this letter is in the Bancroft Library, University of California; printed in Cleland, *op. cit.,* 207-08.

the deep snows of the terrible winter of 1849-50; and his sister, whom I met in Missouri eleven years after, told me that that was the last account she had ever received concerning him. I suppose he perished in the deep snows, or was killed by the Indians.[14]

[14] William Waldo, "Recollections of a Septuagenarian," in Missouri Historical Society *Glimpses of the Past* (St. Louis, 1938), V, nos. 4-6, p. 80.

Louis Robidoux

by DAVID J. WEBER *
San Diego State College

Born at Florissant, near St. Louis, on July 7, 1796,[1] Louis Robidoux was one of seven sons of Catherine Rollet, of Cahokia, Illinois, and Joseph Robidoux II, who had come to St. Louis from Canada in 1771 and had thrived there as an Indian trader. Of the seven boys, six survived infancy and all went into the fur business; Joseph III, François, Isidore, Antoine, Louis, and Michael. Of these, Antoine, who served as an interpreter for Stephen Watts Kearny during the Mexican War, is best known.[2] He has so overshadowed his brothers that one historian recently identified Mount Robidoux, near Riverside, California, as being named after Antoine.[3] Clearly, however, it was named for Louis who also played a significant and fascinating role among the vanguard of those Americans who filtered into northern Mexico in the turbulent decades before the Mexican War.

Little is known of Louis Robidoux's youth or of his involvement in the fur trade until late 1823 when he showed up at Taos, the northernmost village in New Mexico.[4] Ap-

* Preparation of this manuscript was facilitated by a grant from the San Diego State College Foundation and through the assistance of Mark A. Nelson. To each I am grateful.

[1] John William Nelson, "Louis Robidoux: California Pioneer" (unpublished M.A. thesis, University of Redlands, 1950), 9.

[2] William S. Wallace, *Antoine Robidoux, 1794-1860: A Biography of a Western Venturer* (Los Angeles, 1953), outlines the career of Antoine and discusses the Robidoux family.

[3] Andrew F. Rolle, *California: A History* (New York, 1963), 174. Rolle has corrected the error in the latest edition of his book (2nd ed., 1969, pp. 177, 179), but overcompensated by ascribing one of Antoine's accomplishments to Louis.

[4] Testimony of Louis Robidoux, Santa Fe, Dec. 9, 1825, in papers relating to the confiscation of the merchandise of François Robidoux, Mexican Archives of New Mexico, State Records Center, Santa Fe, New Mexico. Hereinafter cited as MANM.

parently he was traveling with a group of trappers outfitted by his older brother, Joseph III, which had set out from Council Bluffs on the Missouri, on August 1, 1823, headed for "the mountains." [5] Somehow the trappers made their way to New Mexico, on the edge of newly-independent Mexico. There, Louis Robidoux would make his reputation as a Mountain Man and merchant.

Louis Robidoux probably remained in New Mexico through that first winter of 1823-1824. When the annual caravan of Missouri merchants arrived at Santa Fe in the summer of 1824, Mexican officials knew and trusted Robidoux enough to accept him as a bondsman for the caravan's captain, Alexander Le Grand. After Le Grand was gone, in the spring of 1825, one of his creditors collected a fifteen-peso debt from Robidoux which was paid in produce rather than in cash. Still Robidoux continued to act as a bondsman for American merchants. [6]

In the 1820s Louis Robidoux, like other Missouri merchants, plied the trails between St. Louis, Santa Fe, and Chihuahua. In the summer of 1825 he traveled home to St. Louis, then returned to Taos in the fall with three of his brothers – François, Michael, and Antonio. [7] In January, traveling with François "Siore" or "Siote," Louis Robidoux headed south, reportedly toward "the states of Chihuahua and Sonora." He apparently did not go as far as Sonora, for business was good at nearby El Paso. On May 19, 1826, Robidoux sent, or ordered to be sent to El Paso, a shipment of merchandise under the care of one Manuel Martín. [8]

---

[5] Benjamin O'Fallon to Joshua Pilcher, Fort Atkinson, Aug. 1, 1823, in Dale L. Morgan (ed.), *The West of William H. Ashley, 1822-1838* (Denver, 1964), 51, 243, 157 n.

[6] Felipe Sandoval to Manuel Marquis of Santa Fe, San Fernando [de Taos], May 19, 1825, MANM. Louis Robidoux, *fiador* for McMahan and Fisher, Santa Fe, Aug. 5, 1830, Ritch Papers, no. 116, Huntington Library, San Marino, California.

[7] Report of Foreigners, Feb. 1, 1826, and Santa Fe Treasury Report, 1826-1827, in David J. Weber (ed.), *The Extranjeros: Selected Documents From the Mexican Side of the Santa Fe Trail, 1825-1828* (Santa Fe, 1967), 19-22, 26.

Robidoux was on the road again in 1827, leaving Taos for Missouri with a party of traders. By July he was in St. Louis making plans to return to New Mexico. Robidoux may have become trail-weary after these strenuous years, for his name appears less frequently on lists of merchants. He continued, however, to import goods over the Santa Fe Trail to New Mexico from time to time. In 1830, for example, he and Charles Beaubien shipped merchandise to Santa Fe with the annual caravan.[9] Robidoux may not have traveled with that caravan, however, for by then New Mexico was his home.

In 1829, when Louis and his brother Antoine applied to become Mexican citizens, New Mexico officials acted with uncommon speed. The brothers asked to be naturalized on July 16, and the next day it was accomplished.[10] For Louis, the transition from French-American to Mexican must have been an easy one. He was already a Roman Catholic and apparently spoke Spanish fluently even before migrating to New Mexico.[11] Furthermore, his marriage to Guadalupe García of Santa Fe, which took place sometime before he became a Mexican citizen, must have hastened his acculturation.

The daughter of one Pedro García, Guadalupe was not, as family tradition suggests, "of a very eminent Spanish family."[12] Nevertheless, the marriage was both enduring

---

[8] Report of Feb. 1, 1826, and book of trade permits, 1826-1828, Santa Fe Custom House, in Weber, *Extranjeros,* 22 and 31. For Siote see Angélico Chávez, "New Names in New Mexico, 1820-1850," in *El Palacio,* v. 64, nos. 11-12 (Nov.-Dec. 1957), 375.

[9] Weber, *Extranjeros,* 36-37. List of persons who entered merchandise with the 1830 caravan, in Albert W. Bork, *Nuevos aspectos del comercio entre Nuevo México y Misuri, 1822-1846* (Mexico, 1961), 117.

[10] L. and A. Robidoux, request for naturalization, July 16, 1829, and list of persons naturalized in New Mexico, 1829, Ritch Papers, nos. 111 and 113.

[11] In his previously cited Dec. 9, 1825, testimony, Louis spoke without the aid of an interpreter and claimed to be Spanish!

[12] Guadalupe's father is named in an entry of Aug. 14, 1835, Santa Fe Baptismal Book B69s, Archives of the Archdiocese of Santa Fe. Orral M. Robidoux, *Memorial to the Robidoux Brothers: A History of the Robidouxs in America* (Kansas City, 1924), 209.

and productive. Guadalupe, who outlived her husband, bore eight of Robidoux's children: Mariano, Luis, Catarina, Carmelita, Adelaide, Benina, Abundo, and Pascual.[13] At least four of these children were born in Santa Fe: Catarina on August 12, 1835; José Luis on December 17, 1837; and Pascual and Mariano whose birth dates have not yet come to light. At least two of the children, Adelaide and Carmelita, were born after the family had moved to California in 1844.[14] Between 1833 and 1841, Robidoux and his growing family lived at 31 Calle Principal, then Santa Fe's main street. Next door, probably in the same building, Robidoux operated a *ferrería* or iron works. Today his address would be on San Francisco Street, perhaps in what is now called the Ortiz House.[15]

As a Mexican citizen, Robidoux participated actively in community affairs, including politics. His political career in Santa Fe began modestly in 1830 when he served as fourth secretary of his election district. Four years later he was elected to serve as a *regidor,* or alderman, on the Santa Fe *ayuntamiento,* or town council.[16] By 1839, he had become first *alcalde* of Santa Fe, an office that his brother, Antoine, had previously held. In this position, Louis dispensed justice

13 Felipe Banks to Ysabel López de Fages, Riverside, Calif., Mar. 10, 1943, copy in the Robidoux Folder, Riverside Public Library. Banks received his information from his father-in-law, Celso Robidoux, a grandson of Louis, who was born in 1867. The children are not named in order of age.

14 Santa Fe Baptismal Book B69s, entries of Aug. 14, 1835 and Dec. 20, 1837. Alice Bryant, "A Daughter of the Old Regime," unidentified newspaper clipping, Apr. 28, 1917, containing the reminiscences of Adelaide Robidoux Estudillo, Robidoux Folder. Robidoux to Manuel Alvarez, Jurupa, May 1, 1848, Benjamin Read Collection, no. 260, State Records Center, Santa Fe.

15 List of property owners in Santa Fe compiled by Juan Bautista Vigil y Alarid, Jan. 26, 1836, Federal Land Office Archives, no. 1314, Santa Fe. Entries of Feb. 20, 1833, and Mar. 20, 1841, in Deed Book J, pp. 48-51, Santa Fe County Courthouse, record the dates of purchase and sale of this property. I am obliged to Dr. Marc Simmons, of Cerrillos, New Mexico, who located these deeds for me.

16 Manzana 1 and 2, Santa Fe, to Cura Juan Felipe Ortiz, Dec. 5, 1830, MANM. Lansing B. Bloom, "New Mexico Under Mexican Administration, 1821-1846," in *Old Santa Fe,* v. I, no. 4 (Apr. 1914), 362.

regarding a myriad of local problems, as evidenced by numerous documents preserved in the New Mexico archives bearing the signature "L. Rubidú." He seems to have won a reputation for fairness – so much so that native New Mexicans trusted him in cases involving Americans – and he allowed no nonsense in his courtroom.[17]

A reporter from the New Orleans *Picayune,* Matt Field, who visited Santa Fe in 1839, wrote that Louis Robidoux "shares the rule over the people almost equally with the Governor and the priests." Robidoux had entertained Field at his home and had introduced him to such local luminaries as Governor Manuel Armijo and the notorious female gambler, "La Tules." Clearly, Field was impressed with Robidoux's position in the community and offered a simple explanation for his rise to prominence: "when an American remains long in the place, and obtains a facility in the language, he becomes a man of great importance." Yet, other Spanish-speaking Americans had lived in New Mexico nearly as long as Robidoux without having achieved his influence or prestige. One suspects that Robidoux was more than the "jolly old fellow" characterized by Field, but was also a shrewed, aggressive, and ambitious man of high intelligence. On the primitive Mexican frontier, even Robidoux's literacy was of inestimable advantage.[18]

Despite his participation in New Mexico politics, Robidoux did not take Mexican citizenship too seriously. In December 1840, for example, he signed a letter as a "citizen" of the United States which praised the activities of the American consul in Santa Fe. After Robidoux had moved

---

[17] See, for example, Robert Morris vs. Manuel Doroteo Pino, Nov. 22, 1836-May 9, 1837, MANM, and John E. Sunder (ed.), *Matt Field on the Santa Fe Trail* (Norman, 1960), pp. 213-14.

[18] Sunder, *Field,* 205-06, 213, 243-44. Robidoux's letters reveal that he wrote with ease in Spanish. He apparently had considerable linguistic ability. After moving to California, he learned to speak the language of the Cahuilla Indians and served as an interpreter.

to Mexican California, he continued to admire American initiative and institutions.[19] His chief motive for becoming a Mexican citizen and politician probably had been economic.

As a Mexican citizen, for example, Robidoux received permission from the ayuntamiento of Santa Fe, on April 9, 1839, to place a grist mill on the Santa Fe River. His political connections apparently helped him to continue to run the mill when, a year later, Antonio Matías Ortiz began composing a torrent of letters protesting Robidoux's operation. Ortis complained that the mill, which was located next to his property, interferred with his business and asked to have Robidoux's permit rescinded. The ayuntamiento appointed a special commission to look into the charges and concluded that Robidoux's "new industrial establishment" was beneficial to the community. Very modern, the mill used far less water than any other in the territory. Ortiz, the commission reported, harbored a grudge toward Robidoux and the complaints were without substance.[20]

The greatest economic advantage which Mexican citizenship offered Robidoux was that it allowed him to trap legally for furs, an activity forbidden to foreigners in New Mexico after 1824. Robidoux revealed his continuing interest in the fur trade in 1831 when he complained to New Mexico officials that an American, Ewing Young, was trapping in Mexican territory.[21] Yet, evidence that Robidoux himself continued to trap, or to outfit trapping parties, remains circumstantial. Mexican documents of the period

---

19 James Giddings *et al* to Manuel Alvarez, Santa Fe, Dec. 8, 1840, Read Collection, no. 9. Alvarez to Daniel Webster, Washington, Feb. 2, 1842, U.S. Consular Dispatches, Santa Fe. Robidoux to Alvarez, Jurupa, Calif., June 17, 1848, Read Collection, no. 261.

20 Robidoux to the Ayuntamiento, Santa Fe, Mar. 9, 1839, and attached papers, Read Collection, no. 259. Various letters from A. M. Ortiz in communications of local officials, Apr. 30-Aug. 25, 1840, MANM.

21 Governor José Antonio Chávez to Louis Robidoux, Aug. 6, 1831, in Governor's Letterbook, Oct. 21, 1830 to Aug. 31, 1831, MANM.

reveal more about trappers who broke the law than those who abided by it; as a citizen, Louis Robidoux fell into the latter category.

Antoine Robidoux, who had trapped and traded out of New Mexico in the 1820s, continued to do so in the 1830s and it seems likely that Louis was associated with him. As the older and better-known brother, Antoine may have been remembered for activities in which his younger brother was an active participant. For example, in the winter of 1833-1834, Kit Carson recalled meeting on the Uinta River a "Mr. Robidoux" who "had a party of some twenty men that were trapping and trading." Scholars have assumed that Carson had run across Antoine Robidoux. But, Antoine seems to have been back in Santa Fe that winter,[22] so it must have been another Robidoux and Louis stands out as the likely candidate.

Sometime in the 1830s, Antoine constructed two trading posts to the northwest of the New Mexico settlements: Fort Uncompahgre, on the Gunnison River near the mouth of the Uncompahgre; and Fort Uinta (or Robidoux), on the Uinta near its junction with the Green, perhaps built in the winter of 1837-1838.[23] Louis probably served as the New Mexico agent for these posts, for they depended on New Mexico for supplies and sometimes as a market for furs.[24] On at least one occasion, in the spring of 1841, Louis Robidoux made the long journey to Fort Uinta. In April, before leaving Santa Fe, he stopped at Manuel Alvarez's store and pro-

[22] See Carson's memoirs in Harvey L. Carter, *"Dear Old Kit": The Historical Kit Carson* (Norman, 1969), pp. 58-59. On Dec. 6, 1833, Antoine's signature appears on a list of members of a commission in charge of the formation of election districts, Santa Fe, MANM. On Feb. 19, 1834, Antoine purchased a mine near Santa Fe. Certificate of sale cited in Ralph E. Twitchell, *The Spanish Archives of New Mexico* (2 vols., Cedar Rapids, 1914), I, p. 215.

[23] Wallace, *Antoine Robidoux*, 14. LeRoy R. and Ann W. Hafen, *Old Spanish Trail* (Glendale, 1954), 102. See the map in vol. I of this *Series*.

[24] LeRoy R. and Ann W. Hafen (eds.), *Rufus B. Sage: His Letters and Papers, 1836-1847* (2 vols., Glendale, 1956), II, pp. 89, 97-98.

visioned himself with a fusil, two pistols, two mules, and a pair of spurs. Sometime in May, as he approached the Green River, he took the trouble to inscribe his name on a cliff in the Willow Creek drainage, some thirty-five miles south of Ouray, Utah.[25] Perhaps Antoine and Louis made this trip together, for Antoine had been in Missouri the previous autumn.[26]

Louis Robidoux's stay at Fort Uinta was brief. By November 1841, he had returned to Santa Fe where officials were pleased to see him. He owed the government fifty pesos in customs duty on goods that he had imported that spring. Cash was in short supply and the governor was anxious to receive payment.[27]

Robidoux's 1841 venture to the mountains cannot yet be satisfactorily explained. Why he went and what he did remain unknown. To add to the puzzle, Robidoux had sold his house, land, and grist mill in Santa Fe in March 1841, just before his departure.[28] Perhaps he was already planning to abandon New Mexico as he would do in 1843. Clearly, tension between foreign-born residents and native New Mexicans had been increasing since the Texas Revolution of 1836. In September 1841, while Robidoux was away, the well-known Texas-Santa Fe expedition had been captured and marched off to Mexico City the following month. Anti-foreign feeling had been particularly high that summer and fall, and continued to flare up in the next years. Commercial

[25] Alvarez Ledger Book, 1840-1842, p. 79, State Records Center, Santa Fe. Letter to this writer from O. Dock Marston, Berkeley, Calif., Jan. 4, 1969, who graciously sent me a photograph of the Robidoux inscription taken by George E. Stewart of Roosevelt, Utah.

[26] Joseph J. Hill, "Antoine Robidoux: Kingpin in the Colorado River Fur Trade, 1824-1844," in *Colorado Magazine,* VII, no. 4 (July 1930), 125.

[27] Cuaderno de ingresos y egresos, 1841; Ambrosio Armijo, Gefe de Hacienda y Tesoria, to Administrador General de Rentas, José Antonio Chávez, Santa Fe, Oct. 30, 1841; and Chávez to Prefecto Juan A. Archuleta, Santa Fe, Nov. 4, 1841; all in MANM.

[28] Deed of sale, Robidoux to Roque Tudesqui, Mar. 20, 1841, County Deed Book J, copy of the original in Deeds File, State Records Center, Santa Fe.

conditions also deteriorated as hostilities increased. In September 1843, Governor Manuel Armijo even closed Santa Fe temporarily to foreign commerce.[29]

How these events affected Robidoux, who had many friends in Santa Fe, is not clear. He remained in New Mexico through the summer of 1842, carrying out business as usual: in March he presided over an election in his district; in May he won twenty-five pounds of beaver fur from Tomás Ortiz in a billiard game; and in August, Lieutenant Escuipulas Caballero sued him for twenty pesos.[30] In February 1843, Robidoux still seems to have been in Santa Fe,[31] but sometime after that he headed for California, leaving his family behind.

Perhaps Louis Robidoux's departure from New Mexico was motivated less by worsening conditions there, than by the lure of California. If Louis had not seen California himself before 1843, he had certainly heard of it from acquaintances in Santa Fe and even from his brother. Antoine had reportedly told a group of Missourians in the fall of 1840 that California was a "perfect paradise," land of "perpetual spring." There, "it was such a curiosity to see a man shake with the chills" that when such a man was discovered, "the people of Monterey went eighteen miles to see him."[32] Soon Louis would share his brother's enthusiasm for California.

By March 16, 1844, Louis Robidoux had reached California and had managed to complete the purchase of two leagues of land to the east of Los Angeles: part of the rancho de Jurupa and the rancho San Timoteo at San Gorgonio,

[29] Max L. Moorhead, *New Mexico's Royal Road* (Norman, 1958), 127-34.

[30] Elección para deputados de electores primarias de San Juan de los Caballeros, Mar. 6, 1842; case before Anastasio Sandoval, 2nd Alcalde of Santa Fe, May 28, 1842; Libro de jucios verbales, 1842, Aug. 18, 1842; all in MANM.

[31] In February, 1843, Robidoux was said to be serving as an attorney for one Montaño. Bent to Alvarez, Feb. 15, 1843, in "Notes and Documents," in *New Mexico Historical Review*, XXX, no. 2 (Apr. 1955), 166.

[32] Hill, "Antoine Robidoux," 125, quoting John Bidwell, who did not specify which Robidoux made this statement.

both of which he bought from James Johnson. Robidoux's familiarity with Mexican law and customs no doubt facilitated the purchase, but perhaps an acquaintance from New Mexico, Benjamin Wilson, also helped. Wilson had originally owned the portion of Jurupa that Johnson sold to Robidoux, and Wilson continued to live on the other half of the rancho until Robidoux bought him out in 1848. Although Robidoux had paid $1,500 to Johnson for Jurupa and San Timoteo, he still had money left, for on April 2, 1844, he also bought the rancho San Jacinto.[33] Financial ruin, then, had not driven him from New Mexico.

After making these purchases, perhaps in the summer of 1844, Robidoux returned to Santa Fe for his family and whatever possessions he could haul. Then, in November 1844, he started back to California. Although he and his family traveled in the safety of a company of traders, the journey was still difficult; his young son, Mariano, died during the crossing.[34] Robidoux never saw New Mexico again. An adobe on the northwest side of the Santa Ana River at rancho Jurupa became his home for the rest of his life. He and his family must have settled onto the ranch very quickly, for by 1846, just as in Santa Fe, Robidoux had a grist mill in operation – one of the first in southern California.[35]

California remained Mexican for only a short time after Robidoux's arrival. In 1846, with the outbreak of the Mexican War, American forces quickly "liberated" California. Robidoux played no part in the initial struggle, but in Sep-

---

[33] Nelson, "Louis Robidoux," 33, 36-37. Copies of the documents pertaining to these land transfers are in the Robidoux File, Riverside Public Library.

[34] On October 8, 1844, Robidoux received a passport to go to California with the caravan scheduled to leave on November 10. Hafen and Hafen, *Old Spanish Trail*, 189. Banks to López de Fages, Mar. 10, 1943, Robidoux File.

[35] Mildred B. Hoover and Hero E. and Ethel G. Rensch, *Historic Spots in California*, rev. by William N. Abeloe (3rd ed., Stanford, 1966), 293-94. Stephen C. Foster, "Reminiscences," in *Annual Publications of the Historical Society of Southern California*, v (1900-1902), 267.

tember 1846, when *Californios* retook Los Angeles from the Americans, foreign-born residents living in outlying areas began to fear for their safety. As Robidoux later described it, on September 25 eighteen foreigners gathered at Jurupa to defend themselves: "the rumor was that the insurrectionists would not spare the life of any foreigner." The next day this band moved to Chino, hoping eventually to reach Los Angeles and join a small American force there. On the 27th, however, what Robidoux later described as a "superior force" of two hundred men attacked the eighteen foreigners. After an hour of fighting, Robidoux's group was "obliged to succumb to discretion" or be burned alive, for the roof of the Chino ranch house had been set ablaze. Taken prisoner, the foreigners were marched off to Los Angeles, all fearing the worst.[36] When a priest came to administer to the wounded, according to Benjamin Wilson, Robidoux exclaimed: "My God men they are going to shoot us, the priest's coming is a sure sign," and Robidoux asked to be confessed. In telling the story in later years, Wilson took delight in Robidoux's fear, but he was probably equally afraid at the time. After a few fretful months in jail, the men were released on January 8, 1847, just before American forces recaptured Los Angeles.[37]

The change of government seems to have pleased Robidoux who cooperated fully with his American "conquerors." He sent flour to help feed members of the Mormon Battalion and served as an "American" alcalde in his area from August 20, 1846, through 1848 and perhaps longer. After civilians took over the government of California in 1850, Robidoux was elected justice of the peace for the township of San Bernardino and was appointed to the county court of

---

[36] Robidoux to Manuel Alvarez, May 1, 1848, Read Collection, no. 260.

[37] Arthur Woodward (ed.), "Benjamin David Wilson's Observations on Early Days in California and New Mexico," in *Hist. Soc. of So. Calif., Annual Publication,* XVI (1934), 110-14, 117.

Los Angeles.[38] In 1853, when San Bernardino County was formed, Robidoux was elected to the County Board of Supervisors, then chosen to be the board's first chairman. He remained on the board until 1861. Part of Robidoux's political power stemmed from the influence that he had over the community of Agua Mansa, just to the west of Jurupa, whose settlers were chiefly from New Mexico and voted as Robidoux directed.[39]

Perhaps more important to Robidoux than poltical office was the increased prosperity which also followed the American conquest. As early as 1848, Robidoux enthused that "the progress that has been made in the commercial arts in California in the short time that it has been in possession of the Americans is a thing of admiration." [40] Yet, California itself was responsible for much of Robidoux's well-being.

In May 1848, Robidoux sent a letter via Kit Carson to Manuel Alvarez at Santa Fe, in which he announced that California "will be the land from which I will leave for the eternal journey." He praised California's moderate climate and the fertility of the land which "pays a man's work well; it is not ungrateful like the land of New Mexico." He described the abundant food and water on his ranch and expressed general satisfaction with everything, admitting that "I do not have much money, but I never want for anything." His wife, on the other hand, was not as pleased. "Notwithstanding all of this," Robidoux told Alvarez, "Guadalupe says that she does not like California." Although her house was finer than in New Mexico and there

---

[38] Foster, "Reminiscences," 267. Hubert Howe Bancroft, *History of California* (San Francisco, 1886) v, pp. 625-26. Walter R. Bacon, "Pioneer Courts and Lawyers of Los Angeles," in *Annual Publication of Hist. Soc. of So. Calif.*, VI (1905), 217.

[39] Nelson, "Louis Robidoux," 51-54. George William and Helen Pruitt Beattie, *Heritage of the Valley, San Bernardino's First Century* (Oakland, Calif., 1951), 230. Major Horace Bell, *Reminiscences of a Ranger, or Early Times in Southern California* (Santa Barbara, 1927), 61-63. Robidoux was a Whig in 1852 according to Bell.

[40] Robidoux to Alvarez, Jurupa, June 17, 1848, Read Collection, no. 261.

was more and better food to eat, Guadalupe complained that "there is no diversion; the *fandangos* are rare because the people are scattered; the churches are very far, since we live fifteen leagues from the Pueblo of Los Angeles, so that we have no other diversion than our work." Yet, these problems were not of great consequence to Guadalupe's contented husband whose only regret, he told Alvarez, was that he lived too far to send his children to school. Clearly, however, his letters also reveal that he missed many of his friends in Santa Fe.[41]

As settlement increased in the valley in the 1850s, life became less lonesome. One of his daughters, Adelaide, remembered how the house was always open to passers-by, and how "there were lively house parties – lasting for days at a time." By the late 1850s, apparently, an English tutor held classes on the ranch and a priest came to say Mass there once a month.[42]

During the 1850s Robidoux's rancho continued to prosper. In 1860, a visitor described Jurupa as excellent pasture land supporting one thousand cattle, and two thousand sheep which produced a large crop of wool. Robidoux had some three hundred acres of his fertile ranch under cultivation, including a large orchard, thirty acres of vinyard, and corn and wheat. Among the by-products of this enterprise was a yearly production of two thousand gallons of wine and five hundred gallons of peach brandy,[43] a good portion of which must have been slated for Robidoux's personal use.

Since his early days in New Mexico, Robidoux had apparently been a heavy drinker. In 1830 he spent several days in the Santa Fe *cárcel* after a drunken night in which he in-

---

[41] Robidoux to Alvarez, Jurupa, May 1, 1848, Read Collection, no. 260. The letter is written in good Spanish.

[42] Bryant, "Daughter of the Old Regime."

[43] Paul W. Gates (ed.), *California Ranchos and Farms, 1846-1862, Including the Letters of John Quincy Adams Warren of 1861.* . . (Madison, Wisc., 1967), 121-22.

sulted several of his friends and the alcalde of Santa Fe. From jail Robidoux wrote an obsequious apology to the alcalde, explaining that his insults were "only inspired by influence of aguardiente," and promising to reform. In California he continued to drink heavily. "Business" trips to Los Angeles often left him incapacitated and in 1856 he was again thrown into jail when his drinking led to a fracas with some Mormons who owed him money.[44]

During his last years, Robidoux relied heavily on alcohol to provide escape from his rapidly-multiplying problems. To build a successful ranch, Robidoux had withstood flood, drought, earthquakes, plagues of grasshoppers, Indian attack, and costly litigation which resulted in the loss of his land at San Jacinto and San Timoteo.[45] Beginning in 1861, however, when a fall from a horse fractured his hip and permanently disabled him, Robidoux's fortunes steadily declined. In 1862 an unusually destructive flood washed away some of his best bottom land where vegetables and grain had been planted. On the heels of flood came three years of drought which destroyed his herds. Thus, Robidoux's last years saw his modest "empire" disappear, while he remained frustrated and helpless to resist the ravages of a formerly-generous nature. On September 24, 1868, in his seventy-second year, Louis Robidoux died a natural death and was buried, in what is now an unmarked grave, at the cemetery of Agua Mansa overlooking his portion of the valley.[46]

Clearly, Louis Robidoux's career does not fit the standard image of the Mountain Man as a semi-barbaric, inarticulate

[44] Robidoux to the 1st Alcalde, Santa Fe jail, Nov. 8, 1830, MANM. Harris Newmark, *Sixty Years in Southern California* (New York, 1930), 176. Beattie, *Heritage of the Valley,* 259-60.

[45] Nelson, "Louis Robidoux," 59.

[46] Robidoux's misfortunes are discussed and sources cited in Nelson, "Louis Robidoux," 55-64. An interview with eighty-eight-year-old Peter Peters, reported in the Riverside *Press,* Nov. 8, 1935, by Miles Cannon, describes Robidoux's last years. See also Bryant, "Daughter of the Old Regime."

social misfit. Robidoux, instead, was an aggressive, public-spirited entrepreneur who seems to have valued family, friends, and fireside over wilderness. After the fur trade had brought him onto a foreign frontier where he could use his skills profitably, Robidoux quickly traded the life of a Mountain Man for that of a merchant, a politician, a miller, and finally a rancher.[47] Yet, Robidoux continued to relive the adventures of his younger days. One visitor to Jurupa, in 1852, remembered falling asleep while "Old Louis," with bottle and pipe in hand, lectured "on his Anglo-Norman ancestry, their domiciliation in the Rocky Mountains, the exploits of mountain men in Indian fighting, of Bridger, of Carson, Godey, Sublett [*sic*], of Jim Beckworth, and of Pegleg Smith."[48] Most contemporaries in California, however, saw Robidoux only as "Don Luis," a "gentleman of fine education, and much extended information." Within his own family, Robidoux's beginnings as a Mountain Man became so forgotten that one of his daughters boasted that he had been born in France and educated in Paris: "Besides being a scholar – he spoke seven languages and he understood law – my father was a man of great enterprise."[49] Only the latter part of her recollection was correct.

[47] Robidoux seems to fit William Goetzmann's analysis in "Mountain Man as Jacksonian Man," in *American Quarterly,* xv, no. 3 (Fall 1963), 402-15.

[48] Bell, *Reminiscences of a Ranger,* 283.

[49] Gates (ed.), *California Ranchos,* 122. Bryant, "A Daughter of the Old Regime."

Ewing Young

by HARVEY L. CARTER
Colorado College, Colorado Springs

Ewing Young, one of the most considerable figures of the fur trade of the Far West, was born near Jonesboro, Washington County, in eastern Tennessee, at least as early as 1794 and, more probably, as early as 1792.[1] He was the son of Charles and Mary Rebecca (Wilkins) Young, who had taken up land there in 1790. His grandfather, Robert Young, was an early Watauga Valley settler and a veteran of the battle of King's Mountain.[2] Although his father died in 1796, it is evident that his son, Ewing, received some education and it is also known that he was apprenticed to learn the carpenter's trade.

When and under what circumstances Young left his native state are unknown but, on January 18, 1822, he bought a farm, in partnership with Thomas P. Gage, at Charitan, Missouri, on the north bank of the Missouri River. On May 24, 1822, they sold the farm and, on the next day, Ewing Young joined William Becknell, who was about to set out on his second trip to Santa Fe.[3] Becknell had twenty-one

---

[1] Kenneth L. Holmes, "Ewing Young, Enterprising Trapper" (Unpublished doctoral dissertation, University of Oregon, 1963), 4-5. The researches of Dr. Holmes turned up a will of Charles Young dated May 28, 1794 (Will Book no. 1, Washington County, Tennessee, p. 176) in which mention is made of his "sons Wilken and Ewen and dater Giny." Thus, Ewing Young's birth was prior to May 28, 1794 and, if an inference may be drawn from the order of the mention of the children, Ewing was probably born during the year 1792. Prior to the investigations of Dr. Holmes, the date 1796 had been accepted for Young's birth because of his baptismal record in Taos in 1831, which gave his age as 35 years at that time.

[2] Samuel C. Williams, *Tennessee during the Revolutionary War* (Nashville, 1944), 157, reports the legend that Robert Young shot Major Ferguson at the battle of King's Mountain, with his rifle, "Sweet Lips."

[3] Holmes, *op. cit.,* 16-22. Here again Dr. Holmes has discovered material enabling a correction to be made. Young could not have been with the first Becknell expedi-

men and three wagons for this trip. This was undoubtedly
the first use of wagons on the Santa Fe trail. Young had
invested whatever he had from the sale of his farm in trade
goods and thus made the journey as a partner in the venture.
The only other members known are William Wolfskill and
John Ferrell. The latter had been in the gunpowder-making
business at Boone's Lick with John Day and Benjamin
Cooper, and he and Young proposed to engage in this business in New Mexico.[4] The route they followed left the
Missouri at present Kansas City and struck the Arkansas at
the Great Bend. Joined by a party under John Heath, they
continued on the Cimarron route and arrived at San Miguel
twenty-two days after leaving the Arkansas.[5] The gunpowder scheme with Ferrell failed to materialize for lack
of an adequate supply of nitre. Young turned instead to
beaver trapping, inviting Wolfskill to join him. They trapped the Pecos River in the fall of 1822 and thus was begun
his notable career as a trapper and trader.[6]

There is no record of Young's movements in the year
1823 but it is likely that he trapped on some of the more
frequented streams of New Mexico and matured his plans
for going farther afield, for he told Wolfskill that he wanted
"to get outside of where trappers had ever been."[7] In pursu-
ance of this aim, he organized and led a party westward to
the San Juan River in February, 1824. The party was loosely
organized and gradually broke up, but Young, Wolfskill,
and Isaac Slover stuck together until June, 1824, when they
returned to Santa Fe with over ten thousand dollars worth
of furs.[8]

tion in 1821, as had previously been believed, because his involvement with land
transactions precludes such a possibility.

  [4] Ibid., 24-5.

  [5] William Becknell, "Journal of Two Expeditions from Boone's Lick to Santa Fe,"
in Missouri Historical Review (January, 1940), IV, pp. 79-80.

  [6] Holmes, 42.   [7] Ibid., 44.

  [8] Joseph J. Hill, "Ewing Young in the Fur Trade of the Far Southwest, 1822-
1834," in Oregon Historical Society Quarterly (March, 1923), XXIV, p. 7.

Ewing Young now had some capital with which to operate and he returned to St. Louis in the fall of 1824, possibly with Augustus Storrs, although this is conjectural. Here he purchased a supply of trade goods worth $1,206.40 in Mexican dollars. He made the return trip to Santa Fe very early in the spring of 1825 and paid $301.50 customs duty on the goods, which were itemized and valued by the Mexican authorities on April 11, 1825. The goods consisted chiefly of cotton and silk cloth, handkerchiefs, ladies' slippers, metal buttons and combs, but also included knives and hoes.[9] Young returned to Missouri with M. M. Marmaduke, leaving Santa Fe May 31, 1825, which may indicate that his goods found a ready market and that his stock needed replenishing. This time he took a number of mules, some of which were stolen by the Osage Indians. He received $216, the amount he requested, from the federal government as indemnification. The Marmaduke party arrived in Franklin, Missouri, on August 5, 1825.[10] Young must have returned to New Mexico after a very short stay in Missouri, for Major Sibley recorded in his *Journal* that he permitted one of his men, Benjamin Robinson, to go trapping with "Mr. E. Young" on November 27, 1825. Robinson died before they had gone far, and Young himself returned to Taos in ill health by January 22, 1826.[11]

While recovering his health, Young again teamed up with his old partner, William Wolfskill, who set out to trap the western rivers while Young returned once more to Missouri, this time with Major Sibley. They set out on February 26, 1826, and reached Missouri early in April. Young started back with more goods from Fayette, Missouri, on May 20,

---

[9] Young's list of trade goods is in the Ritch Collection of the Henry E. Huntington Library, doc. no. R181. See Holmes, 47-8.

[10] M. M. Marmaduke, "Journal," in *Missouri Historical Review* (October, 1911), VI, pp. 1-10.

[11] A. B. Hulbert, *Southwest on the Turquoise Trail, Overland to the Pacific Series,* II, pp. 147, 153.

1826.[12] Arriving in Taos in the late summer he found that
Wolfskill's trapping venture had been unsuccessful because
of trouble with hostile Indians.[13]

Young now decided to organize a trapping party strong
enough to defend itself against the Indians and to recover
the losses suffered at their hands. However, he was by no
means the only leader of a fur brigade headed for the tributary streams of the Colorado River in the year 1826.
Governor Narbona had issued licenses by August 31 of that
year to Isaac Williams, Ceran St. Vrain, Michael Robidoux,
and John Rowland as well as to "Joaquin Joon," as Young
is styled in the Mexican documents. These separate parties
amounted to over a hundred men, and probably more went
than were actually licensed to go.[14]

Young originally led a party of eighteen licensed trappers
in 1826, including Milton Sublette and Thomas L. (later
"Peg-Leg") Smith. But he had consolidated with a group of
sixteen men, of whom George Yount was one, who accepted
his leadership. This large party was in the neighborhood of
the junction of the Salt and Gila rivers when it encountered
three survivors of a group of thirty French-American trappers, the rest of whom had been set upon and killed by
Papago Indians. These three, Michael Robidoux, the leader,
young James Ohio Pattie, and one other were glad to join
Young's band.[15]

Stirred by the news of the massacre of the Robidoux
party, Young set a successful ambush for the Papagos and

12 Holmes, 53-4.   13 *Ibid.,* 55.

14 See Thomas Maitland Marshall, "St. Vrain's Expedition to the Gila" in *Southwestern Historical Quarterly* (January, 1916), XIX, pp. 251-60. Marshall over-
estimates the role of St. Vrain. The New Mexico records usually refer to Young as
Joaquin Joon, Jon, or Jong; the California records used also the designation of
Joaquin or Joachim Joven.

15 Joseph J. Hill, *op. cit.,* 9-15. This reconstruction of events, first made by Mr.
Hill, has been accepted universally by historians. There seems to be no doubt that
Young was the "genuine American leader" referred to by Pattie. See also Robert
G. Cleland, *This Reckless Breed of Men* (New York, 1952), 179-81.

exacted a heavy toll of lives for those of the dead trappers, whose mutilated bodies they gathered and buried. Having done this, Young divided his band into two equal groups to trap the Salt and Gila rivers to their headwaters. Both groups then returned to the junction of these rivers and were reunited. They then trapped down the Gila to its junction with the Colorado, which brought them among the Yuma Indians, with whom they had no trouble. As they moved up the Colorado River they enjoyed good beaver trapping. However, when they came among the Mojave Indians, Young was aware at once that they were menacingly hostile, and he built a stockade in anticipation of trouble. When a chief shot an arrow into a tree, Young put a bullet into the arrow with his rifle. The Indians, unimpressed by this display of marksmanship, attacked the trappers at daybreak but were repelled with a loss of sixteen. Young continued up river for four days, keeping men posted at night. Then, thinking the Indians had given up the chase, he relaxed his guard. Immediately the Mojaves attacked, killing two and wounding two before they were driven off. Eighteen of the trappers pursued them on horseback and killed a number, whom they hanged from trees to discourage the others. At the confluence of the Bill Williams Fork with the Colorado, Young lost three more men, who were scouting for beaver sign. The Indians were found roasting and eating their victims but managed to get away.[16]

Young now led his men along the south rim of the Grand Canyon until they reached the Navajo country south of the San Juan River. Here, for reasons not very clear, it was decided to continue northward and trap the Grand River (now the Colorado). Pattie's narrative becomes extremely vague and untrustworthy from this point. It is certain they could not have been on the Yellowstone and on Clark's Fork

---

[16] *The Personal Narrative of James Ohio Pattie,* ed. by Milo M. Quaife (Chicago, 1930), 136-50.

of the Columbia as he declares. The most probable reconstruction is that they crossed the continental divide from the
headwaters of the Grand (Colorado) in the vicinity of
Long's Peak and got upon the South Platte. Then they may
have swung in a big circle, going to the Laramie, the North
Platte, the Sweetwater, the Little Snake, the Yampa, and
finally, up the Eagle to the headwaters of the Arkansas in
the central Colorado Rockies.[17] In the process, four more
men were lost to Indians, but the remainder of the party
crossed from the Arkansas to the Rio Grande and so, back
into New Mexico, heavily laden with furs worth perhaps
$20,000.

Young must have learned that Narbona was no longer
governor and that the new governor, Armijo, was hostile to
American trappers, for he left twenty-nine packs of beaver
in the village of Peñablanca, in the care of a Mexican named
Cabeza de Baca, before proceeding to Santa Fe.[18] Governor
Armijo learned where the furs were and, in June, 1827, sent
men to confiscate them. They did so, killing Cabeza de
Baca in the process. At Santa Fe, Milton Sublette managed
to seize the two bales of beaver belonging to him and to get
away with them. Young was thereupon thrown in jail for a
time. When questioned he gave no information that would
aid in apprehending Sublette and was soon discharged.
Meanwhile, the beaver pelts had received poor care and
were sold at a low rate, but it is not thought that Young and
his men ever recovered anything despite the fact that they
had been duly licensed to trap.[19] In order to protect himself
better in the future, Young procured a passport from the
American State Department signed by Henry Clay, then
Secretary of State. He also applied for Mexican citizen-

[17] *Ibid.*, 150-9. Pattie's dates are unreliable as well as his geography. See also
Hill, *op. cit.*, 17-18.

[18] Cleland, *op. cit.*, 218-19.

[19] *Ibid.*, 219-24.

ship, in company with four other Americans, on April 26, 1828.[20]

Meanwhile, he opened a store in Taos in partnership with Wolfskill, who had just brought in a fresh lot of goods from St. Louis, and outfitted a trapping party which he sent to the Gila River. This party, not having Young's redoubtable leadership, soon returned because of trouble with the Apaches.[21] He now began to make plans for an extensive trapping expedition, which he would lead in person, all the way to California. Doubtless the recent return of his good friend Richard Campbell from California had made him acquainted with the opportunities that lay in this direction. But before he set out he was to perform a signal service for other traders. The regular Santa Fe caravan had been escorted to the border by Major Bennett Riley and there turned over to the protection of Mexican troops. Although the Mexican guard was 120-strong and the traders themselves numbered sixty, word came in to Taos that the caravan was beleagured by a much larger force of Indians. Young set out, with forty men, to the rescue, but on receiving fresh news, returned and augmented his force to ninety-five men. The Indians rode off when Young and his hunters appeared; the wagon train was saved and decided to go to Taos instead of Santa Fe.[22]

In August, 1829, Young led forty trappers north from Taos into the San Luis Valley. This was to give the impression that they planned to trap in the central Rocky Mountains on American soil. Actually they never got out of Mexican territory but doubled back across western New Mexico to the Zuni pueblo. From here they went to the

---

[20] Ritch Collection, Henry E. Huntington Library, doc. R199. Young's passport was dated March 20, 1828. He applied for Mexican citizenship in order to get a Mexican provincial passport as well.

[21] Holmes, 85.

[22] William Waldo, "Recollections of a Septuagenarian" in *Missouri Historical Society Quarterly* (April, June, 1938), v, pp. 64, 77, 78.

familiar trapping waters of the Salt River. They trapped down that stream and up the Verde River with considerable success, driving off and killing some interfering Apaches along the way. Now Young divided his party and sent half of the men back to New Mexico with the furs, while he himself led the other half to California. Among the latter was young Kit Carson, who had worked as a cook for Young in Taos and who was now out on his first real trapping expedition.[23]

Leaving the headwaters of the Verde (San Francisco) River, they struck out for the Colorado just below the Grand Canyon, camping at a place long after known as Young Spring, near present Truxton, Arizona. After crossing the Colorado, finding themselves short of food, they bought from the Mojaves a mare about to foal and ate both the mare and the foal. Their route lay up the dry course of the Mojave River for several days, then down through Cajon Pass to the mission at San Gabriel, California. Here they stayed only for one night, so eager were they to get upon the beaver streams of California.[24]

They passed on to the San Fernando Valley and over the Tehachapi range to the San Joaquin River. This was the beaver paradise for which they had been heading, but as they worked down the stream they became aware that it had been trapped by another party. This turned out to be Peter Skene Ogden and his Hudson's Bay Company brigade, whom they overtook after a while. They trapped the Sacramento, as far as what is now Redding, together with Ogden's group without any argument developing. Here they parted and Young returned downstream with his party, augmented by a man who had left British employment to join him.[25]

It was now July of 1830. Young aided the San José mis-

[23] Kit Carson, *Autobiography,* ed. by Milo M. Quaife (Chicago, 1935), 9.

[24] *Ibid.,* 10-14. Young was the fourth American to lead an overland party to California. He was preceded by Jedediah Smith in 1826, the Patties in 1827, and by Richard Campbell in 1827.

[25] Hill, *op. cit.,* 25.

sion to recover runaway Indians, who had run off into the Sierra Nevada Mountains, sending Carson with ten men to accomplish this service for the mission. He also sold his furs to a ship captain, Don José Asero, and purchased more horses and mules. Soon after this, Indians stole sixty horses but, by swift pursuit, all but five were recovered. At this time also, three of Young's men went to Monterey to secure passports to return to Taos, but they were forced by the others to rejoin the party.[26]

In September, 1830, they started back to New Mexico, but went by way of Los Angeles where most of the men got drunk. In the course of this spree, James Higgins shot and killed James Lawrence. Young, who was not drunk, sensed bad trouble with the authorities and got the men to ride out of Los Angeles in a hurry. They went down the Colorado River to the Gulf of California, then up the river to the Gila and up that river to its source, trapping with considerable success as they went. Young now employed a stratagem by going to the Santa Rita copper mines and leaving the furs with Robert McKnight, who was working the mines. He then proceeded to Santa Fe, where he procured a license to trade with the Indians at Santa Rita. He then sent back for the furs. There was over a ton of beaver skins, and he was taking no chances of losing this catch by confiscation.[27]

It was April, 1831, when Young paid off his men in Taos. During the twenty months that had elapsed since he had set out for California, three other expeditions had made their separate ways there – those of Antonio Armijo, William Wolfskill, and Peg-Leg Smith. Young's first California expedition, besides being profitable, must be credited with the effective opening of trade with California. It is also notable that Kit Carson served his apprenticeship as a Mountain Man under so experienced a leader as Ewing Young and

---

[26] *Ibid.,* 23. The three would-be deserters were Francois Turcote, Jean Vaillant, and Anastase Carier.

[27] *Ibid.,* 27.

that Young was quick to recognize both the ability and the reliability of the younger man.

On May 11, 1831, Young was baptized by Father Martinez at Taos, but he did not apply for naturalization. He lived with Maria Josepha Tayfoya, but did not contract a legal marriage with her. Young was planning to go to California a second time and considering whether he wanted to settle there. While at San José on his first trip, he had become acquainted with John R. Cooper, with whom he had since had some correspondence in which was discussed both the possibility of developing the mule trade between California and New Mexico and the possibility of Young's settling in California.[28]

On July 4, 1831, the wagons of Smith, Jackson, and Sublette reached Santa Fe. Jedediah Smith had been killed by Indians on the Cimarron, but the other two partners brought in the goods. On July 31, 1831, William Sublette paid Ewing Young $2,484.82 owed to him by William H. Ashley. About the same time, Young formed a partnership with Dr. David Waldo and David Jackson for the purpose of beginning the mule trade Young had in mind and continuing the trade in beaver pelts.[29]

David Jackson went ahead with a letter from Young to John R. Cooper which was to facilitate his buying of mules. He set out on August 25, 1831, and arrived in San Diego early in November of that year with eleven men. Meanwhile, Young had received a passport on August 21 to travel to Chihuahua, but instead of using it he organized a party of thirty-six trappers and set out for California in October, 1831. Among them was Job F. Dye, to whom we are indebted for the following list of men who were in the party: Sidney Cooper, Moses Carson, Benjamin Day, Isaac Sparks, Joseph Gale, Joseph Dofit, John Higans, Isaac Williams,

28 Holmes, 126-7.
29 Sublette Papers, Missouri Historical Society, St. Louis, Missouri.

James Green, Cambridge Green, James Anderson, Thomas Low, Julian Bargas, José Teforia, and John Price. They stopped at the Zuni pueblo for supplies and then trapped down the Salt River, catching beaver in large numbers. There were other adventures as well. Young and Dye had a scrape with a grizzly bear. They fought Apaches and Young himself killed their chief. Then Cambridge Green, usually called Turkey – a small man, but mean – killed big Jim Anderson, who bullied him once too often. By January 1, 1832, they had moved down the Gila and were camped on the Colorado River.[30]

Young took ten men and went to Los Angeles, arriving February 10, 1832. He turned Green in to the authorities for homicide. The rest of the men did not come in until March 14, 1832. Where they spent the intervening time is not known. Early in April, Jackson came in from the north with six hundred mules and one hundred horses. This was only about a fourth of what they had hoped to buy. So instead of all driving them to New Orleans, as had been planned originally, Jackson drove them to Santa Fe and Young remained in California to hunt sea otter.[31] Father Sanchez at the San Gabriel Mission had a vessel built for this purpose which was transported now by ox-cart to San Pedro harbor and assembled there. Young and Jonathan Warner and several others, including two Kanakas, engaged in the otter hunt; but Young did not like being dumped in the surf and, after being spilled several times, left the hunt and went to Monterey.

This was in early July and, by early October, Young had organized fourteen men to trap the San Joaquin. There is no record of Young's movements during this three-month period. It has been supposed that he stayed in California.

---

[30] Job F. Dye, *Recollections of a Pioneer, 1830-1852* (Los Angeles, 1951), 18-29.

[31] Holmes, 142-52. Professor Holmes points out that Alfred Robinson, *Life in California* (New York, 1846), 140-41, almost certainly describes Young's landlubber experiences while hunting sea otter, although Young is not identified by name.

However, Maria Josepha Tafoya, back in Taos, on April 8, 1833, gave birth to a son whose paternity was attributed to Young and never denied by him. It would have been possible for Young to have returned to Taos during the summer of 1832, and if he was the true father of Joaquin Young, who later inherited his property, it is essential to assume that he did so.[32]

Regardless of Young's whereabouts during the summer it is clear that in early October, 1832, he led fourteen trappers out from Los Angeles into the San Joaquin Valley. When they reached the Fresno River they saw signs indicating that a large band of trappers had been there very recently. So they hastened on to the Sacramento, where they found a Hudson's Bay Company brigade under Michael La Framboise, who was soon joined there by another band under John Work. The combined Hudson's Bay Company party amounted to 163 persons, although only forty were trappers, the rest being women and children and Indians.[33] John Turner, one of the survivors of the massacre of Jedediah Smith's men on the Umpqua in 1827, was working for La Framboise but, after talking with Young, he openly transferred to him. Turner interested Young in going farther north than he had intended. In March, 1833, they went to the Pacific coast, about seventy-five miles above Ft. Ross, and continued north as far as the Umpqua River. Ascending

---

[32] The alternatives to the conclusion that Young revisited Taos in the summer of 1832 are: (a) Father Martinez, Maria Tafoya, Kit Carson, Richard Campbell, and Manuel Lefevre were all mistaken in certifying Young's paternity; or (b) Maria Tafoya experienced a pregnancy of eighteen months. The baptismal record is dated April 12, 1833, and states that the infant was four days old at that time. It is in the Chancery office, State Records Center, Santa Fe, New Mexico. However, the entry does not appear in the normal consecutive order for that date but is written on an insert, stuck in at the bottom of the page. This irregularity may provide still a third alternative, namely, that this insert was made some years later than the normal entries and that it may not be accurate as to the date of birth and baptism of Joaquin Young.

[33] Alice Bay Maloney, *Fur Brigade to the Bonaventura* (San Francisco, 1945), 22 ff.

this to its source, they crossed to the northwest shore of Klamath Lake and thence to the Klamath and the Pitt rivers, past Mt. Shasta and back to the upper waters of the Sacramento, thus completing a big circle through most difficult country. By November 13, 1833, the night of the great meteoric shower, they were camped on the shores of Tulare Lake, whence they returned to Los Angeles.[34] Young had some conversation at San Pedro with Abel Stearns about starting a sawmill, but soon they went on to trap once more on the Gila, in the winter of 1833 and 1834.[35]

When he returned to San Diego and Los Angeles, Young was discouraged by the poor results of his last trapping expedition and by his inability to get either men or tools to engage in lumbering. It was at this time, near San Diego, that he met the eccentric Oregon enthusiast, Hall J. Kelley of Massachusetts, who was temporarily stranded on his way to "the promised land." Nevertheless, after listening to Kelley expound the wonderful future of Oregon, Young declined to accompany him thither. Kelley went on to Monterey and was surprised to have Young, with seven men, turn up there during the last of June, 1834, with the declaration that he was ready to go and settle in Oregon and that, if Kelley had deceived him, "woe be unto him." [36]

They started their northward journey with over forty horses and mules belonging to Young. At San José, they stopped for five days to secure provisions, and Young went to San Francisco to get more horses, which he had contracted for before leaving Monterey. When they left San

34 Holmes, 161-7. Both in the Sacramento and San Joaquin valleys, where Indian population had been plentiful, they now found many dead of a great pestilence which had ravaged those regions during their absence in Oregon.

35 Abel Stearns Papers, Henry E. Huntington Library. A letter of Young's to Stearns dated March 14, 1834, indicates that Young had not yet given up the project for a sawmill at that time.

36 Fred Wilbur Powell, *Hall J. Kelley on Oregon* (Princeton, 1932), 100. Kelley wrote that they first met "in Pueblo, near the port of St. Diego." This may refer to Los Angeles.

José, Young had seventy-seven horses and mules, and Kelley and the other men with Young had twenty-one, all of which Young swore were fairly bought. However, either at San José or just north of it, they were joined by nine men with fifty-six horses, of which Young said he did not know whether they were bought or stolen.[37]

This accession to the party was to be the cause of much trouble for both Kelley and Young upon their arrival in Oregon. Governor José Figueroa wrote on September 9, 1834, from Santa Clara Mission to Dr. John McLoughlin at Fort Vancouver, charging Young and the members of his party with having driven two hundred stolen horses out of California and asking McLoughlin's aid in recovering them.[38] There is no proof that Young acquired any of his stock dishonestly. On the contrary, he had always shown a disposition to cultivate good relations with the authorities in California, had helped the missions to recover stock and Indians, had given up a number of horses in his possession in 1833 upon identification of brands, and had refused to give up others.[39] This would seem to be adequate refutation of the charge that Young was a horse thief. His mistake lay in allowing the marauders to join up with him.

Young's party was overtaken in the Umpqua valley by La Framboise and his returning Hudson's Bay Company brigade. At this time, Kelley was extremely ill and Young was glad to allow him to travel with the Hudson's Bay Company captain, who was better equipped to give him medicinal care. Kelley thus arrived at Fort Vancouver a little before Young did, late in October, 1834.[40]

---

[37] *Ibid.,* 300, 351. These are the men whom Kelley called "marauders." There is not much doubt that their animals were stolen. Two of them were deserters from Joseph R. Walker's famous expedition to California in 1833. Kelley says further that these marauders tried to kill him but were prevented by Young. Their number is variously given as five, seven, and nine.

[38] A copy of this letter is in the Archives of the Hudson's Bay Company in London. The transcript of it was furnished to me by Professor Kenneth L. Holmes.

[39] Hubert Howe Bancroft, *History of California,* III, pp. 394, 410.

We do not know precisely what occurred between Ewing Young and Dr. John McLoughlin, but we know that McLoughlin had circulated Figueroa's charge of thievery against Young and that he refused to have any business dealings with him. Young felt a keen resentment over this treatment. He denied the charge and eventually received a retraction of it. But meanwhile, he had to shift for himself. It is no small tribute to his character and ability that he was able to survive in spite of the tremendous power and influence of the Hudson's Bay Company. Looking about for a likely place to settle, he pre-empted fifty square miles of land in the Chehalem valley and built a hillside cabin overlooking his domain. Here for the next two years he managed to exist, entirely independent of the hostile fur company, which refused all his overtures to trade, though willing, on occasion, to offer charity, which Young was too proud to accept. He told Lt. Slacum, in 1836, that "a cloud hung over him so long, through Dr. McLoughlin's influence, that he was almost maddened by the harsh treatment of that gentleman." [41]

But doubtless he was able to trade furs for supplies from American ships that came up the Columbia from time to time and, in 1836, he began the erection of a sawmill with Sol Smith, who had come to Oregon with Nathaniel Wyeth in the same year that Young had arrived. Also, in 1836, he announced his plans to start a whiskey distillery, with Lawrence Carmichael as partner, and bought from Wyeth's trading post, after Wyeth's departure, a large cauldron or

---

[40] Powell, 262-4. Kelley remained in Oregon until March, 1835, when he took ship for the Hawaiian Islands. He was given adequate care by Dr. McLoughlin but was segregated and not admitted to table at the fort. His account of this period is found in Powell, 181-9. It should be said that McLoughlin's treatment of Young and Kelley was an exception to his usual policy of open handed hospitality. Young's spread was located southwest of modern Portland and about twenty miles almost directly west of Oregon City.

[41] "Slacum's Report on Oregon, 1836-1837" in *Oregon Historical Society Quarterly* (June, 1912), XIII, p. 196.

copper kettle for this purpose. A temperance society was already in existence among the American settlers, having been organized February 11, 1836. Jason Lee and other missionaries asked him to abandon his plans to operate a distillery. The Hudson's Bay Company had a strict monopoly of liquor, as well as nearly everything else, up to this time. Young may have seriously intended to break into this monopoly. Or he may have foreseen the objection of the American temperance people and acted as he did for the purpose of winning their good opinion and so lessening the power of the company. At any rate, he consented to their request and stopped the erection of the distillery. He refused to take $51 which the temperance society had raised to compensate him, but later he sold the kettle to them for $50, which was a high price. It is not certain that Lt. William A. Slacum had arrived before this matter was settled, but if so he may have influenced Young's decision not to persist against the wishes of the community.[42]

Slacum, a naval lieutenant, had been ordered by President Jackson to look into affairs in Oregon. He noted the dependence of American settlers on the British company, especially in the matter of cattle. The company would lend a cow to a settler but refused to allow any to pass into private hands. In discussing the situation with Ewing Young, Slacum learned that there were many cattle in California and that some might be brought to Oregon from there. Thus was organized the Willamette Cattle Company. Young agreed to take ten men and go to California, purchase cattle, and drive them to Oregon. Slacum would transport the men to California. Settlers subscribed money for the purchase, and even Dr. McLoughlin was drawn into the scheme by the able lieutenant.[43] The *Loriot,* Slacum's brig, reached the

---

[42] Miss A. J. White, *Ten Years in Oregon* (Ithaca, 1848), 78-9. See also Courtney Walker, "Sketch of Ewing Young," in *Transactions of the Oregon Pioneer Association, 1880, 56-7.*

Russian Post, Fort Ross, February 20, 1837, and a week later sailed into San Francisco Bay, carrying Young and the cattle company treasurer, Philip Leget Edwards, and their men.[44]

In the course of his negotiations with California officials regarding the cattle deal, Young found it necessary to continue to Monterey, where he landed March 2, 1837. To secure final permission, he had to go overland to Santa Barbara. The officials wanted their palms greased and apparently Young applied the unguent by purchasing more cattle than he actually took out of California. At all events, he returned to Monterey, where he met Edwards on May 10, 1837, and took time out to visit his old friend and employee, Job F. Dye, at his still house near Monterey.[45] Then, having been authorized by General Vallejo to purchase one thousand head of cattle, he seems to have bought seven hundred at three dollars per head at San Solano and five hundred more at San José, both purchases being negotiated through the government. However, after they started north on July 27, 1837, Edwards estimated, on August 14, that they were driving 729 head. On September 9, near Mt. Shasta, they still had about 680 head. The cattle were mostly heifers and Young refused to allow any to be killed for food until August 27. They followed the Hudson's Bay Company fur brigade's old trail over the Siskiyous and reached the Rogue River, where they encountered some Indian trouble.[46] Here Edwards ceased keeping his diary but we know they reached the settlements on the Willamette early in October

[43] "Memorial of William A. Slacum" in *Senate Document no. 24, 25* Cong., 2 sess., pp. 12-13.

[44] Philip Leget Edwards, *California in 1837* (Sacramento, 1890), 7.

[45] *Ibid.,* 20. See also Doyce B. Nunis, editor, *The Diary of Faxon Dean Atherton* (1964), 55-6.

[46] *Ibid.,* 20-47. The route lay over rough country where, as Edwards wrote, the mountains "appear every day to grow more difficult. Hills peep over hills, and Alp on Alp."

with about 630 head. The total cost amounted to about $8.50 per head.[47]

Of the cattle he brought through, 135 head belonged to Young himself, making him the most considerable owner of livestock in the Oregon settlements. He was now able to expand his lumbering operations on Chehalem Creek, where he cut planks from Douglas fir and oak. He built himself a larger cabin. He constructed a grist mill, too, since he farmed more than 150 acres of wheat himself and since other settlers had need of one. Of course, he continued his fur trade on a small scale. The business records that he kept were very complete and they indicate that he acted in the capacity of banker for many of the settlers.[48] There was every indication that he was the leading citizen among the American settlers and that his old troubles with the Hudson's Bay Company were over.

In 1838 he was visited by John Augustus Sutter, who was soon to settle in California on a more princely domain than Young had carved out for himself in Oregon. Father Blanchet arrived in that year and borrowed money from Young. Thomas Jefferson Farnham came overland to Oregon in 1839 and visited Young on November 12 of that year.[49] One of Farnham's men, Sidney Smith, went to work for Young and lived with him. Through the Hudson's Bay Company, Young made arrangements to import some Kanakas from Hawaii, in 1839, to augment his labor force. In 1840, he found some gigantic bones of prehistoric animals and arranged to send them by ship to Boston, where they could and did receive study from those versed in such matters.[50]

[47] Hubert Howe Bancroft, *History of Oregon*, I, pp. 139-150.

[48] F. T. Young, "Ewing Young and his Estate" in *Oregon Historical Society Quarterly* (September, 1920), XXI, pp. 197-315. Young's "Day Book" and his "Register" are given here.

[49] Thomas Jefferson Farnham, *Travels in the Great Western Prairies, the Anahuac and Rocky Mountains, and in the Oregon Territory* (New York, 1843), 95.

[50] Holmes, 249-60.

However, Young had for several years been troubled with what was called dyspepsia. The ailment seems to have persisted from the time of his first arrival in Oregon. His records show that he received medicine for it from several doctors. Early in February, 1841, he had a particularly bad attack. He lingered a short while in delirium before he died. A post mortem examination was made and it was reported "that a sack of water had formed on his brain" and "that his stomach was destroyed by acid he was accustomed to take for his indigestion." [51] It is difficult to avoid the conclusion that he had suffered for years from an ulcer of the stomach, which probably also caused his death.

Ewing Young was at least forty-seven but probably not more than forty-nine years of age when he died. His death raised a problem in the American settlement in Oregon. There was no governmental authority to take charge of the disposition of his property. His death caused the first steps toward a provisional government to be taken. His property was disposed of at public auction, with Joe Meek acting as auctioneer. Sidney Smith bought up his land claim and much of his livestock. Old Mountain Men like Doc Newell, Joe Gale, and John Turner bought tools and livestock. George Gay bought seven books for a dollar and Courtney Walker paid $3.50 for a two-volume set of Shakespeare.[52] Some have supposed that Young carried this set with him in all his wanderings, but the price indicates it was in good condition and it seems more likely that he had bought it off some New England ship during his Oregon years. His estate was probably worth a good bit more than it actually sold for.

The government used some of the money to build a jail, as it was allowed to use it until final disposition could be made. Finally, in 1854, a young man arrived in Oregon

---

[51] *Ibid.*, 266.
[52] F. T. Young, *op. cit.,* 171-97.

bearing the name Joaquin Young and armed with creden-
tials from Taos setting forth that he was the son of Ewing
Young and Maria Josepha Tafoya. In addition to these
documents, sworn to by Charles Beaubien, Christopher
Carson, and Manual Lefevre, of Taos, testimony was heard
in Oregon. Joseph Gale certified that he knew of Young's
connection with Maria Tafoya and that the young man
resembled Young very much. Robert (Doc) Newell testified
that Young had told him he had a son in New Mexico. So
Joaquin Young was awarded and paid $4,994.64 by the
Territory of Oregon.[53] Joaquin Young left Oregon for
California, where his inheritance was soon dissipated.

The only physical description that has been recorded of
Ewing Young is that of the Oregon missionary, Elijah
White, who said he was "a large finely built man six feet
and perhaps two inches in height." [54] Farnham referred to
him as "the excellent old Captain" and evidently enjoyed his
company, but told nothing of his appearance. Hall Kelley
refers to him as "bold and enterprising" and speaks of having listened to the thrilling events of his eventful life but
unfortunately he did not set down any of these events in his
writings. Kelley considered that Young had lost some of the
refinements of civilization and more than once indicates that
he stood in some fear of him. At the same time, he admired
the way Young stood up to McLoughlin and he characterized him as of undoubted patriotism.[55] In this connection,
it is to be remembered that, although Young applied for

[53] *Ibid.*, 199-202. During the summer of 1954, while teaching a course in Western
History at Western State College, Gunnison, Colorado, the writer had in his class
two women named Romero, the wives of a grandson and a great-grandson of
Joaquin Young. They knew of his Oregon inheritance and said that he lost most of
it in gambling. They did not know of Ewing Young except through learning of him
in my course.

[54] White was interviewed by Frances Fuller Victor in San Francisco, February
18 and 21, 1879. W. H. Gray referred to Young as "a stirring ambitious man" and
Courtney Walker characterized him as "a candid and scrupulously honest man
. . . thorough going, brave and daring."

[55] Powell, 183-4.

Mexican citizenship for business reasons, he did not complete the process.

Young's attitude towards Indians was condemned by Hall Kelley, who gave instances of the death of Indians he believed to be innocent, at the hands of men traveling with Young. Two things need to be said regarding Kelley's charges. First, Kelley, who believed the Indians innocent, was afraid to speak up in their behalf. Secondly, Young merely permitted the action of others and did not initiate it himself.[56] Young's attitude with regard to Indians was much the same as that of other Mountain Men. He did not trust them because his experience told him this was a mistake. He also believed, and acted upon his belief, that Indians should never be allowed to have the upper hand and that retaliatory action should be swift and sure. Young was not, by choice, an Indian fighter or an adventurer. He was a business man. He took only so much action in the discipline of Indians, or for that matter, the discipline of his own men, as would enable him to continue with his business in an unhampered manner.

As a business man, Young was successful in a modest way from beginning to end. Had he lived longer he might have been successful in a much bigger way. He started with very little capital and succeeded in spite of some hard financial reverses. He was extremely independent and had the habit of command. It is notable that he was the leader of every expedition that he accompanied after his arrival in New Mexico. Sometimes he sent out men whom he did not accompany but, when he was along, he was in charge. When he acted in partnership with others, he seems to have been always at least an equal partner and more often a dominating one, after his first expedition with Becknell, where he was a minor partner.

---

[56] Powell, 351-3.

Young had a good eye for business opportunity. He sensed the necessity of exploiting new and untrapped areas for the fur trade. His mule venture, though not highly successful, was soundly based. He was the pioneer Oregon cattleman, wheat man, and lumber man.[57] These were the three products for which the Pacific Northwest became most famous, and that one man should have been responsible for the beginning of all three is an indication of a high degree of business acumen on the part of that man. Young's most outstanding traits were his unerring business judgment, his marked organizational ability, and his unyielding determination in the face of adversity. For this last quality, a rare one among men, he is much to be admired.

Except for a few letters, preserved by those to whom he wrote, Ewing Young left no records to aid the historian, beyond his expense accounts in Oregon. Had he left a journal of events on even one of his many trapping expeditions, he would loom much larger in the fur trade than he does. He operated in Mexico where such records might be a liability in relations with the government and, being his own boss, he did not need to render a report to anyone.[58] But the fact that we know as much as we do about his career, and that our knowledge comes almost entirely from those who crossed or joined his path in one way or another, are indication of the magnitude of his importance in the history of the American frontier. It is also significant that what was recorded about him by others was never what he said, but what he did.

Only Jedediah Smith and Peter Skene Ogden can be said to have surpassed Ewing Young in terms of penetration of wide areas of the Far West and sheer distance covered. They

---

[57] F. T. Young, op. cit., 171 ff. Small amounts of wheat had been grown by French-Canadians prior to Young's acreage. He was the first American to grow wheat in Oregon.

[58] Cleland, op. cit., 215-16.

surpassed him in terms of priority in time, but Young surpassed them in terms of independent individual enterprise as opposed to company enterprise. Even in chronological sequence, Young was right on their heels and probably more effective in opening routes to be followed by others.[59] In the southwest, he was already experienced before such eminent characters as St. Vrain and Carson had got started. He cannot be said to have furnished so dramatic a leadership as many of the principal characters of the fur trade were able to give. Nor can it be said that he was the hero of celebrated individual exploits to the extent that even minor characters were at certain stages of their careers. But it is doubtful if anyone connected with the fur trade touched the historical development of the American Far West at more frequent or more vital points than Ewing Young.

When we think of this grandson of a pioneer on the Watauga in eastern Tennessee coming to the end of his career in the Chehalem valley of far-off Oregon, before that land had become part of the United States, and when we consider that he came to that extreme westerly spot by strenuous marches through the borderlands of what was then northern Mexico, we must realize not only the enormous geographical distance traversed but also the tremendous span of American history encompassed in the career of Ewing Young.[60]

---

[59] Holmes, 3.

[60] Archer Butler Hulbert, *Frontiers; The Genius of American Nationality.* (Boston, 1929), 56.

David E. Jackson

by CARL D. W. HAYS
Columbus, New Mexico

One of the men who signed up with William H. Ashley to go along on his fur trading and trapping venture up the Missouri River in April 1822, was David E. Jackson.[1] Jackson was not, however, one of Ashley's "enterprising young men" as far as age went among that group of adventurers. He was already well into his thirties and was a settled family man with a wife and four growing children.

He had just recently decided to settle permanently near his brother, George E. Jackson, in what was then Ste. Genevieve County, Missouri.[2] George had already settled on a homestead in what later became Jackson Township, Ste. Genevieve County. Like most Jacksons anywhere in the United States in pioneer times, George was also the proprietor of a mill, on the Fourche de Clout [Fourche a du Clos] branch of Establishment Creek near his home. His was a saw mill.

---

[1] This outline sketch of David E. Jackson is extracted from a work in progress covering the complete story of Jackson and other members of his family who took part in the major westward movements.

A portrait of David E. Jackson, owned by family descendants, will appear in the above-mentioned work by the author of this sketch.

The main authorities relied on for this sketch for the period 1822-1830 can be found in Dale Morgan, whose research in the original documents has paralleled that of this writer every step of the way. Those works to which the reader is referred are: Dale L. Morgan, *Jedediah Smith and the Opening of the West* (Indianapolis, 1953), Dale L. Morgan, ed., *The West of William H. Ashley, 1822-1838* (Denver, 1964), and Dale L. Morgan and Carl I. Wheat, *Jedediah Smith and his Maps of the American West* (San Francisco, 1954).

It is believed that the above references are so well known that it will be unnecessary to repeat them in each instance here.

[2] All references to the Jackson family or the personal business of David E. Jackson, including court records, are from what I shall call the *Hays Family Papers,* the originals or copies of which are in the possession of this writer. That citation also will not be repeated in this paper.

David was not the first member of his family to enter or engage in the Indian trade. George had already been up the Mississippi River as early as 1810-11 trading with the Sauk and Fox Indians for the firm of James Gamble & Co. of Ste. Genevieve.

According to some members of the family, David Jackson is said to have fought in the Battle of New Orleans under Andrew Jackson, or at least to have been present at that battle. That tradition remains unverified. It is certain, however, that Jackson did visit New Orleans at least once in his career. If it was before his entrance into the fur trade, the two most likely times were in the winter of 1814-15 or in the spring of 1820. Some of the Jackson relatives were engaged seasonally in flatboating produce to the New Orleans market and David could have accompanied them on one of those trips.

It is not known whether David Jackson made arrangements to become a member of Ashley's party as a result of the much discussed advertisement in the Missouri papers or whether it was arranged through personal contact with Ashley or Henry. He and his brother George were living in the region adjacent to the lead mines of Missouri and George had known Ashley at least since 1810. It was not far from George's home to present Potosi in Washington County where Andrew Henry resided. George had clerked in Ste. Genevieve in at least one store which was engaged in furnishing supplies to the lead mines and could have known Henry also. At any rate David Jackson's plans for settling down as a farmer were altered abruptly in that spring of 1822.

A far greater number of men were recruited by Ashley from the Ste. Genevieve and Washington county areas of Missouri than has generally been supposed. Many employees so far unidentified by writers had settled in those areas. Several were known to the Jacksons personally.

Not much is known of David Jackson's movements during his first season in the Rocky Mountains. He made all preparations to start up the Missouri in early April and I have seen no evidence that he did not do so. In that case he would have been a member of Andrew Henry's group which started to leave St. Louis by April 3, 1822.

Jackson must have been employed to serve in a clerical capacity rather than as an expedition leader as he assumed the function early of maintaining a sort of temporary headquarters in the field. He became a steadying influence among the more boisterous spirits of the younger men in the group.

The first published information which has come to light in all these years on Jackson's presence with Ashley's men is William Waldo's account of Jackson's participation in the fight with the Arikara Indians when Ashley's men were attacked at the Arikara villages on June 2, 1823, while ascending the Missouri.

Waldo in his "Recollections of a Septuagenarian," says:

> . . . Sublette and Jackson after fighting bravely around the animals, until all were either killed or dispersed, fought their way through the crowded ranks of Indians, leaped into the river, and under a hail storm of arrows and balls, swam to the boats.[3]

William Waldo was an employee of David Jackson over a period of two years and should have known whereof he spoke. In addition the two families had known of each other for many years and David Jackson was associated with David, William, Lawrence L. and Daniel Waldo at various times or engaged in enterprises at the same places.

If Jackson had not returned to Missouri with Ashley from the 1822 expedition, he must have been accompanied by Jedediah Smith down the Missouri in 1823 in order to have been present at the fight, as Dale Morgan pointed out to me in a private letter.

---

[3] William Waldo, "Recollections of a Septuagenarian," in *Glimpses of the Past,* Missouri Historical Society (St. Louis, 1938), 82.

The next reference which can be applied to David Jackson is from Hiram Martin Chittenden.[4] After the first battle with the Arikara, Ashley and his men dropped down the river a safe distance and sent for reinforcements. In answer they were joined by Colonel Leavenworth with a contingent of men and Joshua Pilcher with a group of men of the Missouri Fur Company. Ashley's men were formed into a semi-military organization consisting of two groups. A man named as George C. Jackson was appointed a lieutenant in one group. The combined forces of Leavenworth, Ashley and Pilcher attacked the two villages on August 9-10, 1823, and the Arikara sued for peace.

The identity of the above George C. Jackson has given rise to several conjectures. My own personal opinion is that the name was meant for George E. Jackson, David's brother. I have several specimens of his signature and in them the "E" can easily be mistaken for a "C." That was the usual way in which he signed his name.

However, from what I know of the movements of the two brothers at that particular time, it is more likely that David was the one at the battle and that Ashley, having known George for a longer period of time and being familiar with his signature, was thinking of him when he submitted the names of his officers to Colonel Leavenworth.

George E. Jackson was busy raising a family at home along about that time, but he could have joined a relief group sent up the Missouri to help Ashley after the first battle and then returned home after their mission was accomplished. Such a group is said to have been formed and several names cannot be accounted for otherwise.

Family tradition places David Jackson in a fight with Indians along the Missouri during his fur trade experience and it is assumed that it was in the engagements with the Arikara.

---

[4] Hiram Martin Chittenden, *The American Fur Trade of the Far West* (New York, 1935 edition), 586.

The first written report that indicated Jackson's presence in the mountains with any reasonable degree of certainty was at the first annual rendezvous, held on Henry's Fork of Green River, present Utah, in July 1825.

General Ashley says in his letter to General Henry Atkinson, dated "Saint Louis, dec. 1, 1825":

> On the 1st day of july, *all the men in my employ or with whom I had any concern in the country,* together with twenty-nine, who had recently withdrawn from the Hudson Bay Company, making in all 120 men, were assembled in two camps near each other about 20 miles distant from the place appointed by me as a general rendezvous . . .[5] (Italics mine.)

If *all* of Ashley's men were present at the rendezvous that year, David Jackson was present, as he was one of them.

The first positive identification of Jackson in the fur trade which has been published, is his presence on Bear River in 1826 right after the summer rendezvous in Cache Valley that year. There William H. Ashley sold out his interest in the fur trade to J. S. Smith, D. E. Jackson and Wm. L. Sublette who began business as partners in a new firm to be known as Smith, Jackson & Sublette. On July 18, 1826, an agreement was entered into between General Ashley and the new partners "concerning goods to be brought to the mountains" the next year. That is the first preserved record of David E. Jackson's signature in the fur trade business.

That new partnership marked the beginning of the second era in the history of Ashley men in the Rocky Mountain fur trade.

From the moment the new partnership was formed the functions of the three partners became more specialized. Jedediah Smith became the explorer; David Jackson became the field manager, trying to keep a more or less settled

---

[5] Harrison Clifford Dale, "The Ashley Narrative," in *The Ashley-Smith Explorations and the Discovery of a Central Route to the Pacific, 1822-1829* (Glendale, Calif., 1941 edition), 152.

headquarters from which to direct the operations of the men in the field and to which the men could report; and to Bill Sublette fell the task of making the annual trip back to Missouri to deliver the year's catch of furs and bring back supplies.

Perhaps to Jackson fell the task of holding the men and business together because of his being somewhat older than the average employee, and partly because he had already apparently spent some time in that capacity under Ashley.

Certain it is that a guiding hand was necessary in the field in order to keep the business going and the men contented and satisfied. Without Jackson's personal supervision Jedediah Smith would not have been free to make his explorations, and Sublette would not have been wise to abandon the business in the mountains in order to bring in supplies. The importance of Jackson's contribution in this matter has been almost entirely overlooked by historians. Without a central location of some kind with someone in charge neither Smith nor Sublette would have had any place to report back to, nor would their business have lasted very long. So it became "the regular practice for Jackson to spend almost all his time in the mountains." [6]

During the winter of 1826-27, Jackson is said to have stayed in Cache Valley. Sublette left there on January 1, 1827, and started for St. Louis for the purpose of confirming the order with Ashley for a new outfit for the following season.

The annual rendezvous for 1827 was held at the south end of Bear Lake in present Utah. General Ashley had sent out supplies for that year. His caravan was accompanied by a small cannon on a carriage which was drawn by two mules. That was the first wheeled vehicle to cross South Pass. The trappers were practically all assembled by July 1 and the rendezvous broke up on July 13, 1827. Jedediah Smith ar-

6 Chittenden, *op. cit.*, 310.

rived from California on July 3 and planned another trip there. On his arrival he was met by a salute fired from Ashley's cannon. He planned to meet his partners again in one or two years at the head of the Snake River.

In the four years between July 1826 and August 1830, Jackson, according to family tradition, is said to have been back to Missouri at least once. Morgan states that Jackson accompanied Bill Sublette down to the States in the late summer of 1827, and that they returned to the mountains that fall.[7] If so, that would account for the tradition.

In this connection it may be noted that on October 5, 1827, Governor John Miller of Missouri issued a commission appointing George E. Jackson as justice of the peace of the newly created township of Jackson in the County of Ste. Genevieve. David may have had something to do with it.

Under date of October 1, 1827, Wm. H. Ashley issued a quitclaim to the firm of Smith, Jackson & Sublette for the sum of a note in his favor in the amount of $7,821, which he says has since been paid. So, Jackson and Sublette had reached the settlements by that date. Their party had been encamped near Lexington about the first of October, 1827.[8]

The rendezvous of 1828 was again held at Bear Lake in July and Jackson presumably was there. Smith had not yet returned from California.

After that rendezvous Jackson accompanied or led a party north and northwest into the Flathead and Kutenai lands of present western Montana and northern Idaho. Jackson and his men probably wintered near Flathead Lake, Montana. He was still in that area in the spring of 1829 when he was joined by Jedediah Smith back via Fort Vancouver from his second disastrous trip to California.

Smith met Jackson along the Flathead River north of

---

[7] Morgan, *West of Ashley*, 169.

[8] Sublette Papers, Mo. Hist. Soc.; and Morgan, "James B. Bruffee, Statement, October 1, 1827," in *West of Ashley*, 171.

Flathead Lake. The two worked their way down to Pierre's Hole on the west side of the Tetons in present Idaho and met Sublette there about the 5th of August, 1829. A general rendezvous was held that month. The gathering seems to have lasted two weeks or more.

Jackson's movements have not been definitely worked out for the remainder of that year of 1829, but when he cannot be accounted for otherwise he was almost always somewhere in the Snake Indian country along the Snake River or in Jackson Hole. The Snake country seems to have been his favorite grounds. It was also a more central location for use as a vantage point in overseeing the work of the various parties in the field and expediting the business. Jackson joined his partners at winter quarters on Wind River, present Wyoming, just before Christmas 1829.

Immediately after January 1, 1830, Sublette set out for St. Louis while Smith and Jackson decided to spend the rest of the winter on the Powder River to the northeast of their location on Wind River. They remained in that place until the first of April. Jackson then returned to the Snake country while Smith and party trapped farther to the northwest.

Sublette reached Missouri safely and set about making preparations at once for the return journey. His party left St. Louis in April, 1830. It consisted of eighty-one men mounted on mules. He also took along ten wagons, drawn by five mules each, and two dearborns, drawn by one mule each. This was the first time that wagons were ever taken to the Rocky Mountains by way of the overland route, thus demonstrating the practicability of that mode of travel. The caravan reached the meeting place in the Wind River Valley on July 16, 1830.

Jackson arrived at the rendezvous with a good catch of beaver.

At this rendezvous the firm of Smith, Jackson & Sublette

sold out to a new group called The Rocky Mountain Fur Company. It was made up of Thomas Fitzpatrick, Milton G. Sublette, Henry Fraeb, Jean Baptiste Gervais and James Bridger. The transfer was concluded August 4, 1830.

Various reasons have been advanced for this rather sudden action on the part of the three partners. The theory has been advanced that the death of Jedediah Smith's mother may have caused him to decide that he was needed at home and that the remaining partners were more or less forced to accede to his wishes. However, Jackson had lost four immediate relatives while in the mountains. Perhaps they all wanted to go home and mail which had been brought out by Sublette influenced their decision. Judging by their subsequent plans it seems more reasonable that the controlling factor in their decision was the fact that they would now be out of debt and financially able to set themselves up as landed proprietors.

Whatever the reason, the partners set out for Missouri the same day that the final transfer of the business was made. The ten wagons were brought back with them but the two dearborns were left behind. The return trip was uneventful and the route followed was good for wheeled vehicles. The last of the caravan arrived in St. Louis on October 11, 1830.

The value of the furs brought back by this last caravan of Smith, Jackson & Sublette netted the partners $84,499.14.[9] This was their best season financially in the mountains.

The partners set about almost at once drafting a letter to the Secretary of War, the Honorable John H. Eaton, detailing the significance of their accomplishments in the mountains. This was a five page letter dated St. Louis, October 29, 1830. The letter went to some length outlining the extent of their explorations in the West, the ease with which transportation could be accomplished to the Rocky Mountains and beyond, a description of the country, and

[9] Morgan, *Jedediah Smith*, 323.

suggested methods for dealing with the British in the Oregon country. Its contents were deemed of such importance that it was immediately printed as a Senate Executive Document and made available to the Congress and to the public.[10]

The authorship of this letter is still in doubt. The original has not been located. It obviously is a combination of the information and experience of all three partners and they may have availed themselves of the services of someone in St. Louis close to the government in its preparation or in its final form.

That winter of 1830-31 Jedediah Smith set about preparing a map of the western regions of the United States showing all the travels and geographical discoveries of the Ashley men. It was a landmark in mapping of the American West.

David Jackson contributed information and the results of his own explorations for that map. His greatest contribution is for the Snake River drainage basin. The originals of Smith's map have been lost, but the information from his was found superimposed on a base map of Fremont's in the files of the American Geographical Society of New York by Carl I. Wheat a few years ago. The transcription work has been ascribed to George Gibbs.[11]

That map bears a notation along the middle course of the Snake River across present southern Idaho reading as follows:

Most of what is known of this section of country has been derived from Mr. Jackson and such Partisans as have travelled through it. Apply this note to the opposite waters of Lewis river and the Owyhee River. *Smith.*

After Smith's death a eulogy was printed in the *Illinois Magazine* for June 1832. It was by an unknown writer and signed "Alton, March, 1832." That writer said in part:

[10] *Senate Exec. Doc. 39, 21* Cong., 2 sess., 21-23.
[11] See copy of that map in Morgan and Wheat, *op. cit.,* in back pocket.

. . . convinced as Smith was, of the inaccuracy of all the maps of that country, and of the little value they would be to hunters and travellers, he has, with the assistance of his partners, Sublitt [*sic*] and Jackson, and of Mr. S. Parkman, made a new, large and beautiful map; in which are embodied all that is correct of preceding maps, the known tracts of former travellers, his own extensive travels, the situation and number of various Indian tribes, and much other valuable information. This map is now probably the best extant, of the Rocky Mountains, and the country on both sides, from the States to the Pacific. . .[12]

Although David Jackson's contribution to the Smith map has been discounted, it might be but fair to point out that Jackson had learned the rudiments of surveying under his father while still a boy. He also, like most members of his branch of the Jackson family, possessed a true sense of direction and distance and the faculty of proper perspective.

Smith's map shows a "Sublette Lake" for what is now Yellowstone Lake and a "Jackson Lake" for the body of water in Jackson Hole which still bears that name, although those two lakes are not shown in their proper position with reference to each other and Jackson Lake is shown too large in proportion.

Smith's map is the first known time that David Jackson's name was applied on a map to a feature of the landscape.

In 1839, David H. Burr, geographer to the House of Representatives in Washington, published a map of the United States of North America which embodied all the features of Smith's map and showed his discoveries. Burr's map continued the use of the name "Jackson Lake."

"Jacksons L." is also shown on the "Map of the Oregon Territory, 1841" used by Commander Charles Wilkes, and from that time on David Jackson's name on the maps of that region was secure. The name "Yellowstone" was subsequently substituted for that of "Sublette Lake."

---

[12] " Captain Jedediah Strong Smith, A Eulogy . . .," in *Illinois Magazine,* June 1832, as reprinted in Edwin L. Sabin, *Kit Carson Days* (New York, 1935 edition), 823.

At some unspecified time during his career in the mountians the name "Jackson's Hole" had come to be applied by his comrades to the beautiful valley surrounding Jackson Lake. The first written record which has survived of that name being attributed to David Jackson is that by Warren Angus Ferris in the *Western Literary Messenger* of Buffalo, New York, in its issue dated July 29, 1843. Ferris published a series of articles in that magazine entitled "Life in the Rocky Mountains" relating his experiences in the fur trade in the Rocky Mountains. In that issue Ferris states:

> On the 4th [July 1832] we crossed the mountain, and descended into a large prairie valley, called Jackson's Big Hole. It lies due east of the Trois Tetons, and is watered by Lewis River. . . The Hole is surrounded by lofty mountains, and receives its name from one of the firm of Smith, Sublett and Jackson.[13]

Ferris also drafted a map in 1835 or 1836, apparently for publication with his narrative of "Life in the Rocky Mountains." On that map the name "Yellowstone L." appears on a map for the first time and the name is substituted for that of "Sublette Lake." "Teton L." is substituted for the name "Jackson Lake," but the name "Jacksons Hole" and "Little Hole" for Jacksons Little Hole appear for the first time on any map anywhere. Unfortunately the Ferris map was not published at that time, so it escaped public attention.[14]

Jackson Hole is still known by the name first given it. The name embraces the whole valley along the eastern base of the Teton Mountains.

From that time onward the names Jackson's Big Hole (now Jackson Hole), Jackson's Little Hole, Jackson Lake, and eventually the town of Jackson, Wyoming, came into general usage. They are all memorials to David E. Jackson.

Both Jackson and Sublette must have left St. Louis imme-

---

[13] Courtesy of The Grosvenor Library, Buffalo, New York.

[14] See copy of the Ferris map in W. A. Ferris, *Life in the Rocky Mountains,* ed. by Paul C. Phillips (Denver, 1940), insert between xiv-xv.

diately after furnishing Smith whatever information they contributed for his map. They both had urgent business elsewhere.

Jackson was trying to establish a homestead near his brother in what is now St. Francois County, Missouri. It was directly on the old original road north from Farmington to the Valle lead mines in present Jefferson County. David's brother, George, was in active management of his affairs during his absence, but George was now seriously ill and unable to do anything. David had four or five slaves and it is assumed that they were working on this homestead part of the time. During his absence he had transferred the slaves to his brother to be in his custody and be put to whatever use he saw fit. It is probable that David's personal servant, Jim, accompanied him in the mountains the latter part of his stay there.

On March 26, 1831, George E. Jackson deeded all the real estate owned by him in Ste. Genevieve County to David E. Jackson. This consisted of a half interest in the Establishment Trace (an old Spanish Land Grant) and the homestead on which George lived. George Jackson was on his deathbed and the reason for the transfer was to be sure to save the property for the family and save costs and uncertainties of administration of his estate.

George E. Jackson died on that same day. David subsequently deeded these same properties back to George's children. Return of custody of the slaves to David had already been arranged for and was subsequently carried out.

David had been quite busy that winter arranging for a merchandising trip to Santa Fe, New Mexico, with his partners. By April 7th he was back in St. Louis and executed a power of attorney to Joseph D. Grafton of Ste. Genevieve to act in his stead in all matters pertaining to the estate of George E. Jackson. That paper was witnessed by a clerk, E. S. Minter.

By that time plans for the Santa Fe expedition must have already been agreed upon and the merchandise purchased. The last wagons of the partners left St. Louis on April 10, 1831. They assembled for two weeks at Lexington, Missouri, to conclude their business and make final arrangements for the trip.

Among the new personnel was a young man from Connecticut named Jonathan Trumbull Warner. He hired out as clerk to Jedediah Smith. Smith's two brothers, Peter and Austin, and his friend Samuel Parkman, were also along. Mr. Minter went as clerk to Jackson and Sublette. Thomas Fitzpatrick arrived from the mountains for his yearly supplies just as they were leaving the settlements. It was decided that he too should accompany them as far as Santa Fe where he could be provisioned.

On setting out the caravan consisted of eighty-five men and twenty-three mule drawn wagons. Ten of the wagons belonged to Jackson and Sublette, eleven are credited to Smith, one belonged to Samuel Flournoy of Independence, and the last was the joint property of Smith, Jackson & Sublette. It carried a small cannon which could be unlimbered and quickly made ready for use. Another wagon, drawn by oxen, was the property of two men named Wells [sometimes called Mills] and Chadwick.[15]

The caravan broke camp on May 4th, 1831, near the Big Blue and headed out over the prairie for Santa Fe. Before reaching the Pawnee Branch of the Arkansas a band of several hundred Comanche and Gros Ventre Indians attempted to charge them but were driven off by the use of the small cannon. Mr. Minter, the clerk, next fell slightly behind to hunt antelope and was surprised and killed by a party of Pawnees on May 19th.

The leaders of the caravan decided to try what has since become well known as the Cimarron cutoff in order to

---

15 Morgan, *Jedediah Smith,* 326 and 434, note 42.

shorten the distance; however, that was usually a two day trip without water. Water had to be hauled in barrels for the men and mules. On this trip the wagons were heavily laden and the deep sand slowed them to a snail's pace.

On the third day the men were crazed with thirst and Smith and Fitzpatrick set out in search of water. Jackson and Sublette kept on with the wagons over what appeared to be the trail. On May 27th Smith and Fitzpatrick separated in their search. Smith reached a dry hole in the bed of the Cimarron and began to dig for water. He was surprised by a small band of hostile Comanches and killed.

That evening, the main caravan, which had kept on, encamped on the Cimarron at a place where they found some water. The next morning a large party of about fifteen hundred Blackfeet and Gros Ventres approached as if to attack them. Fortunately Sublette was able to negotiate with them and they passed on without further molestation.

The caravan continued along the Cimarron for that day and encamped. A band of Gros Ventres surrounded them before dawn, but were successfully frightened off.

The first signs of civilization were reached at the small village of San Miguel, New Mexico. The caravan continued on and entered Santa Fe, July 4, 1831.

Changes had to be made in the organization on account of the death of Smith. A new partnership was entered into by Jackson and Sublette to handle the business in the mountains formerly conducted by Smith, Jackson & Sublette. The latter duly entered their merchandise at the custom house in Santa Fe on July 8, 1831, and proceeded to dispose of it as rapidly as possible.[16]

David Waldo was living in New Mexico at the time and was engaged in the Santa Fe trade and purchasing furs. He was a long-standing acquaintance of David Jackson. Jack-

---

[16] Customs Manifest of Jackson and Sublette dated July 8, 1831, Mexican Archives of New Mexico No. 2878, State Records Center and Archives (Santa Fe),.

son learned of the lucrative possibilities of purchasing mules in California for the Missouri and southern market from one Henry Hook, a fellow member of the Masonic Order. Hook was from the same part of the country as Jackson, had just recently arrived in New Mexico from California via Guaymas, Sonora, and was convinced of the profits to be made from such a venture. Jackson had already been thinking of making a trip to California and, since this would furnish him with an opportunity, he was easily persuaded to do so.

In order to provide for the disposition of his remaining merchandise and in order to continue in business in the Santa Fe trade, which promised to be profitable, Jackson formed another partnership in which David Waldo was to attend to that part of the business.

By the latter part of August, Jackson, Sublette and Fitzpatrick had all been in Taos, New Mexico, which was the headquarters for American trappers in the Southwest. There Jackson met Ewing Young who had returned from California in April from a trapping and trading expedition the preceding year. Young had also become aware of the possibilities of the mule trade with California and, having met Captain Cooper of Monterey, had discussed it with him in San Jose during the previous year. Young must have convinced Jackson that his knowledge of the route and his fur trading experience in the Southwest would be indispensible to him. He was taken in as junior member of a temporary partnership known as Jackson, Waldo and Young for purposes of the trip. There is no evidence that Young invested any money in the partnership, but he had an interest in the outfits of some of the trappers. He was put in charge of one group of men to do the trapping along the way and meet Jackson later in California.

On August 18, 1831, in Santa Fe, Henry Hook wrote a letter of introduction for David Jackson to Captain Cooper in Monterey requesting his assistance in purchasing mules. Captain Cooper may also have belonged to the Masonic Order as Hook ends his letter "I remain yours Fraternally." [17]

On August 24, Ewing Young also wrote a letter to Captain Cooper from Taos requesting aid for Jackson in the mule buying venture.[18] The following day, August 25th, Jackson left Taos for Santa Fe, and on August 29th, he and a party of ten men planned to set out from Santa Fe for California. They did all finally get on the road by September 6th.

Jackson planned to reach California as expeditiously as possible without stopping to trap along the way. For that reason he chose the southern route by way of the Santa Rita del Cobre mines, Tucson and the Gila.

As finally composed, the party consisted of Mr. Jackson, his negro slave Jim, and nine men. One was Peter Smith, a younger brother of Jedediah, who had accompanied the caravan from Missouri. Another was probably William Waldo. It was about this time that William entered the employ of David Jackson which continued for a period of two years. He may have joined the caravan upon leaving Missouri or he could have been in New Mexico with his brother, David, and joined there. Another was Jonathan Trumbull Warner, the historian of the trip. After the death of Jedediah Smith and the arrival of the caravan in Santa Fe, Warner had found himself without employment and his health being improved he decided to continue on to California. Still another may have been Moses Carson. Job Dye lists Carson as a member of Young's group. However, in 1850 in California, Moses Carson told David Jackson's nephew that he and David "came together to this coast trapping and that (Jackson) took away 80 mule loads of furs and that he never heard from him after that." As will be

<hr />

[17] The original of this letter is in the Vallejo Documents, Bancroft Library, Univ. of Calif., Berkeley.   [18] Original letter in Vallejo Documents, *loc. cit.*

explained later, another member may have been Antoine
Leroux, at least for part of the way. At least two were said
to be native guides from New Mexico. Leroux could have
been classed as one of those. The remainder of the party is
still anonymous.

The main authority for the overland trip to California is
found in various versions of the "Reminiscences" of Jonathan Trumbull Warner.[19] These are rather confusing if read
independently, but by combining them with an expert
knowledge of the available routes it can be worked out
satisfactorily.

The party started south down the Rio Grande by way of
the old Spanish Camino Real as far as the vicinity of Valverde. Each man had a riding mule; there were seven pack
mules, and what interested Warner most was the fact that
five of the pack mules were loaded with Mexican silver
dollars. From Valverde they took a newer route down the
west side of the river. This route had been used for some
time by American parties on their way to trap the Gila, to
reach the Copper Mines, and even to go back and forth to
the province of Sonora by way of the presidio town of
Janos, Chihuahua.

Just south of Hot Springs the route left the river somewhat and bore southwest toward the Santa Rita Copper
Mines. That route was later followed by General Kearny
with the Army of the West in 1846.

The copper mines were still being worked by Robert
McKnight and Stephen Courcier and it is probable that

---

[19] There are several versions of Warner's reminiscences in manuscript in the
Bancroft Library; a printed version entitled "Reminiscences of Early California
from 1831 to 1846," in *Annual Publications of the Historical Society of Southern
California, 1907-1908* (Los Angeles, 1909), 176-93; and still another version, the
original of which was consulted by this writer, in the Holliday Collection, Arizona
Pioneers' Historical Society (Tucson). There are also some newspaper accounts.
I have also consulted Job F. Dye, "Recollections of a Pioneer of California," in
the *Santa Cruz Sentinel* (California), May 1, May 8 and May 15, 1869. I have relied
on Warner for the most part.

James Kirker and other former trapper friends and acquaintances were also there. The party should have reached the mines easily well before the end of September.

From there the route led southwest over the old Janos Trail as far as the Ojo de Vaca (Cow Springs) in the northwest corner of present Luna County, New Mexico. That part of the route was later followed by Colonel Philip St. George Cooke and the Mormon Battalion in 1846.

From Cow Springs to the abandoned mission of San Xavier del Bac, David Jackson's party was opening a new direct route between New Mexico and Arizona. Their route proceeded from water hole to water hole by way of Doubtful Canyon, Apache Pass, and Dragoon Wash to the San Pedro River just north of present St. David, Arizona. There they crossed the north end of the old San Pedro Ranch on the west side of the river and proceeded to the Cienega Creek and thence to the San Xavier Mission.[20] From there they reached the presidio and settlement of Tucson over the old Indian and Spanish trail from the south.

This direct route from Cow Springs to San Xavier had been traversed in sections over its complete length by various Spanish and Mexican military parties under military members of the Elias-Gonzalez family of the northern frontier of New Spain and Mexico, but it had not been traversed in its entirety on any one particular expedition on account of Indian hostility. After Jackson opened that route there is no record of its having been used again until the Frémont Association party, of which Robert Eccleston was a member with Colonel John C. "Jack" Hays as guide, passed over it

---

[20] Warner is here speaking in general terms when he refers to the San Pedro Ranch. That ranch as originally constituted was a Spanish land grant which was never fully confirmed. It was first granted to Don Ygnacio Pérez of Sonora, Mexico, who also received the San Bernardino grant. Under Pérez the San Pedro Ranch extended from the plains of Cananea north along the San Pedro River to Tres Alamos.

In the period 1822-1834 under the new Mexican regime the San Pedro Ranch was broken up into several parcels and granted to various members of the Elías-Gonzalez family. One of those was a much smaller San Pedro ranch.

with minor deviations in October and early November, 1849.[21]

Jackson's party should have reached Tucson by early October, 1831. Jackson must have been one of the first American citizens to have ever seen the mission of San Xavier and the old walled pueblo of Tucson. He may have been the first.

In Tucson, Jackson made an attempt to procure a native guide from that place to the Colorado River and beyond. No one in Tucson could be found who had any knowledge of the route. A messenger was sent to the Altar district in present Sonora, as it was thought that would be a more likely place to procure a guide. None could be found there either.

It is supposed that Jackson sent some native person from Tucson to Altar to make inquiry, and it is likely that he would also have dispatched some Spanish speaking person from his own party to accompany him. In this connection it is noted that on July 22, 1852, in the vicinity of the abandoned ranch of Calabasa [Calabasas] [22] John Russell Bartlett, boundary commissioner, noted in his journal: "This Calabasa, I was told by Leroux, was a thriving establishment when he visited it twenty years ago." [23] That statement puts Antoine Leroux in that vicinity close enough to the time the Jackson party was in Tucson for Leroux to have been with him either going to or returning from California. Leroux could have remained on the Colorado or in Arizona while the rest of the party proceeded on to California. Leroux had gone up the Missouri with Ashley's men in 1822 and remained there for two years. He would certainly

---

[21] George P. Hammond and Edward H. Howes, eds., *Overland to California on the Southwestern Trail, 1849: Diary of Robert Eccleston* (Berkeley and Los Angeles, 1950).

[22] The old ranch of Calabasas here referred to was thirteen miles north of the international boundary at present Nogales, Arizona.

[23] John Russell Bartlett, *Personal Narrative of Explorations and Incidents in Texas, New Mexico, California, Sonora, and Chihuahua* (New York, 1854), Vol. II, p. 307.

have been recognized by Jackson when seeing him again in New Mexico.

It was found impossible to procure a guide while in Tucson so the party started out for the Pima Villages on the Gila. From Tucson to "the Red River of the West" [the Colorado] the route was the same as that followed in 1775 by Juan Bautista de Anza and his band of colonists en route to found the city of San Francisco.

Upon approaching the Gila River the party must have noticed off to their right what appeared to be the ruins of a large building on the horizon. Their curiosity may have been aroused enough that they detoured to visit it. This was the famed Casa Grande, visited by Father Kino and all early Spanish and Mexican explorers who traveled that route.[24]

The Gila River had been followed and trapped by bands of American trappers all the way to its junction with the Colorado, but it is unknown whether any who had been over that part of the route were along with Jackson.

The Colorado was crossed at the lower crossing six miles downstream from its junction with the Gila, and within sight of Pilot Knob. From that point onward Jackson's route deviates somewhat from that of Don Juan Bautista de Anza. The route Jackson opened was followed by Colonel Cooke with the Mormon Battalion and later by the Butterfield Overland Mail. On this section across the Colorado Desert and on to the Warner's Ranch area, Jackson was again a pathbreaker as far as Americans were involved.

---

[24] I have never noticed it pointed out in this connection, but "P. Weaver" scratched his name on the walls of Casa Grande with the date "1832." Job Dye in his *Recollections* (Los Angeles, 1951) lists a Powel Weaver as accompanying the same party as himself from Arkansas to New Mexico in 1830. Again, a Paulin de Jesus Guiver (Weaver) was baptized at Taos, New Mexico, Aug. 26, 1832, and married Maria Dolores Martin there on Sept. 10, 1832 – Fray Angélico Chávez, "New Names in New Mexico, 1820-1850," in *El Palacio* (Santa Fe), Nov., Dec., 1957, p. 379.

It is possible that Pauline Weaver was one of the members of Young's party and that on the return trip with Jackson he left his name on the walls of Casa Grande.

His party passed by way of First Wells (later Cooke's Wells), the water hole of Alamo Mocho, on past the site of Calexico, California, thence across to and up the Carrizo Creek to Vallecito and over the divide to the present Warner Valley.

Jonathan Warner was so impressed with the beautiful valley filled with majestic oaks and surrounded by lofty mountains and possessed of hot and cold running water that he remained in California; later, having procured a large grant of land including the entire valley, he came back to it and settled down. It is now the site of the famous resort of Warner's Hot Springs and of the giant size Warner Ranch.

The party continued on through the groves of oaks in the direction of Los Angeles as far as the Indian village of Temecula. There they decided to change their course for the Mission of San Luis Rey and San Diego. The Mormon Battalion later did the same.[25]

They paused at Mission San Luis Rey and proceeded on to San Diego which they reached in early November 1831. From there they retraced their steps to San Luis Rey, passed on by way of the Mission of San Juan Capistrano and reached the pueblo of Los Angeles on December 5, 1831.

Jackson was still in the Los Angeles-San Gabriel area when he dispatched a letter dated December 24, 1831, to Captain Cooper at Monterey requesting his aid in arranging up and down the coast to purchase up to one thousand mules at up to eight dollars a head, depending on quality.[26]

As soon as he could conveniently do so, Jackson started up the coast himself by way of the old Camino Real from mission site to mission site. He left Mr. Warner and one other

---

[25] The city of Temecula, California, now has a monument to the memory of "those who passed that way." Among others, the names of Cooke, Jackson and Warner are proudly inscribed. *They Passed This Way, Biographical Sketches, Tales of Historic Temecula Valley at the Crossroads of California's Southern Immigrant Trail* (Laguna House, Temecula, 1970), sponsored by Temecula Valley Chamber of Commerce.   [26] Vallejo Documents, Bancroft Library.

man in Los Angeles to look after his property already acquired.

He traveled as far north "as the missions on the southern shores of the bay of San Francisco." The wording of Mr. Warner here is somewhat ambiguous. Except for that statement there is no definite evidence that Jackson actually reached as far north as San Francisco. He did visit the missions of Santa Clara and San Jose, both of which were opposite the extreme southern end of the bay. If his success in purchasing mules was only moderate, it is very likely that he proceeded on to San Francisco where he would have a double opportunity, that being the location of both a mission and a presidio. He undoubtedly stopped at Monterey on his way north to visit Captain Cooper and transact his business with him.

On the return journey the party was detained for fourteen days opposite the mission of Soledad on account of high water in the Salinas River. They were at the mission of San Miguel by February 22, 1832, and reached Los Angeles again in the latter part of March.

Here the Jackson party met up with the party of Ewing Young which had arrived in the pueblo about the same time. The combined forces rendezvoused at the Sierra Ranch on the Santa Ana river. They had about six hundred mules and one hundred horses out of the thousand or more that had been anticipated. They set out for the Colorado River in May and reached it in June over the same route used in going to California.

When they arrived at the Colorado they found the river in flood and nearly bank full. They experienced considerable difficulty and it took twelve days to get all the animals and men across the river at the lower crossing below Yuma.

Here Jackson gave Young three thousand dollars in cash to purchase additional mules and follow him later; Young also received a large outfit of arms, ammunition, tobacco, steel traps, etc. (said to be valued at around seven thousand dollars), belonging jointly to Jackson, Waldo and Young. Young and five men, including Jonathan Warner, Job F. Dye and Moses Carson, then returned to Los Angeles.

Six and one-half bales of skins were turned over to Jackson. With these Jackson and the remainder of the combined Jackson and Young parties set out on their return journey to New Mexico over the same route used by Jackson on the outward trip. It was during the month of June, the weather was hottest of the season and water was scarce. Several mules are said to have been lost on account of the heat. Lieutenant Colonel Philip St. George Cooke with the Mormon Battalion, writing in his journal fourteen and a half years later on the evening of December 20, 1846, at a point sixty-two miles from Tucson and ten from the Gila River said:

> . . . but on the other hand it is said to have been an extraordinary drought here for several years. A Mr. Jackson once lost many of a small drove of mules he took through in an imprudent manner in July.[27]

It should be noted that at least two men thought to have been with Jackson were with Cooke as guides, Antoine Leroux and Pauline Weaver. That may be one of the reasons Cooke was guided over the same identical route.

Jackson's party continued on in spite of the heat and lack of water and reached Santa Fe the first week of July, 1832, with a large part of their herd and the six and one-half bales of beaver skins. The mules were probably held in the vicinity of Santa Fe while the bales of beaver skins were said to have been concealed temporarily in a hiding place near there. Information to that effect was given to the authorities about July 12, 1832, by one Manuel Leal who seems to have been one of those who returned with Jackson.[28]

27 Ralph P. Bieber, ed., "Cooke's Journal of the March of the Mormon Battalion, 1846-1847," in *Exploring Southwest Trails, 1846-1854* (Glendale, Calif., 1938), 166.

28 Statement of Francisco Rascon(?), Santa Fe, July 12, 1832, Mexican Archives of New Mexico, 3209, State Records Center and Archives.

This action aroused suspicion on the part of the New Mexican authorities. As a result several very confidential statements were taken from various natives in regard to the movements of Yaqueson, Baldo & Juiaquin Yon [Jackson, Waldo and Young] and the extent and value of their cargo.[29] The trouble with the authorities was evidently worked out satisfactorily in some manner.

Jackson and Waldo had some commercial dealings with Alexander LeGrand in the summer of 1831. In the late fall of 1831 a newcomer had arrived in New Mexico. His name was Albert Pike, late from New England. He was still in New Mexico in July 1832, when Jackson's party arrived there. LeGrand seems to have exerted some influence on the immediate future destination of both Jackson and Pike.[30]

If he ever seriously entertained the idea in the first place, Jackson abandoned the plan of driving his mules through Texas to Louisiana. While it was still summer, Jackson apparently started back in the direction of Missouri with that part of his livestock which had not been disposed of in New Mexico. Young Ira G. Smith, Jedediah's younger brother, had arrived in Santa Fe in the summer to meet his brother Peter. Peter had forty-five mules left from his share in the California venture. Ira was delegated to conduct these mules to Missouri.[31] It is assumed that he was a member of the Jackson party.

Somewhere along the route, probably along the Arkansas, Jackson must have sent some of his mules on to Missouri and directed some to the Cherokee lands. He was at Fort Gibson by the fall of 1832, supposedly at the same time that

---

[29] Statements relating to the embargo of the furs of Juiaquin Yon (Ewing Young), Santa Fe, July 12-25, 1832, Mexican Archives of New Mexico, 3209. Courtesy of Dr. Myra Ellen Jenkins.

[30] Since both Jackson and Pike were headed for the same destination upon leaving New Mexico that summer, I have never been able to understand why Pike did not accompany Jackson's party.

[31] Stella D. Hare, "Jedediah Smith's Younger Brother, Ira," in *The Pacific Historian* (Stockton, Calif.), vol. 11, no. 3, Summer 1967, p. 44.

Washington Irving was there.[32] It is possible that some mules were being held elsewhere, or Jackson could have sent for more from New Mexico.

David Jackson's movements are difficult to reconstruct for the next year. On February 22, 1833, he was back in Ste. Genevieve where on that day he deeded the George E. Jackson homestead back to George's son, Edward G. Jackson. A month later, on March 20, 1833, Jackson was in St. Louis where he and William L. Sublette settled their old accounts.[33]

Jackson's health had been poor ever since he had left Santa Fe and he wanted to return there or to the mountains at the first opportunity. He always planned to return at least to the Santa Fe trade personally, and he nursed a secret desire to settle in California at some future time. He had money invested in the Santa Fe trade with David Waldo, and continued to do so up until the time of his death.

In the meantime William Waldo had been tending a great number of mules for Jackson somewhere in the area of the Cherokee lands. Jackson was somewhere in Tennessee and adjoining territory. In the fall of 1833 Jackson sent his son, W. P. Jackson, across from Memphis, Tennessee, to Fort Smith-Van Buren, Arkansas, area where Waldo had been holding about two hundred animals for him. The son crossed 133 mules to one hundred miles beyond Memphis and had sold some in Arkansas.[34]

For the next four years Jackson's movements were dictated more by the state of his health than his wishes. He had

[32] For Irving's visit to Fort Gibson see Washington Irving, "A Tour on the Prairies," in *The Crayon Miscellany* (New York, 1835, and subsequent editions).

[33] David E. Jackson's Receipt for Accounts Settled, March 20, 1833, Sublette Papers (Mo. Hist. Soc.).

[34] It must have been as a result of this employment with Jackson that William Waldo met his future wife. He married Elizabeth Ely Vaill, daughter of a missionary to the Osage, at Union Mission, about 25 miles from Fort Gibson, Jan. 23, 1834. See "Introduction," p. 60, in Waldo's *Recollections of a Septuagenarian* (1938 reprint).

money invested in Tennessee and the South, proved up on his homestead in Missouri, invested money in lead mines at Rundlettsville in the Virginia Mines district in Union County, Missouri, and was planning on active participation in the Santa Fe trade and another trip to California the moment his health permitted. In the spring of 1834 he had definitely expected to start for Santa Fe or the mountains again. In the late fall of 1835 he was planning to go to the California coast in the spring of 1836 and take one of his sons along. Poor health intervened in both projects. Jackson never saw or heard from Ewing Young again after leaving him on "the Red River of the West." One of the reasons for his interest in a California trip was probably to force a settlement with Young.

As a result of the order issued by President Jackson in the summer of 1836 forbidding the treasury to accept anything but gold or silver in payment for further sales of public lands, there was a tightening of credit already being felt in the western areas where David Jackson had his investments. The result was the financial panic of 1837 which swept the country.

In January 1837, Jackson went to the Paris, Tennessee, area to attempt to make some collections on outstanding investments which he had made with citizens there. He arrived at the home of one of his partners just at the time they were all down with typhoid fever. He contracted the disease himself and was forced to put up at a tavern in Paris. In the meantime Jackson's creditors in his mining ventures were being sued by their own creditors. They in turn instituted suits against Jackson in order to get money to pay off their own suits. However, Jackson was unable to attend to any business on account of his physical condition. His son, W. P. Jackson, was dying in Missouri that same year.

Due to his weakened condition and his chronic poor health Jackson was unable to throw off the typhoid fever.

He lingered for eleven months during which time he was unable to do anything. He died from the effects of that illness at Paris, Tennessee, on December 24, 1837.[35]

An attempt was made to settle Jackson's estate at various times in four different states without any apparent references to each other. The settlement of his affairs was also dragged over a period of several years in at least three different places in Missouri.

At the June 1846 ('45), term of the Clackamas County Court in Oregon, Daniel Waldo in behalf of his brother David Waldo, brought suit against the administrator of the estate of Ewing Young for a settlement of the amount owed by Young to Jackson and Waldo. That court found that the deceased was one of the partners of the plaintiff and that the estate was indebted to the plaintiff, but in an amount uncertain. The court then appointed the presiding judge of the court to examine the books and papers of the plaintiff and ascertain the amount due said plaintiff.[36]

At a subsequent meeting of the court (apparently in August, 1846) a report was submitted "stating that there appeared to be due from said estate to the plaintiff the sum of four thousand three hundred and Eighty dollars fifty Eight cents."

The Court proceeded to rule as follows:

It is therefore considered by the Court that the said plaintiff recover of and from the Administrator of the Estate of Ewing Young the sum of four thousand three hundred and Eighty dollars and fifty Eight cents, together with his costs in this behalf laid out and expended.[37]

The Provisional Government of Oregon had been organized to take charge of Young's estate. They controlled

---

[35] I have been told by genealogists that there was no typhoid epidemic in that part of the South at the time and therefore Jackson could not have had that disease. Nevertheless, that was diagnosed as the cause of his death.

[36] Case of David Waldo vs. Administrator of the Estate of Ewing Young, Clackamas County Court Records, p. 17 (State Archives Center, Salem, Ore.).

[37] *Ibid.*, 20.

the money and property of the estate and had been instrumental in appointing the administrator. Daniel Waldo then petitioned the legislature of Oregon in behalf of his brother David and Thomas Jeffreys his attorney, for payment of the above judgment against the estate of Ewing Young.

The legislature failed to take any positive action even though suit was brought for settlement in the supreme court of the territory. The supreme court delayed a decision. The remaining money from the estate had been used to construct a jail and was no longer available. The court decided that the claim was not properly presented, or at least they were so advised. The Mexican War was now imminent and David Waldo had been appointed a captain in Colonel Doniphan's Missouri Regiment. As a result the claim was never brought to a definite conclusion in the Oregon courts.[38]

David E. Jackson's contributions have thus far gone unrecognized mostly because they were the result of joint efforts of his partners and partly because his individual accomplishments have been unknown and he has had no champion to plead his cause.

However, through the joint efforts of all, the Southern Pass through the Rockies was first identified correctly and crossed, a wheeled vehicle crossed the continental divide for the first time, wagons were first used on the Oregon Trail as far as the continental divide, Americans reached the Pacific coast overland, the whole country was explored from the Canadian to the present Mexican border throughout the Rocky Mountains, the first map was made which showed the correct drainage pattern in the Rocky Mountains, and the Oregon country was saved for the Union.

Individually, Jackson first opened the direct route from New Mexico to Arizona through the Apache country; he

---

[38] See F. G. Young, "Ewing Young and his Estate," in *Oregon Historical Society Quarterly*, XXI, no. 3, September 1920, and compare with original documents in Oregon State Archives (Salem).

laid out the best watered course across the Colorado desert which was later followed by the Army of the West, the Mormon Battalion, used by the Butterfield Overland Mail and by the '49ers who came that way. He took Jonathan Trumbull Warner to California and first showed him the Warner Ranch country and lastly he unwittingly provided the money to set up the first organized government in Oregon.

Of all the memorials to the Rocky Mountain fur traders, that to David E. Jackson is the most sublime. Jackson Hole, "the crossroads of the fur trade," and Jackson Lake, both lying at the eastern base of the Teton Range in Wyoming, have together been called one of the most beautiful areas in nature. (Along with the Vale of Kashmir, Jackson Hole has been listed as one of the seven most beautiful spots in the known world.) A great part of it is still in its primeval state. Jackson's passing went unnoticed except by members of his immediate family, but his memorial lives on.

Milton G. Sublette*

by DOYCE B. NUNIS, JR.
University of Southern California

The *Daily Missouri Republican,* in its issue of June 16, 1837, carried a somber announcement:

> Died – On 5th of April last, at Fort William, River Platte, Milton G. Sublette, long known as one of the most enterprising Indian traders of the Rocky Mountains. The deceased first embarked in the Indian trade as early as 1822, and by his intrepid bravery soon acquired an influence amongst his associates which he retained until the hour of his death. The hardy pioneers of the Rocky Mountains, in his death have met an irreparable loss, which they will long mourn.[1]

Milton Green Sublette, "Thunderbolt of the Rocky Mountains,"[2] at the age of thirty-six, was dead.

The second son of Phillip Allen Sublette, Milton was born in Somerset, Kentucky, probably in 1801. His mother was Isabella Whitley, daughter of a famed Kentuckian, Colonel William Whitley.[3] The Sublettes were descendants of French Huguenot refugees who settled at Manakin Town, Virginia, in 1700. During succeeding generations, the Sublettes migrated to Kentucky in search of the advan-

---

* This biographical sketch first appeared in *Montana Magazine,* XIII (Summer 1963), 52-63. It is here republished in a revised form by permission.

[1] Hiram M. Chittenden, *American Fur Trade of the Far West,* volume I, incorrectly dates Milton's death – the 1902 and 1954 editions (p. 254) stating Dec. 19, 1836; the 1935 edition (p. 252) stating Dec. 19, 1838. This error has found continued vogue in much of the literature dealing with the fur trade.

[2] William Waldo, "Recollections of a Septuagenarian," in *Glimpses of the Past,* v, pp. 65-71 (hereinafter cited *Waldo Mems.*), quotes this nickname for Milton.

[3] John E. Sunder, *Bill Sublette, Mountain Man* (Norman, Okla., 1959), ch. 1; Doyce B. Nunis, Jr., "The Sublettes of Kentucky: Their Early Contribution to the Opening of the West," in *Register* of the Kentucky Historical Society, LVII (Jan. 1959), 21. (Hereinafter cited as Nunis, "Sublettes of Kentucky.")

tages offered on the frontier – land and opportunity – moving west after the Revolutionary War.[4]

Eventually, Phillip Allen Sublette and his family settled at Crab Orchard, Kentucky. There he reared his children: William Lewis, Milton Green, Pinckney, Andrew Whitley, Solomon Perry, Sophronia Fullen, Mary (Polly), and Sally.

In the fall of 1817, the family moved to Missouri, settling at St. Charles. Within a few years, the parents died, leaving their offspring in the charge of near relatives and their eldest son, William.[5]

For the five Sublette sons, life at St. Charles was a splendid training ground for frontier survival and existence. There they were exposed to the hardships of primitive living on the fringe of American civilization. At the same time, they grew up watching enterprising fur traders go forth to harvest the riches of the upper Missouri, for St. Charles was a significant port of call for such expeditions. Destined to play a large part in forging the paths of empire for America, the experiences afforded by the Sublettes' childhood and environment fittingly prepared them to meet the frontier's challenge.

By 1822, St. Louis was the undisputed gateway to the trans-Mississippi West. The Santa Fe trade already beckoned the adventuresome southward, while the upper Missouri basin awaited the threatening onslaught from ambitious and enterprising frontiersmen. Wealth and empire were on the western horizon.

Responding to that attractive lure, William H. Ashley

---

[4] Doyce B. Nunis, Jr., "The Sublettes: A Study of a Refugee Family in the Eighteenth Century," in *Virginia Magazine of History and Biography*, LXIX (Jan. 1961), 42-66. A detailed genealogy will be found in Cameron Allen, "The (Soblet, Subley) Sublette Family of Manakintown, King William Parish, Virginia," *Detroit Society for Genealogical Research Magazine*, 27-29 (1963-66), beginning in the Fall 1963 issue.   [5] Sunder, *Bill Sublette*, Chs. I-II.

formed a partnership in 1821 with Andrew Henry, an experienced, longtime fur trader and Missouri resident, for the exploitation of the upper Missouri basin's fur fields. Both William and Milton heeded his call for volunteers. At least by 1823 both of them made their debut as trappers in the employ of Ashley and Henry. From that moment on, the name of Sublette became a by-word on the fur frontier.

Standing well over six feet, large of stature, strong of arm, audacious, "reckless of life and money," Milton was the prototype of a fictionalized fur man.[6] By 1828, his name and exploits secured to him an envied frontier fame.

Milton's activities prior to 1826 are none too clear. In all probability he gained his apprentice experience alongside his brother, William, in trapping and trading on the upper Missouri under the Ashley-Henry banner.[7] His legendary reputation, however, was earned in the fur trade of the Southwest. It began in 1826.

In September of that year, Milton was engaged in trapping the Gila Valley as a member of a group of Mountain Men who had been recruited that spring in St. Louis by an experienced Southwesterner, Ewing Young. Milton's party was commanded by Le Duke and Thomas L. Smith. During the course of the hunt, while taking up beaver traps, the Coyotero Apaches surprised the trappers. In the ensuing fight, Milton was hit in the leg, but was saved from an Indian death by the quick action of Smith, who carried him off to safety. Driven back to the Rio Grande by the avid

---

[6] *Waldo Mems.*, 70-71; Dale L. Morgan, *Jedediah Smith* (Indianapolis, 1953), 239, who labels Milton, "rambunctious"; David Lavender, *Bent's Fort* (Garden City, N.Y., 1954), 70.

[7] The evidence on the date of entry of William and Milton into the fur trade is argumentative, and is summarized in my article: Nunis, "Sublettes of Kentucky," *notes* 30 and 34, pp. 30-31. Sunder, *Bill Sublette*, 36, places William in the 1823 party, and on p. 30, suggests that Milton, "if we may believe the available evidence – had entered the fur trade before 1823."

hostility of the Indians, Young consolidated his field men into a single fur battalion.[8]

Young's company roster included Isaac Williams, Ceran St. Vrain, John Rowland, Sylvestre Pratte, James Pattie, and Miguel Robidoux, as well as Smith and Milton. Some ninety-odd trappers operating more or less as independent parties, yet dependent because of Indian hostility, emboldened Young to lead the hunters back into Apache territory in search of beaver.[9]

The 1826-1827 season proved to be a dangerous one. After trapping up the Salt and Verde River, as reported by James Ohio Pattie, the Young company followed down the Gila to the Colorado. Going up the latter, they entered Mohave Indian country. When they refused to pay the tribute demanded, the trappers fought their way clear, leaving sixteen natives dead. From there Young's men continued upstream to the mouth of the San Juan. After journeying along the banks of the San Juan, the party returned to the Colorado, following it for some distance. Then crossing over to the South Platte near the vicinity of present-day Denver, the company moved on to the Upper Arkansas. In their descent

[8] There is a conflict in the evidence bearing on which party Milton served with first. H. D. Barrows, "The Story of an Old Pioneer [the life of William Wolfskill]," in Wilmington [Calif.] *Journal,* Oct. 20, 1886, states Milton served in a party of eleven under Wolfskill. Also, see Barrow's article, "William Wolfskill, The Pioneer," in *Annual Publications of the Historical Society of Southern California,* v (1902), 290-91. "The Story of an Old Trapper. Life and Adventures of the Late Peg-leg Smith," in San Francisco *Bulletin,* Oct. 26, 1886, states that Milton was with him [Thomas L. Smith] and Le Duke in a party of five. Since Smith reports the wounding of Milton, this writer tends to lean toward his version, for ten years later, Milton was to succumb from a "fungus" in his leg. (This will be discussed later.) Morgan, *Jedediah Smith,* 238, says Milton was with Pratte in a party of fifteen in 1826.

[9] For details of the various hunting parties in the Southwest, 1826, see: Thomas M. Marshall, "St. Vrain's Expedition to the Gila in 1826," in *Southwestern Historical Quarterly,* vii (Jan. 1916), 251-60; Joseph H. Hill, "New Light on Pattie and the Southwestern Fur Trade," in *ibid.,* xxvi (Apr. 1923), 245-54, and Hill's "Ewing Young in the Fur Trade of the Far Southwest," in *Oregon Historical Quarterly,* xxiv (Mar. 1923), 9-22; Lavender, *Bent's Fort,* 67-70, for a concise summary of events.

of that river, they had to fight off an attack from the Black-foot, losing four of their own men in the encounter. Moving rapidly, Young led his battalion over the divide to the Rio Grande back to Santa Fe, arriving with a modest fur catch.[10]

The hazards of the hunt had not deterred the trappers. Their profits, however, evoked considerable envy among the native New Mericans. Ironically, it was an American com-patriot who was responsible – James Baird. In a damning letter, he denounced his fellow countrymen, pointedly ob-serving that the trappers were annually taking some $100,000 in furs from Mexican territory. Alexandro Ramirez, com-mandant of the El Paso district, to whom Baird remon-strated, hastily informed the Mexican authorities. With dispatch, Governor Antonio Narbona, who had indulged the Americanos, was replaced, and stringent regulations were promulgated.[11] The fur men, except for one – and that was Milton Sublette – subsequently lost their fur catch; a year's labor went for naught.

The occasion was noted by Josiah Gregg. The newly-arrived governor for New Mexico, Manuel Armijo, began to enforce the prohibition of fur trapping in Mexican terri-tory. In so doing, "he was . . . obliged to 'knock under' to one of those bold and daring spirits of the Rocky Mountains whom obstacles rather energized than subdued." This was Milton Sublette.[12]

When the trappers returned from the field that year, they heard of the new governor's edict of enforcement. To pre-vent the seizure of their catch, they secreted the furs in the village of Peñablanca, trusting them to the care of Luis

---

[10] James O. Pattie's, *Personal Narrative of James O. Pattie of Kentucky,* in Reuben G. Thwaites (ed.), *Early Western Travels* (Cleveland, 1905), XVIII, 119-44, details much of this trip. However, Pattie's *Narrative* is in error both as to date and the extent of the hunters' geographic wandering. Charles F. Coan, *History of New Mexico* (Chicago and New York, 1925), I, pp. 302-03, presents the best surmise, and places the fur catch at 29 packs, worth $20,000.

[11] Marshall, "St. Vrain's Expedition," 255-60.

[12] Thwaites (ed.), *Early Western Travels,* XX, pp. 23, 246.

María Cabeza de Baca.[13] On order of Armijo, a search and seizure order was issued. The governor dispatched Agustin Duran, the Substitute Commissary of the territory, and Juan Estevan Aragon, Alcalde of Cochiti, in company with nine soldiers, to find the hidden cache. The expedition was successful – and it cost Baca his life when he attempted to resist the confiscation.[14]

Because the furs were found to be damp when brought back to Santa Fe, they were spread out to dry in the quadrangle of the Guardia. Milton approached Ewing Young and inquired where his packs of fur were. When Young pointed to them, Milton sprang forward and picked them up, carrying them triumphantly away "before the eyes of the whole garrison." As a result of this open defiance, Armijo mobilized the garrison to search out the offender. But Milton and his furs were not to be found.[15] Ewing Young was brought to trial for disobeying the political chief of the territory "and [for] the part he took in the daring action of his fellow-citizen Soblet, in the robbery committed by the latter of a load of beaver skins." Sentence, however, was never executed.[16]

Hiding out the rest of the summer months, Milton joined the expedition of Sylvestre Pratte and Ceran St. Vrain in the fall of 1827. Although forbidden by law, the objective

---

[13] De Baca claimed to be a descendant of Alvar Nunez Cabeza de Vaca. In hiding the furs, de Baca was probably motivated by the money he would receive for his service: he was desperately poor. After two years of petitioning, May 29, 1821, he had been granted the "Vegas Grandes" Rancho, being officially put into possession. Later, Indian hostility robbed him of his assets and drove him from his land. Destitute, he moved to Peñablanca. Verna Laumbach, "Las Vegas Before 1850," in *New Mexico Historical Review*, VIII (Oct. 1933), 244-45; Lansing B. Bloom, "New Mexico Under Mexican Administration, 1822-1846," in *Old Santa Fe*, I (Jan. 1914), 260-61.

[14] Official report made by Armijo, June 6, 1827. Printed in Robert G. Cleland, *This Reckless Breed of Men* (New York, 1950), 219.

[15] Thwaites (ed.), *Early Western Travels*, xx, pp. 23-24. Sublette sought refuge in the house of Cristobal Torres, later fleeing.

[16] Cleland, *This Reckless Breed of Men*, 220, cites the charge against Young.

of the company was fur trapping. Thomas L. Smith and other old friends were among the battalion's members. Their travels during the season of 1827-1828 are uncertain, but in all likelihood the company trapped northwestward to avoid both the Apache and the Mexicans.

Again, the hunt proved modestly successful. And as in the previous year, the hardships and dangers of the trail exacted their toll. Sylvestre Pratte died at Park Kyack on September 1, and was succeeded in command by Ceran St. Vrain. Later, Thomas L. Smith lost a leg in an Indian skirmish, probably in the vicinity of present-day North Park, Colorado. It fell to Milton's lot, it is said, to amputate the shattered leg, an action which probably saved "Peg-leg" Smith's life.[17]

After Pratte's death, the company, already with some three hundred beaver, moved on to the Green River to winter. In April 1828, part of the company under St. Vrain determined to return over the mountains and down the Platte to St. Louis with Pratte's property. But striking a large Indian trace, lacking ammunition, and fearing a hostile Indian party, most of the company headed for Taos, which they reached on May 23. When the battalion's catch was disposed of, Milton's share (second only to that of St. Vrain), came to $919.07.[18]

Milton, however, probably in company with a few more daring hunters, had headed for St. Louis, leaving the rest of the company to make for Taos. For by the spring of 1828, Milton was on his way to Santa Fe with the party of Colonel Meredith M. Marmaduke. In the course of this journey, the party had a close call. While in the vicinity of the Arkansas River, they were attacked by two hundred Comanches, "and

---

[17] Lavender, *Bent's Fort*, 72-76.

[18] Trapper Agreement and Division of the Estate of S[ylvestre] S. Pratte, by Ceran St. Vrain, Taos, Sept. 1; St. Vrain to B[ernard] Pratte & Co., Sept. 28, 1828. Pierre Chouteau-Maffitt Collection, Missouri Historical Society (hereinafter cited MHS); *Missouri Republican*, Sept. 30, 1828.

were only saved from certain death by the skill and long experience of Milton Sublette in Indian warfare."

The Marmaduke company did not tarry long in New Mexico – just long enough to recruit a herd of twelve hundred horses. Enroute back to St. Louis, the company was not so fortunate. On August 28, the Comanches struck the herd on the north bank of the Arkansas near the mouth of Pawnee Fork, driving off over half the stock. The rest of the animals were driven on to Missouri without further incident, arriving in late September.[19]

By early spring of 1829, Milton entered the employ of his brother. Leaving behind the Southwest, he joined his elder brother William's supply caravan to seek his fortune in the transmontane region.[20] In the wake of the annual rendezvous held that year on the Popo Agie, Milton joined Henry Fraeb and Jean Baptiste Gervais as company trappers, and with them spent the ensuing season in Bighorn country.[21] That year's association, 1829-30, was to lay the basis for a new development in Milton's life – his involvement in the Rocky Mountain Fur Company, the concern that succeeded the firm of Smith, Jackson and Sublette in 1830.

After an eventful career, first as a trusted lieutenant in the employ of Ashley and Henry, William Sublette had joined Jedediah Smith and David Jackson in a partnership in 1826 to continue the fur harvest of the Rocky Mountains when Ashley retired from the scene. During the four years that followed, the young partisans blazed many of the trails over which subsequent generations of pioneers would travel to the Pacific slope: they were heralds of *Manifest Destiny*.

---

[19] *Waldo Mems.*, 65, 70-71.

[20] The Sublette caravan left St. Louis, March 17, and arrived at the rendezvous, July 1. Sunder, *Bill Sublette*, 79-80.

[21] J. Cecil Alter, *James Bridger* (Salt Lake City, 1925), 105-06; LeRoy R. Hafen and W[illiam] J. Ghent, *Broken Hand: The Life Story of Thomas Fitzpatrick* (Denver, 1931), 72; Frances F. Victor, *River of the West* (Hartford, Conn., 1870), 80.

Their final achievement climaxed their partnership in 1830 – the firm was responsible for taking the first wagons west of St. Louis to the vicinity of South Pass. They proved, dramatically, the feasibility of a wagon road west.[22]

Whatever their motives may have been, Smith, Jackson and Sublette decided at the 1830 rendezvous (again held on the Popo Agie) to dispose of their business interests to a new partnership called the Rocky Mountain Fur Company. On or about August 4, for the approximate sum of $16,000 the transaction was completed. The new partners were Thomas Fitzpatrick, James Bridger, Henry Fraeb, Jean Baptiste Gervais, and Milton Sublette.[23]

For the next four years the new firm struggled to gain financial success. They were adventuresome and exciting years, and marked the flowering of Milton's career.

When the 1830 rendezvous disbanded, Milton captained one of the firm's two battalions, trapping on the Lewis Fork of the Columbia River. They boldly entered the fur-rich Blackfoot country. Milton was joined in this enterprise by a new-found friend and recruit, Joseph L. Meek, who had journeyed to the mountains with William Sublette's 1829 mule caravan.[24] Associated with Milton in the 1830-31 season were Thomas Fitzpatrick, James Bridger, and a company of eighty men. They hunted extensively in the basin of the Missouri's Three Forks until March 1831. At that time, Fitzpatrick headed east to procure the coming season's supplies in preparation for the Rocky Mountain Fur Company's first rendezvous.[25]

---

[22] Morgan, *Jedediah Smith*, 315-17; Carl P. Russell, "Trapper Trails to the Sisk-Ke-Dee," in [Westerners] *Brand Book 1944* (Chicago, 1946), 57-79.

[23] Morgan, *Jedediah Smith*, 320-21; Sunder, *Bill Sublette*, 88.

[24] Alter, *James Bridger*, 112; Hafen and Ghent, *Broken Hand*, 78-81; Stephen Hall Meek, *Autobiography of a Mountain Man, 1805-1889* (Pasadena, Calif., 1948), 4-5. Harvey E. Tobie, *No Man Like Joe* (Portland, Ore., 1949), provides a balanced view of Milton and Meek's relationship.

[25] St. Louis *Enquirer*, May 12, 1831; Dorothy O. Johansen (ed.), *Robert Newell's Memorandum* (Portland, Ore., 1959), 31-32.

The first annual rendezvous for the new partnership was held in the summer of 1831 on the Green River. It was hardly a joyous occasion. Although faced with steadily mounting competition from John Jacob Astor's firm, the American Fur Company (directed by shrewd Kenneth McKenzie), the Rocky Mountain Fur Company had a prosperous 1830-31 hunt. However, the challenge offered by the McKenzie men was fraught with potential disaster.

The chief weakness of the Rocky Mountain Fur Company was lack of trading supplies: they could not compete without goods.[26] The firm found its answer when William Sublette, after an abortive and tragic fling in the Santa Fe trade, heeded the plea of his former friends and commenced operations as a fur contractor, conveying goods to the annual rendezvous.[27]

In the fall, James Bridger and Milton Sublette, in company with Meek and some fifty other trappers, established winter quarters on the forks of the Snake. The American Fur Company, whose strategy was based on their fairly recent arrival and unfamiliarity with the transmontane region, followed their opponents. William H. Vanderburgh, McKenzie's chief field man, countered by erecting his camp in Cache Valley. The fight was on.[28]

During the course of the winter, life for Milton was far from tranquil, or so one would be led to believe if Joe Meek's hyperbolous narrative is relied on. While out on a

---

[26] The difficulties Fitzpatrick had in moving supplies to the rendezvous are discussed in volume I of this *Series*, pp. 110-12, 114.

[27] Morgan, *Jedediah Smith*, 326 *et seq.* William Sublette, writing to General William H. Ashley on the return trip at Walnut Creek near the Arkansas River, Sept. 24, 1831, reported that the Santa Fe traders had brought word that Milton's trapper band had acquired 50 packs of beaver in the spring hunt. Robert Campbell Papers, MHS, microcopy through the courtesy of Dale L. Morgan.

[28] Kenneth W. Porter, *John Jacob Astor, Business Man* (Cambridge, Mass., 1931), II, p. 768; Paul C. Phillips, "William Henry Vanderburgh: Fur Trader," in *Mississippi Valley Historical Review*, xxx (Dec. 1943), 386-94; Johansen (ed.), *Newell's Memorandum*, 32; John C. Ewers (ed.), *Adventures of Zenas Leonard, Fur Trader* (Norman, Okla., 1959), 8-9ff.

trapping expedition, according to Meek, Milton got into a fight that almost cost him his life. No doubt the situation was brought on by whiskey, an article of trade which was carried and used by the Rocky Mountain Fur Company. Whatever the cause, Milton tangled in a knife duel with Chief Gray, a Rockaway Indian. When the fracas was over, Milton lay badly wounded. With only Meek to care for him, life and death hung in the balance for forty wintry days. No sooner had the shadow passed than news spread that the Snake Indians would take to the warpath. Again, fortune smiled. Milton and Meek were saved by the intervention and action of an old chief, Gotia. Through his efforts and those of an accomplice, Mountain Lamb, a reputedly beautiful Indian lass, the two fur men found safety. Subsequently, Milton reportedly married Mountain Lamb. And when Milton died, his friend Meek took his widow for wife.[29]

This delightful romantic ending to a knife fight is pure fiction. Milton as a typical fur man had taken a squaw in 1829. By 1831 she had a child and was traveling on horseback with Milton during the hunting season. In 1832 a second child was born. As to Milton's Indian wife's name or tribe, and her eventual fate, nothing is known. But one thing is certain – it was not Mountain Lamb – a figment of Joe Meek's later imagination.[30]

The 1832 rendezvous was held at Pierre's Hole near the foot of the Tetons. Two events transpired there which were to affect Milton's future decisively. First, the competition from the American Fur Company was unabated – indeed, it was increasing. The independent trappers of the Rocky Mountain Fur Company, although successful in their fur

---

[29] Tobie, *No Man Like Joe,* 23-34.

[30] Harvey E. Tobie, "Joseph L. Meek," *Oregon Historical Society Quarterly,* XXXIX (Mar. 1938), 133-34. (Tobie's work supersedes Frances F. Victor, *River of the West,* on Milton's association with Meek.)

harvest, faced the bleak fact of hardening competition, fewer furs, a depressed market, and rising supply costs.[31] Neither firm wanted competition; neither could afford it.

Kenneth McKenzie, the Astor firm's chief factor, put the matter in clear focus. Writing to Pierre Chouteau, he noted the problem and the possible solution:

> [Last Spring, 1832] . . . Fontenelle was empowered by me to make certain propositions to Milton G. Sublett & Co. and communicate the result to me here:
>
> I received a letter from Mr. Fontenelle but he was wholly silent on the subject: Mr. M. G. Sublett arrived here [in the fall of 1833], had seen Mr. Fontenelle but nothing passed on this point: I have good reason to believe he would willingly have entered into some arrangements with me, but it was necessary for him to consult his partners as for me to know if Mr. Fontenelle had abandoned the views suggested & recommended to him in the Spring, thus a chance has been lost of relieving ourselves of a dead weight or perhaps of turning the scale in our favor. [sic] [32]

McKenzie's solution was simple – buy out the competition!

When William Sublette's supply caravan reached the rendezvous on July 8, a New Englander, Nathaniel Wyeth, and a party of easterners accompanied it. Milton's meeting with Wyeth was to bring about a second radical change in his future plans and actions.[33]

The rendezvous disbanded on July 17. Milton, accompanied by a small number of trappers, and Nathaniel Wyeth with a few of his remaining band, struck out from camp. The next day, after making only eight miles, the

---

[31] The total fur catch for that year was estimated variously from $60,000 to $80,000. Thwaites (ed.), *Early Western Travels,* XXI, p. 81; *Arkansas Gazette,* Oct. 31, 1832. On the subject of fur scarcity and market prices, William Gordon to Lewis Cass, St. Louis, Oct. 3, 1831. Fur Trade Collection, MHS. Porter, *John Jacob Astor,* II, p. 769, notes the problem of whiskey.

[32] Written at Fort Union, Dec. 16, 1833, Annie H. Abel (ed.), *Chardon's Journal at Fort Clark, 1834-1839* (Pierre, S.D., 1932), 367.

[33] Thwaites (ed.), *Early Western Travels,* XXI, pp. 47-49; William Sublette to General William H. Ashley, May 12, 1832; Thomas Fitzpatrick to [Robert] Campbell, June 4, 1833, Robert Campbell Papers, MHS.

seventeen-man party was attacked by a large band of Black-foot. Quickly word was sent to the rendezvous for aid. William Sublette led his force of trappers and some friendly Indians to the rescue. What followed was one of the classic trapper-Indian battles – the Battle of Pierre's Hole, second only to the 1823 Arikara fight. In both of these encounters, William and Milton played a part.[34]

Victorious, Milton and Wyeth continued on their western mountain trek. During the course of the season, 1832-33, their adventures were many, and some of these have been recorded in Washington Irving's *The Adventures of Captain Bonneville.*[35] In the course of his year's association with Wyeth, Milton and his new-found friend eventually devised a scheme to rebuild and augment the fortunes of the Rocky Mountain Fur Company. The two would seek eastern capital: Wyeth would embark on a daring plan – revive the strategy of the original Astor supply plan of 1810, send ships around the Horn to the mouth of the Columbia River and bring a party overland at the same time. In such a pincer maneuver, the American Fur Company would be destroyed.

While Milton and Wyeth were thus drawing their plans, William Sublette and his business partner, Robert Campbell, were launching their own competitive attack against the American Fur Company. Sublette and Campbell were motivated by the desire to act as exclusive fur contractors for the transmontane area. They were willing to surrender the upper Missouri basin to their opponents. To implement their scheme, Sublette and Campbell took the fight into the Missouri basin, establishing a series of trader forts in the vicinity of their rivals.[36]

---

[34] For a summary of the battle of Pierre's Hole, see Sunder, *Bill Sublette,* 109-10; volume I of this *Series,* pp. 123-26.

[35] Washington Irving, *Adventures of Captain Bonneville,* ed. with introduction by Edgeley W. Todd (Norman, Okla., 1961), 134 *et seq.*

[36] Sunder, *Bill Sublette,* 126-29.

At the 1833 rendezvous, sensing victory over the American Fur Company, Sublette and Campbell drove harder bargains with the Rocky Mountain fur men for the year's catch. So harsh were the trading prices, Milton and Fitzpatrick retaliated by signing an agreement with Wyeth, August 14, when they met again on the Bighorn, contracting with him for the next season's supplies.[37]

In order to implement the agreement and give direction to Wyeth's preparations and purchases, Milton journeyed east in company with his brother William.[38] William's objective was a settlement with the American Fur Company over boundaires to their respective territory. Milton's purpose was to retrieve and revive the fortunes of the Rocky Mountain Fur Company by assisting Wyeth in purchasing rendezvous goods.

After their arrival in St. Louis, prior to their departure east, Milton stayed on William's St. Louis farm and was treated by Dr. Bernard Farrar for an inflammation in his foot – a result, in all probability, of his arrow wound inflicted during the course of his 1826 Gila River trapping with "Peg-leg" Smith.[39] Undaunted by the infection, Milton traveled east with his brother in December, 1833.

By December 26, Milton and William were ready to leave Philadelphia. There they had tarried for a brief visit with Robert Campbell's brother, Hugh; then on to New York City.[40] From Pittsburgh, Milton wrote to Wyeth informing him that after his arrival in New York, he would journey on to Boston to confer with him in the selection of

---

[37] Wyeth to Milton Sublette, Nov. 20, 1833. F[rederick] G. Young (ed.), *Correspondence . . . of Nathaniel J. Wyeth, 1831-1836,* in *Sources of the History of Oregon* (Eugene, 1899), 83 (hereinafter cited as *Wyeth Corres.*).

[38] Sunder, *Bill Sublette,* 129-30.

[39] William Sublette to Robert Campbell, Feb. 14, 1834. Robert Campbell Papers, MHS; Sunder, *Bill Sublette,* 136.

[40] Wyeth to Leonard Wyeth; same to Milton Sublette, Jan. 2, 4, 1834. *Wyeth Corres.,* 96-97.

trading goods for the forthcoming season.[41] Arriving in New York shortly after New Year's day, William immediately plunged into negotiations with the Astor firm – and won a decisive partition of the fur territory of the trans-Mississippi.[42]

In the interim, Milton made Boston and with Wyeth returned to New York on February 9 to solidify their ambitious plans to cut supply costs and revive the faltering fur trade. After negotiations there, they planned to move on together to Philadelphia toward the end of the month and then on to Baltimore. Openly, Wyeth wrote William of their plans. But Milton's foot was only a bit improved, and was continually troubling him – an ominous sign.[43]

Because the infection was still inflamed, and time was pressing, Milton broke with the plans. On February 13, he left Wyeth in New York, relying on him to complete arrangements, and headed for Philadelphia to rejoin William for the return trip to St. Louis.[44] Other than the excuse of his infected foot, Milton may have been disturbed by the fact that the Wyeth contract would work against his brother's business interests. It was both a matter of family connection and business acumen: Wyeth was a dreamer; William Sublette, a man of practicality.[45]

Unexpectedly, Wyeth's vision as a fur contractor matured. William challenged the newcomer decisively. Probably William believed that the Bostonian would never realize such an ambitious scheme. When Wyeth proved himself, William destroyed him and his venture by dash and daring.

---

[41] Wyeth to Milton Sublette, Jan. 2, 4; same to Leonard Wyeth, Jan. 14, 1834. *Wyeth Corres.*, 97-98, 103.   [42] Sunder, *Bill Sublette*, 136.

[43] Wyeth to William Sublette, Feb. 10, 1834. *Wyeth Corres.*, 109; Sunder, *Bill Sublette,* 137-38.

[44] Wyeth to William Sublette, Feb. 12, 1834. *Wyeth Corres.*, 110.

[45] William and Campbell tried to prevent Milton's participation, but to no avail. Thwaites (ed.), *Early Western Travels*, XX, p. 141; Chittenden, *American Fur Trade,* I, pp. 300-03, 446-49; Sunder, *Bill Sublette*, 139-43.

On his arrival in St. Louis, Wyeth prevailed on Milton to captain the caravan west from Independence in April 1834, a caravan consisting of seventy men. But the company's prospects dimmed considerably when Milton, due to his aggravated injury, was forced to turn back to St. Louis, on May 8, only ten days' march out of Independence. As John K. Townsend, who was a member of the company, relates:

> He [Milton] has been suffering a considerable time with a fungus in one of his legs, and it has become so much worse since we started, in consequence of irritation caused by riding, that he finds it impossible to proceed. His departure has thrown a gloom over the whole camp. We all admire his admirable qualities, and his kind and obliging disposition. For myself, I had become so much attached to him, that I feel quite melancholy about his leaving us.[46]

As if the loss of their guide and experienced captain was not enough to defeat the company's prospects of a successful undertaking, Wyeth failed to reckon with the business shrewdness of Milton's elder brother. By forced march and clever timing, William beat the Wyeth caravan to the rendezvous, thus gaining the year's fur catch.[47]

When Milton turned back to St. Louis on May 8, 1834 – inadvertently leaving the Wyeth party to its bitter commercial defeat – he proceeded to St. Louis for medical treatment for his bothersome leg. There, on the 27th, Doctor Farrar dressed the wound. By early February of the following year, Doctor Farrar amputated. Surgical methods in 1835 were such that only the strong could survive the shock

---

[46] Thwaites (ed.) *Early Western Travels,* XXI, p. 149. For another eye-witness account, Jason Lee's diary, printed in Archer B. Hulbert and Dorothy Printup Hulbert (eds.), *The Oregon Crusade* (Denver, 1935), 147-60.

[47] *Wyeth Corres.,* 131 *et seq.,* gives particulars. He believed Milton's departure ruined the enterprise. William Sublette's caravan passed Wyeth's on May 12 and reached the rendezvous site, Ham's Fork on the Green River, June 14. Robert Campbell Papers, MHS; Chittenden, *American Fur Trade,* I, pp. 302-03 and note, 449-50. Also see Don Berry, *A Majority of Scoundrels* (New York, 1961), 352-53.

and suffering. Milton Sublette's courage cannot be denied, for not only did he survive the surgery, but departed in the spring for the mountains to continue his fur trade activities. On his return to St. Louis in the fall, Hugh Campbell presented him with a cork leg which he had had made in Philadelphia for his admired friend.[48]

At the 1834 rendezvous, under the hard competition of Sublette and Campbell, and recognizing the fact of the loss to the Rocky Mountain Fur Company in the partition of the fur territory between the American Fur Company and Sublette and Campbell, the firm dissolved. In *abstentia,* since his illness had forced him back to St. Louis, Milton gave his proxy to Thomas Fitzpatrick for the dissolution of their four-year-old firm. Instead, a new association composed of Milton, Fitzpatrick and Bridger replaced the defunct company. In a vain effort, two months later, they merged with Lucien Fontenelle and Andrew Drips in establishing the firm of Fontenelle, Fitzpatrick & Company, a firm that was sold at the 1836 rendezvous to Joshua Pilcher, agent of the American Fur Company.[49] These desperate efforts were to no avail – it was too late.

With the 1835 rendezvous (Milton having recovered from his operation was in the field), Sublette and Campbell realized that their days in the fur trade as suppliers and contractors on a monopolistic basis were over. William Sublette's actions in undercutting Wyeth's business venture in 1834 had left much resentment among the important trappers. That event forced a realignment of the fur traders

---

48 The idea that Milton cut off his own foot is fictional. Lavender, *Bent's Fort,* 74-76, 376, note 2, clarifies the story. Chittenden, *American Fur Trade,* I, p. 254, states Milton underwent two amputations; Sunder, *Bill Sublette,* 146, indicates "successive operations."

49 Robert Campbell Papers and the Sublette Papers, MHS, contain the essential documents. Also, see Lucien Fontenelle's letter to Pierre Chouteau, Jr., dated Sept. 14, 1834, in Chittenden, *American Fur Trade,* I, p. 309; Archer B. and Dorothy P. Hulbert, *Marcus Whitman, Crusader* (Denver, 1936), I, 230-31, for the 1836 sale.

and alienated many a former friend of William's, not to mention his own brother Milton. In 1834 when Milton and his friends, Fitzpatrick and Bridger, joined with Fontenelle and Drips, William knew that his position was precarious. It was for this reason that he sold out Fort William on the Platte to Milton and his associates.[50] And further, by 1835, furs were getting more scarce and prices were falling. Always a man of foresight, William Sublette and his partner, Robert Campbell, saw naught but diminishing returns from their fur trade enterprise. Wisely, they transferred their interests to more durable things: banking, real estate, and commercial shops in St. Louis.[51]

In the spring of 1836 when Milton and his longtime friend and trapper partner, Thomas Fitzpatrick, departed for the mountains, they acted as escorts for the first major Oregon immigration, the Whitman-Spalding party. As one of the Oregon-bound travelers wrote, "We are really a moving village – nearly four hundred animals with ours, mostly mules and seventy men [of the fur company]." The fur men had seven wagons, each pulled by six mules. And poignantly the traveler commented that one cart drawn by two mules carried "a lame man, one of the proprietors of the Com[pany]."[52] Valiantly, Milton Sublette was determined to continue his pattern of living, even as a cripple, to the end. And this trip did mark Milton's end – the end of his career on the frontier.

The rigors of the journey, the recurrence of the "fungus" in his leg, forced him to turn back to Fort William. There, surrounded by those things he knew best – the Indians, traders, fort, and furs, things so closely identified with his

---

[50] Sunder, *Bill Sublette,* 145-46; Chittenden, *American Fur Trade,* I, pp. 304-05.

[51] Sunder, *Bill Sublette,* chs. IX-X.

[52] Narcissa Whitman to Sister Harriet and Brother Edwards, Platte River (Just above the Falls), June 3, 1836. "Additional Letters [on the Whitmans]," in *Trans. of Oregon Pioneer Assn.,* 1893 (Portland, 1894), 105.

frontier life – he served, during the closing months of his life, as majordomo of the fort. Less than a year later, April 5, 1837, he died. Fittingly, he was buried in the fort's cemetery, alongside former friends and foes. His epitaph has nowhere been better expressed than in the *Daily Missouri Republican's* announcement of his death, June 16, 1837.[53]

In 1843, Matthew C. Field, an assistant editor on the New Orleans *Picayune,* traveling with the famed "party of pleasure to the Rocky Mountains," led by Sir William Drummond Stewart who was accompanied by William Sublette, recorded in his diary, while visiting Fort William, then renamed Fort Laramie:

> Here, also we found the resting-place of MILTON SUBLETTE, whose story has been told by Irving. A rude pine cross, prostrate and broken, was all the memorial over the brave man's bones; but two of his brothers [William and Solomon] were with us, and one of them remained here while we moved onward in among the mountains. When we returned, we found a monument built somewhat in Christian fashion, marking the spot. Solomon Sublette during our absence paid his fraternal attention to the remains of poor Milton.[54]

Thus did Milton Sublette find his grave, "a few hundred yards from the fort – red men and white reposing, as it were, in each other's arms!"[55]

---

[53] Quoted at the beginning of this article. R. Wharton Gaul, M.D., of *Charlotte,* N.C., is of the opinion that Milton died from "the inexorable course of advanced cancer." See "Death of the Thunderbolt: Some Notes on the Final Illness of Milton Sublette," in *Bulletin of the Missouri Historical Society,* XVIII (Oct. 1961), 33-36.

[54] Matthew C. Field, *Prairie and Mountain Sketches,* ed. by Gregg and McDermott (Norman, Okla., 1957), 78. The entry date was July 5, 1843.

[55] *Ibid.,* 75.

Lucien Fontenelle

by ALAN C. TROTTMAN
Columbus, Ohio

"At Fort Laramie, Fontenelle committed suicide in a fit of *mania a potu,*" wrote Mrs. F. F. Victor in her biography of Joe Meek.[1] Bernard DeVoto, however, in his book *Across the Wide Missouri,* stated that Lucien Fontenelle probably died in 1840, a sober man. Fontenelle has been a shadowy figure in the history of the American Fur Trade, but he was not a suicide.

Lucien Fontenelle was born October 9, 1800, on the family plantation south of New Orleans. His parents were Francois and Marie Louise Fontenelle.[2] Lucien spent his early years on the plantation. When he was attending school in New Orleans a hurricane struck the area of his plantation home, causing the death of his mother and father by drowning. Lucien and his sister, Amelia, remained in New Orleans in the care of an aunt by the name of Madame Merlier. Lucien supposedly rebelled at the discipline he received from his aunt, who was described as a haughty, austere, cruel person. She had found it difficult to raise a boy approaching manhood. Saying goodbye to the family nurse in the early hours one night, Fontenelle departed for St. Louis.[3]

Stephen H. Long noted in his journal in January 1820,

---

[1] Frances Fuller Victor, *The River of the West* (Columbus, Ohio, 1950), 224.

[2] Book of Baptisms, no. 4, page 36b, act., 296. St. Louis Basilica Archives, St. Louis Basilica, New Orleans, Louisiana. A copy of the original entry written in Spanish was sent to me by Mrs. Alice D. Forsyth, corresponding secretary of the Genealogical Society of New Orleans.

[3] I have based the early events of Fontenelle's life upon the short biography in Hiram M. Chittenden, *The History of the American Fur Trade* (New York, 1901), I, p. 391; "Transactions and Reports of the Nebraska Historical Society (Robert Furnas ed.), I, pp. 90-93.

that "Mr. Fontenelle, in the employ of the Missouri Fur Co., who has been absent for sometime trading with one of the bands of the Omahaws called today on his return."[4] Fontenelle was nineteen at the time Long reported seeing him at Council Bluffs. Fontenelle stated several years later that he recalled 1819 as the first year he entered the Lower Missouri country. If Fontenelle left New Orleans in 1816, there are three years for which no trace of him has been found.

From Fort Lisa, Fontenelle moved about trading with the neighboring tribes. The following summer of 1820, the Sac Indians disrupted the activities of the whites, frightening and driving many back down the river to St. Louis. Many horses belonging to the Missouri Fur Company were lost. To add to the company's troubles, 1800 pelts were stolen in St. Louis before Thomas Hempstead could deliver them to the company's supplier, David Stone & Co.,[5] and unhappily, the price of beaver dropped. Then, Manuel Lisa, the driving force behind the company, died on August 12, 1820.

Joshua Pilcher, who succeeded Lisa, decided to enlarge his field of operation. Not until 1821, however, was he able to send Michael Immell and Robert Jones to the Upper Missouri. They rebuilt a post twelve miles from the mouth of the Knife River and named it Fort Vanderburgh. A new post, Fort Benton, was built "near where the Bighorn empties into the Yellowstone."[6] As a result of these successes, an outfit was readied for the spring of 1822. Thomas Hempstead, the acting partner in St. Louis, had concluded an agreement on the 1st of April with O. N. Bostwick for necessary supplies. In turn, the Missouri Fur Company

---

[4] Reuben G. Thwaites (ed.), "S. H. Long's Expedition," in *Early Western Travels* (Cleveland, 1906), XIV, p. 275.

[5] Richard E. Oglesby, *Manuel Lisa and The Opening of the Missouri Fur Trade* (Norman, 1963), 177.

[6] Paul C. Phillips, *The Fur Trade* (Norman, 1961), II, p. 394.

"agreed to deliver him 30 packs of Beaver and 300 pack Robes." [7]

Fontenelle proceeded to St. Louis on the 29th of April. He soon discovered that hiring able-bodied men for the trip up the Missouri in the spring of 1822 would be difficult indeed. William Ashley had come to a decision which would bring about a rich harvest of furs as well as establish new procedures in the fur trade. He, along with the experienced Andrew Henry, had been hiring men and boats for their initial spring expedition to the mountains. Difficult as this made matters, Fontenelle was successful enough to send the company boat, "Mary Jane," up the Missouri by May 13, 1822, with Louis Bompart in charge. [8]

If Fontenelle was on board, it was not recorded. Fontenelle may have remained in St. Louis arranging for further supplies which had not arrived from New York via New Orleans. Also, Andrew Drips and William Vanderburgh were bringing down the previous year's catch. This would require his interest as well. Undoubtedly he lingered and then headed up the river for Council Bluffs and the Lower Missouri trade. That fall of 1822, "the furs sent down the river were valued at $25,000." [9]

In the meantime, overtures were made through Ramsay Crooks to bring the Missouri Fur Company within the arms of the American Fur Company. Joshua Pilcher's group was realizing some success with the operation on the Upper Missouri. But this success enabled the company barely to keep solvent. The competition of the Ashley group as well as Berthold, Chouteau and Pratte strained the company's financial base, and for one reason or another O. N. Bostwick & Co. was often late in sending supplies. Never-

[7] Dale L. Morgan (ed.), *The West of William Ashley* (Denver, 1964), 3.

[8] *Ibid.*, 9.

[9] Phillips, *op. cit.*, 394. See also Morgan, *op. cit.*, 19; Charles Peterson, "Manuel Lisa's Warehouse," *Bulletin* of the Missouri Historical Society, IV (January 1948), 83-84.

theless, Pilcher and his young partners felt confident that their company could withstand the everpresent competition. (Crooks was brushed aside.) Immell and Jones were again in the field trapping in the Yellowstone country. Whether by design or by accident, Pilcher's company received a blow in the spring of 1823 from which it did not recover. This was the year that found Andrew Henry, William Ashley and Immell and Jones in trouble with the Indians in the Upper Missouri country.

Michael Immell and Robert Jones were attacked by the Blackfeet near Pryor's Fork of the Yellowstone, May 31, 1823. Both leaders of the brigade were slain. The Blackfeet made off with all the equipment, beaver pelts, and horses. The loss was irreplaceable. William Gordon, clerk of the brigade, escaped and wrote a complete account of the incident.[10] When the news reached Joshua Pilcher, he was involved in the fight with the Arikara Indians who had attacked William Ashley that same spring. Fontenelle may have joined Pilcher and Vanderburgh in their advance to punish the Arikaras. However, no mention is made of his participation in this punitive expedition under the command of Colonel Henry Leavenworth. In August, Fontenelle was reported at Fort Lisa and in good health. His presence would be needed at Bellevue where a new post had been established during the previous months.[11]

As a result of the disaster on Pryor's Fork, Pilcher hurriedly gathered a small party and sent it off to trade with the Crows in the Wind River region where Ashley had resolved to go overland with a brigade led by Jedediah Smith. Fontenelle remained at Bellevue handling the trade with the nearby tribes. The Omaha Indians were of particular interest to him. The chief of the Omaha tribe, Big

---

[10] *Senate Document 1,* 18 Cong., 1 sess. (Serial 89), 70-71; *Senate Document 90,* 22 Cong., 1 sess. (Serial 213), 26-27.

[11] Morgan, *op. cit.,* 20. As Dale Morgan points out p. 232, note 65, Thomas Hempstead "casually" refers to the new post which is Bellevue.

Elk, had a daughter, Me-um-ba-ne, (meaning The Sun or Bright Sun). She came to live with Fontenelle as his wife sometime in 1824. Me-um-ba-ne was an intelligent woman who returned to her people whenever her husband traveled to the neighboring tribes or the mountains. She learned to live in a house but was always more comfortable in her father's tepee. She evidently was a fearless woman.

Several stories grew from her actions regarding an Iowa brave whom she killed with an ax. He supposedly was about to kill her baby. Yet the story goes that this same brave had helped kill her relatives during a raid. She had recognized him when he appeared at Fort Atkinson; therefore, getting him drunk, she slew him. Perhaps more fiction than fact, but the Indian women were notorious in avenging the loss of loved ones. Bellevue became Me-um-ba-ne's home, however, and it was here that her first child was born in May, 1825. This first born was named Logan, after the famous Indian chief of the Mingo tribe. Logan proved to be an intelligent boy and for a short time became a chief with the Omaha Indians. He was killed by the Sioux during an elk hunt in 1855. The name Fontenelle is remembered in Nebraska from Logan's renown as a chief.

Logan had three brothers and a sister, Albert, Tecumseh (Felix), Henry, and Susan. Both Logan and Albert attended a boarding school operated by Joseph Wells near St. Louis. Tecumseh joined his brothers sometime later. When Wells died in 1835, Joseph Sappington conducted the school. In August of 1836, tuition was paid by the father but sometime after, probably in the spring of 1837, the entire family joined Lucien at Fort Laramie. Albert, who learned the blacksmith trade, died in 1859 of injuries suffered when he was thrown from a mule. Tecumseh was killed by his sister's husband, Louis Neal, during a drunken brawl sometime in 1858. Henry, who ran away from the Indian school near present day Kansas City, Kansas, where he, Tecumseh, and Susan were sent after their father's death, became a respected man of the area.[12]

Prior to these events, however, Thomas Fitzpatrick had returned from the Ashley expedition in the spring of 1824 with the important news of the rich beaver country in and around the Green River country. He had placed his furs "en cache" on the North Platte and traveled east with the news. Immediately, Fontenelle purchased his furs and hired mules so that Fitzpatrick could return for his packs. "So it was that the dying Missouri Fur Company, or its heirs and assigns, reaped the benefit of Fitzpatrick's first returns from beyond the Continental Divide."[13]

Writing to John Daugherty, Indian agent at Cantonment Leavenworth, February 26, 1829, Fontenelle stated that the man who returned with Fitzpatrick's furs passed a Pawnee village. Several of the tribe followed and robbed him of his coat, blanket, and all of his ammunition, but the packs of beaver were not touched. (The following spring, Fontenelle himself lost a valuable horse to the Pawnees.)[14]

Meanwhile, an arrangement had been made between J. P. Cabanné and Joshua Pilcher. This was accomplished to keep each from usurping the other's trade with the Indians by going to them directly. Laforce Papin was stationed at Bellevue where Fontenelle was located. Pilcher stationed someone at Cabanné's post. James Kennerly, Indian agent at Fort Atkinson, noted in his journal that Cabanné complained to him because Fontenelle was trading with the Indians at their camp. In December of 1825, Fontenelle and Andrew Drips were at Fort Atkinson to see Joshua Pilcher. Whether Kennerly discussed Cabanné's complaints with Fontenelle, he failed to note. On January 2, 1826, both

---

[12] J. Sterling Morton, *et al, Illustrated History of Nebraska* (Lincoln, 1907), I, pp. 71-72.   [13] Morgan, *op. cit.,* 97.

[14] Lucien Fontenelle to Major John Daugherty, U.S. Indian Agent Feb. 26, 1829, National Archives, "Letters Received by the Office of Indian Affairs, 1824-81." Micro-copy 234, roll 883.

Cabanné and Fontenelle complained to Kennerly of each other's duplicity.[15] Each wanted the other restrained, but both were after the same item of trade. Deceit was part of the game.

The Missouri Fur Company, however, was for all practical purposes a defunct organization. By 1826, John Jacob Astor had formed an alliance with B. Pratte and Company. Then the Columbia Fur Company merged with Astor's American Fur Company also, and became the Upper Missouri Outfit July 8, 1827. Such powerful opposition, however, did not daunt the efforts of Pilcher and his partners. By September 1827, Fontenelle with Pilcher, Drips, Vanderburgh and Bent, headed for the mountains with goods purchased from the American Fur Company. With them were forty-five other men plus a hundred horses. This venture marked the inaugural trip to the mountains for Fontenelle.[16]

Leaving Council Bluffs, the brigade followed the Platte and Sweetwater rivers. Good fortune was not to be theirs. Winter weather rapidly closed in on the party. Heavy snows hindered their progress. Then, nearing South Pass, a party of Crow Indians stole most of their horses. Forced to cache their goods, the party continued on foot to the Green River, where the men spent the winter. The following spring, with horses obtained from the Snake Indians, a party went back to retrieve the supplies, only to discover that water had seeped through the cache and had ruined most of the goods. This loss caused many of the men to desert, some returning to St. Louis, others joining the outfit of Jedediah Smith, David Jackson, and William Sublette (the successors to William Ashley). Fontenelle and his partners, however, remained in the country, trapping beaver until time for the rendezvous at Bear Lake.

---

[15] Edgar B. Wesley (ed.), "Diary of James Kennerly, 1823-1826," *Missouri Historical Collections,* VI (1928-1931), 91.

[16] I have been unable to locate Lucien Fontenelle in the mountains prior to 1827.

Amazingly enough, the partners picked up from sixteen to eighteen packs of beaver.[17] With the break up of the rendezvous, Pilcher set out for the Columbia River country. A new partnership developed between Fontenelle and Drips, while Vanderburgh joined the American Fur Company, and Charles Bent left for St. Louis where he eventually entered the Santa Fe trade.

Fontenelle and Drips turned to J. P. Cabanné. Unfortunately, Cabanné could not promise much. The number of beaver that Fontenelle brought in would not have given them sufficient funds to establish new credit and pay the debts owed by the partners. Nonetheless, Cabanné assured Fontenelle he would do what he could. Representing the American Fur Company, Cabanné hoped to rid the area of all competition. As he stated, it would "have been just so many fewer fellows to contend with next year."[18]

Thus Fontenelle and Drips became affiliated with the American Fur Company in the fall of 1828 or early 1829. Fontenelle returned to Bellevue, reorganized the post and added new buildings. In the spring of 1830, Fontenelle met the company's westward bound caravan at Cabanné's post. Drips and Joseph Robidoux had been busily engaged buying mules and hiring men for the spring outfit in the St. Louis-Liberty area. They arrived at Bellevue with the caravan in April and then proceeded to Cabanné's post where Fontenelle took charge. From all indications, Fontenelle and Drips owned a part of this expedition of the American Fur Company.[19]

Warren Ferris recorded: "Our traveling code of 'pains

---

[17] J. P. Cabanné to Pierre Chouteau, Jr., September 1828. Chouteau-Papin Collection, Missouri Historical Society.

[18] J. P. Cabanné to Pierre Chouteau, Jr., October 14, 1828. Chouteau-Papin Collection, Missouri Historical Society.

[19] A letter in the Drips Collection of the Bancroft Library, University of California, written by Lucien Fontenelle to Andrew Drips indicates that the partners were still making the attempt to remain independent.

and penalties' was signed by Fontenelle, a veteran leader in the mountain service, who now assumed the direction of affairs, and in all things showed himself to be an experienced, able and efficient commander."[20] The caravan traveled as far as Scott's Bluff by the 27th of May. On the 13th of June, the party reached Independence Rock on the Sweetwater River. Between this date and the 16th of August, Fontenelle sent various parties of men in search of free trappers, Drips leading one group, Robidoux another. Then, "On Harris Fork we cached our goods, and separated into three parties, headed respectively by Messrs. Fontenelle, Dripps and Robidoux, who had each his portion of hunting ground specified, in order to avoid interference with the rest. Fontenelle was to hunt to the southward on the western tributaries of the Green River . . . my unlucky stars having induced me to join Mr. Fontenelle's party, which met with the least of either."[21] Nor did he find much beaver.

Having missed the rendezvous that year, Fontenelle and Drips established themselves for the winter in Cache Valley in company with two of the Rocky Mountain Fur Company partners, Henry Fraeb and Jean Baptiste Gervais.[22] Fontenelle and his men managed to survive the bitter winter months, undergoing several experiences with the Snake and Blackfeet Indians. In April 1831, the main party moved down the Portneuf River where the Hudson's Bay Company brigade, under the leadership of John Work, was camped. The men enjoyed the hospitality of the Britishers for three days. During this enforced stay (the weather had turned severe), one of the "Nor'westers," as Ferris recorded, thought Fontenelle had induced one of the Bay Company's

[20] Warren A. Ferris, *Life In The Rocky Mountains* (Salt Lake City, 1940), 21.

[21] *Ibid.,* 45.

[22] Jedediah Smith, David Jackson, and William Sublette dissolved their partnership at the rendezvous of 1830. Thomas Fitzpatrick, Jim Bridger, Milton Sublette, Henry Fraeb, and Jean Baptiste Gervais formed the Rocky Mountain Fur Company when they bought out Smith, Jackson and Sublette.

men to join his outfit. As a result, the man "presented his gun at the breast of our leader (Fontenelle), but was withheld from firing, by the interference of a more sensible comrade."[23] The party left the Bay Company's camp, sending out trapping parties until Fontenelle and Drips departed for St. Louis, June 19, 1831,[24] Drips to return in the fall with a few supplies. He rejoined Vanderburgh and wintered in Cache Valley. The harassment of the R. M. F. Co. was to begin in earnest.

Preparations were immediately set in motion for the supply caravan of 1832. This year Fontenelle came to the rendezvous by way of Fort Union. He had arrived at Fort Tecumseh with twenty men and a number of horses on May 22, 1832. The steamboat "Yellowstone" carrying supplies was expected daily and finally arrived on the 31st of May. By June 6th, Fontenelle was packed and ready to leave. "Mr. Fontenelle left here with 40 and odd men for Fort Union with 110 or 15 Horses."[25] The delay at Fort Union was costly, as Fontenelle never did make it to Pierre's Hole. He missed the rendezvous and the battle with the Gros Ventres entirely. En route, he had met up with that ill-starred band which gave him no trouble. But, it would seem that Fontenelle was approaching the rendezvous in a very casual manner. By the end of July, Drips was a little frantic. "I have been looking with much anctiaty (anxiety) for twenty days back to see some person from the Missouri but as yet no news the compy of Sublet Frapp & Co has left us yesterday & what Trappers is with us is getting Impatient. . . ."[26] The R. M. F. Co. had departed; therefore Vanderburgh and Drips set out in search of Fontenelle whom they located in the valley of the Green River. Nearby was

[23] Ferris, *op. cit.*, 67.   [24] *Ibid.*, 45.

[25] Fort Tecumseh Journal, January 27-June 1 (1832-1833) Chouteau Collections, Missouri Historical Society.

[26] Andrew Drips to John B. Sarpy, July 27, 1832, from Pierre's Hole. Chouteau-Papin Collection, Missouri Historical Society.

a newcomer – Captain B. L. E. Bonneville. Picking up their supplies, Vanderburgh and Drips hurriedly departed for the rich beaver country that they hoped Jim Bridger and Fitzpatrick would lead them to. Vanderburgh would lose his life in this race for riches. Meanwhile, Fontenelle remained in the area trading and buying what furs were to be had. He returned to Fort Union and then with Kenneth McKenzie descended the Missouri. They arrived at Fort Tecumseh September 30. In December, Fontenelle was at Bellevue.

Fontenelle and Drips prospered well enough. Their credit with the Western Department was established. In June of 1832, $21,841.74 for the sale of goods belonging to them, was credited to the Western Department.[27] This evidently included all furs which belonged to Fontenelle and Drips, delivered from the 1830 and 1831 expedition. The proceeds, amounting to $6,768.40 from the 1832 expedition, were credited to their account in February of 1833.[28] Fontenelle and Drips appeared to serve two interests – the American Fur Company who supplied them and for whom they led the trapping brigades, and their own partnership. They had with them individual trappers engaged to them and those who were engaged to the A. F. Co. The company certainly needed experienced leaders, yet by 1834 Pierre Chouteau, Jr., felt that he could no longer supply Fontenelle and Drips. In doing so, the company was in opposition to itself. The Rocky Mountain Fur Company, whose financial control William Sublette held, provided enough opposition. Therefore, the strain created by the R. M. F. Co. needed no further prodding from within. But Fontenelle continued his partnership with Drips, and the A. F. Co. must have continued to supply them.

[27] William B. Astor to Bernard Pratte, June 23, 1832. Chouteau-Papin Collection, Missouri Historical Society.

[28] William B. Astor to Pierre Chouteau, Jr., February 11, 1833. Chouteau-Papin Collection, Missouri Historical Society.

Pierre Chouteau, Jr., was supposedly an early friend to Fontenelle in New Orleans. Between 1816 and 1819 there is no record of Fontenelle's activities. Therefore, Fontenelle may have been in the employ of Chouteau when he first came to St. Louis. Long after, William Sublette and Joshua Pilcher, *et al,* indicated that Fontenelle was having difficulties, mainly with liquor. Yet Pierre Chouteau continued to support him, whether from sentiment for a sixteen year old he once knew or whether from a desire to have his allegiance to the A. F. Co., knowing the abilities of the man.

Fontenelle had been on the frontier trading for approximately fifteen years. But a good description of him is difficult to locate. Writers have pictured him as saturnine, swarthy in appearance, temperamental, of refined sensibilities, a man of talents, intemperate, a gentleman, and affectionate with his family. DeVoto even wrote that "there had been a mysterious romance in his earlier life." [29] But he did not enlarge on this interesting information. Fontenelle certainly enjoyed the finer things in life, as Alfred Jacob Miller confirmed in 1837.[30] Fontenelle's sarcasm appeared in a letter written to William Laidlaw from the rendezvous of 1833 concerning men hired by the company. "For God's sake if you can find a tight hole to put in Dean I wish you would do it and keep him there untill his time is out it would be rendering a service to humanity – the other five, send them down to their Mamas & Buttermilk." [31] More often than not, however, Fontenelle has been pictured as a refined, well-educated man who did not fit the ordinary description of a Mountain Man.

Fontenelle came into contact with individuals who were perhaps more out of place in the Rocky Mountains than he. While traveling down the Missouri River by canoe from

[29] Bernard DeVoto, *Across The Wide Missouri* (Boston, 1947), 225.

[30] Marvin C. Ross (ed.), *The West of Alfred Jacob Miller* (Norman, 1951), 49.

[31] Lucien Fontenelle to William Laidlaw, Green River Rendezvous, July 31, 1833. Chouteau-Walsh Collection, Missouri Historical Society.

Bellevue, Lucien met the Steamboat "Yellowstone" on its journey up the river May 2, 1833. On board was Maximilian, Prince of Wied-Neuwied, on a trip to the mountains.[32] Fontenelle undoubtedly enjoyed his presence for a while. By the 18th, he left Bellevue for Fort Pierre, where he arrived sometime toward the end of May. On June 8, the caravan with sixty men and 185 horses and Fontenelle headed for Green River Rendezvous.[33] Once again Andrew Drips was kept waiting. Robert Campbell and Bonneville were there also. But Fontenelle achieved nominal successes in the trading, mostly through the efforts of Drips. Etienne Provost was sent east with the returns.

During the rendezvous, an incident with a mad wolf occurred, causing great excitement and fear throughout the nearby camps. Charles Larpenteur recorded in *Forty Years A Fur Trader,* that ". . . we learned that a mad wolf had got into Mr. Fontenelle's camp about five miles from us, and had bitten some of his men and horses."[34] Only one man was named by Larpenteur as being badly bitten and that was George Holmes, who later went mad, according to information Fontenelle gave Larpenteur.

> For some days he could not bear to cross the small streams which they struck from time to time, so that they had to cover him over with a blanket to get him across; and at last they had to leave him with two men until his fit should be over. But the men soon left him and came to camp. Mr. Fontenelle immediately sent back after him; but when they arrived at the place, they found only his clothes, which he had torn off his back. He had run away quite naked, and never was found.[35]

There were many hazards to overcome living in the wilderness; a mad wolf was just one.

---

[32] Reuben G. Thwaites (ed.), "Travels in the Interior of North America" by Maximilian, Prince of Wied, in *Early Western Travels* (Cleveland, 1906), XXII, 264-65.

[33] *Ibid.,* 332.

[34] Charles Larpenteur, *Forty Years A Fur Trader,* Elliott Coues (ed.) (Ross & Haines, Inc. 1962) I, p. 36.   [35] *Ibid.,* 41.

The news that Chouteau would no longer supply Fontenelle and Drips reached Fontenelle at the rendezvous on Ham's Fork in 1834. He and Drips had remained in the mountains the previous fall to trap; Drips in the Snake River country, Fontenelle the Utah country. Étienne Provost, who led the caravan westward that summer, brought a letter from Fontenelle's good friend, J. Charles Cabanné, who stated: "The A. F. Co. will not be permitted to furnish you with any more goods."[36] Cabanné was willing to risk all for his close friend. "But my father is inclined to think that you perhaps would prefer a situation not quite so adventurous . . . he says that he is sertain that he has an offer to make you that will sute you better."[37] He did not elaborate on the elder Cabanné's proposal. The reason behind this news was the fact that the A. F. Co. had made arrangement with William Sublette and Robert Campbell who agreed to abandon the Upper Missouri. Fitzpatrick, Milton Sublette and Jim Bridger formed a new partnership out of the old R. M. F. Co. By the end of the 1834 rendezvous, however, Fontenelle arranged affairs so that all concerned were in the pay of the A. F. Co. "I have entered into a partnership with the others and the whole of the beaver caught by them is to be turned over to us by agreement made with them in concluding the arrangement."[38] Fontenelle, Fitzpatrick, Bridger, and M. Sublette formed the new partnership now called Fontenelle, Fitzpatrick & Company. Fort Laramie became their base, sometimes referred to as Fort John, Fort William and even Fort Fontenelle or Fort Lucien.[39] Drips and Bridger returned to the fall hunt. Fontenelle went east to coordinate his affairs with the new developments.

---

[36] J. Charles Cabanné to Lucien Fontenelle, April 9, 1834. Drips Papers, Missouri Historical Society.   [37] *Ibid.*

[38] Chittenden, *op. cit.*, 305.

[39] Joshua Pilcher to Pierre Chouteau, Jr., June 21, 1836. Chouteau-Papin Collection, Missouri Historical Society. Pilcher refers to Fort William which he has come to take possession of as Fort Lucien.

The historic A. F. Co. caravan of 1835 was led by Fontenelle. Marcus Whitman, doctor and missionary, along with Samuel Parker were members of this expedition. This caravan was stymied at the outset in Bellevue with an outbreak of cholera. Suffice it to state here that through the advice and ministrations of the good doctor, a complete breakdown was prevented, although Fontenelle himself came down with the dreaded disease. When the caravan arrived at Fort Laramie, Fontenelle wrote to Andrew Drips who was waiting at the rendezvous, to give special care and attention to the two gentlemen who had accompanied him, "the Doctor particularly, He has been of great service to us." [40]

The effects of cholera and the long tedious trip undoubtedly overtaxed Fontenelle's strength. Fitzpatrick took the caravan on to the rendezvous. Fontenelle wrote Drips that "I have had a good deal of difficulty in getting up this outfit on account of the heavy expenses that we are under. we ought to try and make them as small as possible if you can so arrange it." [41] The expenses of the westward bound caravan, notes due to creditors, and the wages due the men created great expenses indeed. William Sublette indicated that Fontenelle would have to pay out wages amounting to $40,000. [42]

After Fitzpatrick came back to Laramie, Fontenelle proceeded east to Bellevue (Dr. Whitman again accompanying him) with about 120 packs of beaver. William Sublette commented that "Fontenelle they say leads near about the same life us usual." [43] Fontenelle was drinking heavily. His continuous merrymaking gave Sublette grave doubts. He had a reason for concern as Fontenelle was in debt to him and no settlement in sight. The A. F. Co., however, settled

[40] Lucien Fontenelle to Andrew Drips, August 1, 1835. Drips Papers, Missouri Historical Society.   [41] *Ibid.*

[42] William L. Sublette to Robert Campbell, November 2, 1835. Campbell Papers, Missouri Historical Society.   [43] *Ibid.*

one note due of Charles Cabanné and Fontenelle,[44] but the debts then owed by Fontenelle, Fitzpatrick & Company to him were another matter. Eventually Fontenelle and Fitzpatrick sold Fort Laramie and all of their equipment including wagons, horses, mules, tents, etc. to the A. F. Co. Fontenelle's partnership with Fitzpatrick ended as a total loss for the company. The debt still remained a problem. Pilcher now in the employ of the A. F. Co. arrived at Fort Laramie (Fort Fontenelle – Fort Lucien) June 1836, to bring about the final solution to the debts and the need for the post. Perhaps because of his financial troubles that winter, Fontenelle decided that a visit to New Orleans was needed.

Fontenelle's only sister, Amelia, had remained in New Orleans and married a prominent lawyer, Henry Lockett. During Fontenelle's visit (the first in twenty years) he learned that property which had been appropriated by some individual belonged to his late father. As a result, Lucien was compelled to sue for compensation or recovery of this land, reportedly worth $35,000. Unquestionably he needed money. At this point, Fontenelle even doubted whether Pierre Chouteau would honor a draft drawn on the house of Chouteau so he asked his friend Sarpy to honor it himself.[45] There is little known to indicate the success of this lawsuit or of anything else that may have occurred during the New Orlean's trip.[46]

If Fontenelle traveled with Fitzpatrick that spring the

[44] William L. Sublette to Robert Campbell, February 27, 1836. Campbell Papers, Missouri Historical Society.

[45] Lucien Fontenelle to S. P. Sarpy, New Orleans, May 5, 1836. Chouteau-Papin Collection, Missouri Historical Society.

[46] Fontenelle may have been successful in borrowing money from his sister and brother-in-law. In 1870 a niece inquired of Father DeSmet what he knew of the disposition of her uncle's property. See fn. 54. In 1885, however, this same niece, Mrs. A. L. Thompson, wrote that an ad appeared in a St. Louis newspaper around 1870 or 1871 asking for heirs to property in Bellevue, Nebraska. "Transactions and Reports of the Nebraska Historical Society," Robert W. Furnas (ed.) I, pp. 90-93.

literature does not say. Among the A. F. Co.'s party traveling west May 1836, were Dr. Marcus Whitman and his bride, Narcissa. If Fontenelle was not along, it was too bad as he would have enjoyed the company of the vivacious Mrs. Whitman.[47]

Nevertheless Fontenelle was with Andrew Drips at the rendezvous on the Green River that summer. Joshua Pilcher came on to the rendezvous also. Kit Carson related "I joined Fontenelle's party and we started for the Yellowstone. We trapped the Yellowstone, otter, and Muscle Shell Rivers and then up the Big Horn and on to Powder River, where we wintered."[48] The Powder River area was a favorite wintering ground for the trappers. Most often free of snow, plenty of grass, and plenty of buffalo made this a paradise in winter.

In April of 1837, Fontenelle broke camp and continued the hunt for that (fast becoming) elusive beaver. Returning to the Yellowstone, he led his men to the North Fork of the Missouri. They discovered a large village inhabited by their favorite enemy, the Blackfeet. As Carson stated ". . . the small-pox had not killed all the Blackfeet. . ." With forty-one men including Carson, the trappers attacked the village. For three hours the fight raged until the ammunition began to run out. The Blackfeet soon became aware of the fact and began pressing forward. The trappers retreated and finally were aided by Fontenelle and the rest of the camp. Fighting close at hand, the trappers routed the Indians. "This ended our difficulties with the Blackfeet for the present hunt."[49] Fontenelle left the brigade early and went on to Fort Laramie. Carson does not mention this. In

[47] Also traveling with the caravan were Rev. and Mrs. H. H. Spalding, W. H. Gray, and Miles Goodyear. All were to make their places in the history of the West. C. M. Drury (ed.), *First White Women Over the Rockies* (Glendale, 1963), I, pp. 49-51.

[48] Blanche C. Grant, *Kit Carson's Own Story of His Life* (Taos, 1926), 38-39.

[49] *Ibid.,* 40-42.

the Joe Meek story, *River of the West,* Mrs. Victor says, "About the first of January, Fontenelle, with four men, and Captain Stuart's party, left camp to go to St. Louis for supplies." [50] At this point, by Meek's account, Fontenelle committed suicide. However, Osborne Russell recorded events of the trapping parties led by Fontenelle that summer and winter. When Captain Stewart returned to Fort Laramie, Alfred Jacob Miller, the renowned painter accompanying him, stated that "Fontenel was in command of the fort and received us with kindness and hospitality." [51] Obviously, Lucien was very much alive. After the rendezvous on the Green River, Fontenelle then led another brigade into the Yellowstone country and the Upper Missouri. Sometime in February of 1838, he purchased supplies at Fort Laramie for his trading party in the Crow region. Something was wrong, however. Either Fontenelle was unsuccessful in his trapping or liquor was getting the best of him. He was having difficulty making ends meet. Although Myra Eells recorded in her diary in the spring of 1838 that a horse was sold to "Capt. Fontenelle for forty dollars," [52] by August of 1838, Fontenelle wrote to Peter Sarpy that he did not have any horses, and that articles were left "en cache" at the fort for ". . . those persons who will come to take charge of it. . ." [53]

Lucien Fontenelle must have decided enough was enough. He may have taken another trapping party into the mountains, but with all equipment now turned over to the A. F.

[50] Victor, *op. cit.,* 224.

[51] Ross, *op. cit.,* 49. William Drummond Stewart came from Scotland, son of a Scottish nobleman. He had fought in the Napoleonic Wars; restless, he journeyed to America, traveling to the Rocky Mountains many times. He became quite familiar with the people involved in the fur trade.

[52] "Journal of Myra Eells," *Transactions of the Oregon Pioneer Association* (1889), 73. Drury, *op. cit.,* II, pp. 87-88.

[53] Lucien Fontenelle to P. A. Sarpy, August 5, 1838. Chouteau-Papin Collection, Missouri Historical Society.

Co., he undoubtedly returned east to Bellevue and his family. The effects of his heavy drinking and his failures in the mountains probably broke his spirit. At thirty-nine years of age, Lucien Fontenelle died at Bellevue (today Bellevue, Nebraska).

Father J. P. DeSmet wrote in 1870: "I attended him (Lucien Fontenelle) in his last moments either in 1838 or 1839. . . Shortly after his death I started for the Rocky Mountains." (Father DeSmet traveled with the A. F. Co. fur caravan led by Andrew Drips in the spring of 1840.) "I married Mr. Fontenelle to the daughter of the renowned chief, La Cerf of the Omaha tribe. I baptized four of his children, three sons and a daughter."[54] In the archives of St. Mary's College, St. Marys, Kansas, the record of baptisms shows that Father DeSmet baptized the children January 9, 1839.[55] Henry Fontenelle wrote in 1894 that he was about eight years old when his father passed away. He well remembered that Father DeSmet administered the last rites to his father, Lucien Fontenelle.[56]

The location of Fontenelle's burial plot is reportedly on the bluffs of the Missouri River overlooking the railroad tracks near what was once his home. Buried next to his father is Logan Fontenelle, Chief of the Omaha Indians. Today, Fontenelle Forest covers the area.

[54] DeSmet Papers, v, pp. 14, 157. Archives of the Missouri Province of the Society of Jesus. Pius XII Library, St. Louis University. A copy of this letter from Father Pierre DeSmet to Mrs. A. L. Thompson of New Orleans, September 16, 1870, was sent to me by William B. Faherty, s.j., St. Louis University, St. Louis.

[55] Kickapoo – Council Bluffs Register of Baptisms and Marriages, St. Mary's College, St. Marys, Kansas. A copy of this record was sent to me by Augustin C. Wand, s.j., archivist.

[56] Henry Fontenelle to Mrs. Harriet McMurphy, 1894. Original in the Old Log Cabin, Sarpy County Historical Society, Bellevue, Nebraska.

James Clyman

by CHARLES L. CAMP
University of California, Berkeley

James Clyman's long life span and active career began in post-revolutionary Virginia and extended twice across the continent before the Gold Rush. The course of his pioneering often put him well ahead of the advancing frontier. It took him into Ohio during the War of 1812 and into the Rockies in the early 1820s with the Ashley fur brigade. It sent him back to Illinois and into the Black Hawk War along with young Abe Lincoln; thence across the Plains to Oregon in 1844; over the Umpqua Trail to California the next year; then back across the Sierra and the steppes of Nevada to Illinois in 1846, and finally to return to California in '48. Here he married and raised a family in the final thirty-three years of his life.

Clyman's reminiscences and extensive diaries cover a large part of his remarkable career and provide rich source materials for some of the critical and decisive episodes of westward expansion. An intimate record of early, lesser-known years in the Rocky Mountain fur trade is included in his reminiscences. He had a feeling for history and was himself a part of an expansive history. He also had the luck to be on hand when events took decisive turns.

Clyman's parents and grandparents were tenant farmers in the 1790s in the Blue Ridge country of Virginia. They held a life-lease on land belonging to President George Washington. And James was born there, in the northeastern corner of Fauquier County, on February 1, 1792. Here young Jim received a sketchy education of which he made the most in later life. He learned to read, write, and "cipher," and to express himself poetically in his own individual way.

There were many other things that came by rough-and-tumble experience during his varied life. This was the training that enabled him to survive perilous adventures in the West. He could handle a rifle expertly. He was a supremely good hunter, a hunter of grizzly bear and buffalo, and a bee hunter. He could clear land with axe and mattock, and could plant corn in virgin soil with nothing better than a hoe. He knew how to build a cabin and a mill. He was able to run a country store, trap and skin a beaver, ride a horse, paddle a canoe, build a fire in a blizzard, construct a bullboat, and even manage the quartermaster supplies for a military detachment. He became a qualified surveyor, and in California he successfully undertook the all-round operation of a large ranch, where he raised fruits, walnuts, berries and vegetables, hay, grain and cattle. There he originated the Clyman plum, a variety prized in those days.

He was lithe and quick, with superb powers of endurance. He outran Indians and outsmarted them. His mind was as active as his body. He had poetic and literary tastes and feelings. He read Shakespeare, Byron, and the Bible, kept a diary for years, and wrote verses and reminiscences in his old age.

His writings are full of shrewd wisdom and the experience of the prairies, forests, and mountains. He notices the characteristics of the rocks and soil, the habits of animals, the nature of the Indians and of his pioneer associates. He wastes few words on trivialities. What he says is original, entertaining, historically valuable, often sublime in depth of feeling.

He was about six feet in height – rawboned, slender, a little stooped when he returned from the Rockies. His hair was dark brown, his eyes dark blue and piercing. His face was thin, his lips were thin, his forehead and cheek bones were high and prominent. He spoke clearly and distinctly with a slight Southern accent as a Virginian would, and his manner was courteous and dignified. He was not inclined to be garrulous or overly sociable; he was a little cool to strangers, and especially so to Indians.

He was held in affection and esteem by his friends and relatives, who respected him for his wisdom, enterprise, honesty, and courage. He had an independent spirit, self-confidence, and a love of adventure. The mysteries of the western wilderness were the challenges that led him on his long journeys, and he survived many dangers because of his intelligence, his skill in woodcraft, and his avoidance of harebrained recklessness.

His career as a mountain trapper was short, but it included the lesser-known, critical years 1823-27. And his memories of that era illuminate the pages of that influential period.

Jim Clyman left Virginia at the age of fifteen, with his father and mother and his brothers and sisters. Washington had died and Jim's grandfather had died. The Fauquier County lease was sold and the West beckoned. A quarter section was finally purchased in Stark County, Ohio, and the Clymans settled down to farming just at the time of Harrison's victory at Tippecanoe, November, 1811. Peace was not long to last. Hull's surrender loosed a mob of raiders, and the Clyman boys had to take to the saddle and scout the countryside to ward off skulking Indians who were killing settlers and burning cabins and crops. This was Jim's brief service in the War of 1812.

Clyman didn't take to farming. After four years with his father he decided to set out on his own, drifting finally into Jennings County, Indiana. Here he cleared twenty acres, planted corn with the hoe, traded the crop for Delaware Indian ponies and traveled on into Illinois. He got a job with a surveyor and learned the rudiments of surveying, and he soon became proficient enough to be entrusted with the completion of half a township subdivision.

In the summer of 1821, he was employed at a salt factory at the Salines on the Vermilion River in Illinois. Here he met Col. William S. Hamilton, son of the famous Alexander, who was on a surveying tour. Clyman worked under Col. Hamilton, and was left in the summer of 1822 in charge of finishing the job. That autumn found him still employed as a surveyor on the Sangamon River.

Early in the spring of 1823, James Clyman went down to St. Louis to draw his pay. While there he heard tales of the Ashley expedition of the previous year to the mouth of the Yellowstone River. These stories fired his imagination. So he sought out Lt. Gov. Ashley, just as Jedediah Smith had done the year before, and soon found himself hired to circulate through the grog shops and brothels of the city to flush out boatmen for the second expedition upriver. The motley crew finally assembled would have made Falstaff's Battalion look genteel by comparison – as Clyman quaintly remarked.

Ashley appointed Clyman as his trusted clerk on one of the "cargo-boxes," or clumsy keelboats. These heavy craft were at times propelled upstream by sail. When wind failed, they were laboriously poled, or even more laboriously dragged along by a tow-line, or "cordelle," attached to the mast and pulled by men wading in the water or along the slippery banks.

Supplies were obtained through the generosity of the officers at Fort Atkinson, as well as by night-time raids on the riverbank farms, and finally by hunting along shore. The long months passed. A boat came down the river bearing a messenger from the Yellowstone, Jedediah Smith, no less, to inform Ashley that Andrew Henry at the upriver post was short of horses. Ashley made a fatal decision. He moored at the Arikara Villages to trade ammunition for horses!

After three days of dickering, some twenty horses and over twenty-five men were left encamped on the sand beach or bar in front of the picketed village. That night it had stormed and the horses could not readily be taken to the boats. A few Whites tarried to visit in the village. About midnight a commotion started and one of these visitors was killed. The next morning the Rees began firing at the unprotected men and horses on the exposed sand bar. In a few minutes all the animals had been killed, as well as twelve of the men; and at least fourteen were wounded, three of whom were soon to die. A skiff sent to shore rescued four men.

Smith and Clyman, with others, finally jumped into the river to swim to the boats. Smith made it, but Clyman, hindered by his rifle, drifted downstream and was luckily pulled into one of the skiffs by Reed Gibson, who had bravely come to his rescue. Gibson was then fatally shot. Clyman escaped by running out onto the prairie and hiding. Those killed on the sand bar had to be left there; their scalps were taken "for the squaws to sing and dance over."

Thus ended what has been called "the worst disaster in the history of the Western fur trade." Boats could no longer traverse the river. Relief of Henry's Yellowstone post was delayed. The expedition had to await Army support to subdue the Rees. And when this help finally came, along with the allied Sioux, the results were abortive and unsatisfactory, as most of the seven hundred Ree warriors escaped, abandoning the village and dispersing for further depredations.

Col. Henry Leavenworth at Ft. Atkinson, when apprised of the dangerous situation upriver, determined on his own authority to march against the Rees, and give them cause to respect American enterprise. A sizable expedition was launched in five boats under command of Leavenworth and Joshua Pilcher. Pilcher had good reason to take an active part – one of his own parties under Immell and Jones had recently been massacred on the Yellowstone. Henry had also lost four men at the hands of the Blackfeet. Ashley, too, had good reason to await the coming of the troops. Success of his whole venture now hung on the success of the military campaign.

Ashley went into camp on a small island near the mouth of the Cheyenne River, living on "Scant and frquentle no rations allthough game was plenty on the main Shore," says Clyman.[1]

Perhaps it was my fault in greate measure for several of us being allowed to go on Shore we were luckey enough to get Several Elk each one packing meat to his utmost capacity   there came on a brisk shower of rain Just before we reached the main shore and a brisk wind arising the men on the boat would not bring the skiff and take us on board. . went off to the nearest timber made a fire and dried myself laid down and went to sleep   in the morning looking around I saw a fine Buck in easy gun shot and I suceeded in killing him   then I was in town plenty of wood plenty of water and plenty of nice fat venison   nothing to do but cook and eat   here I remained until next morning   then taking a good back load to the landing whare I met several men who had just landed for the purpose of hunting for me   after this I was scarcely ever allowed to go ashore for I might never return.

[Towards the end of July when the troops arrived, Ashley and Henry's forces joined them, together with men from Pilcher's Missouri Fur Company, and a body of Sioux warriors ready to take vengeance on the Rees.] A grand feast was held and speeches made by whites and Indians. [Three days later,] being 2 or three miles from the village the Sioux made a breake   being generally mounted they out went us although we ware put to the double Quick   and when we arived the plain was covered with Indians which looked more like a swarm [of] bees than a battlefield they going in all possible directions   the Rees having mounted and met the Sioux a half mile from their pickets   But as soon as we came in sight the Rees retreated into their village   the boats came up and landed a short half mile below the village   but little efort was mad that afternoon except to surround the Rees and keep them from leaving   the Sioux coming around one side and the whites around the other   Quite a number of dead Indians streued over the plain   I must here notice the Bravery of one Sioux   A Ree

---

[1] The quotations in this biographical sketch are from Clyman's own narrative. See note 2, at end of the biography.

ventured out some distance from the pickets and held some tantalizeing conversation with the Sioux, one Siox on a fast horse approached him slowly Still bantering each other to approach nearer   at length the Sioux put whip to his horse directly for the Ree and ran him right up to the [village]   then firing at full speed wheeled to retreat   the Rees inside of the pickets firing some 40 or 50 of them covered him completely in smoke but Sioux and his horse came out safe and the Rees horse went through the gate without a rider   the Rees friends came out and carried in the man   Several Rees lay dead and one in long shot of the pickets   the old Sioux chief Brought one of his wives up with a war club who struck the corps a number of blow with [the] club he tantalizeing the Rees all the time for their cowardice in [not] coming out to defend thair dead comrad and allowing his Squaws to strike the braves in gunshot of their village   a common habit of the Indians in war is the first man that comes to the body of a dead enemy is to take his Scalp   the second will take off his right hand   the third his left   the fourth his right foot   the fifth his left foot and hang the trophies around their necks to shew how near they ware to the death of their enemy on the field of Battle   and in this case a number of our Sioux showed Trophies   .   .   .   one large middle aged Sioux blonged to the grizzle Bear medicine came on hand [and] feet to the body of a dead Ree in the attitude of a grzzly Bear snorting and mimican the bear in his most vicious attitudes and with his teeth tore out mouth fulls of flesh from the breast of the dead body of the Ree

But I will not tire you with details of the savage habits of Indians to their enimies but I will merely state that it is easy to make a savage of a civilised man but impossible to make a civilised man of a savage in one Generation

Terms of peace were proposed on the third day. But that night the Rees abandoned their village and fled, much to the disgust of Major Pilcher, Captain Bennet Riley, and the Sioux allies. The Rees were to remain troublesome for years, despite this abortive demonstration against them. All the fur traders except those of Ashley had now been driven from the Upper Missouri.

Ashley got hold of enough horses to start Henry off again overland toward the Yellowstone. Clyman and a small party under Jed Smith and Thomas Fitzpatrick were detailed to go directly west from Ft. Kiowa, across the Black Hills and eventually over South Pass in the spring of 1824. Clyman's account of this makeshift expedition is the only one available. But the route is traced on the Gibbs copy of one of Jedediah Smith's lost maps – along the north side of White River; into the Black Hills probably by way of Buffalo Gap, a natural gateway that can be seen from afar; out of the hills through the narrow gorges at or in the vicinity of Hell Canyon; and thence westward into the Powder River country. Here Jed Smith was attacked by a grizzly. His scalp and ear were badly mangled and Clyman undertook a difficult and painful experiment in plastic surgery:

> I got a pair of scissors and cut off his hair and then began my first Job of d[r]essing wounds . . . I [found] the bear had taken nearly all of his head in his capcious mouth close to his left eye on one side and clos to his right ear on the other and laid the skull bare to near the crown of the head leaving a white streak where his teeth passed   one of his ears was torn from his head out to the outer rim after stitching all the other wounds in the best way I was capabl and according to the captains directions the ear being the last I told him I could do nothing for his Eare   O you must try to stich up some way or other said he   then I put in my needle stiching it through and through and over and over laying the lacerated parts together as nice as I could with my hands   water was found in about one mille when we all moved down and encamped the captain being able to mount his horse and ride to camp where we pitched a tent the onley one we had and made him as comfortable as circumstances would permit   this gave us a lisson on the charcter of the Grissly Baare which we did not forget

This also proved the hardihood of Jed Smith. The miracle was that the wounds didn't become infected. As Jim Bridger remarked when Whitman removed the arrowpoint so long embedded in his back – "meat jest don't spoil in the mountains."

While Smith was recovering, Clyman rode about the country. On one of these excursions he discovered "Quite a grove of Petrified timber standing laying and inclining at various angles . . . one stub in Perticular wa[s] so high that I could barely lay my hand on top sitting in the saddle." Such a standing stump and such a "grove" may be seen on the Timar Ranch, eleven miles east of Buffalo, Wyoming.

From here the party rode up over the broad, elevated backbone of the Bighorn Mountains, descended the western slope by way of Shell River, struck off south across the Owl Creek Mountains and arrived, exhausted, at the Crow Encampment on Wind River, near present Dubois, Wyoming. The early winter of 1823 was spent in grand buffalo hunts on foot and horseback. Hundreds of animals were killed. The meat was preserved by "jerking," or drying, over fires.

An abortive attempt was made to cross the Wind River Mountains at Union Pass. Deep snow blocked that effort. Then, with the help of a sand map that Clyman spread out on a buffalo robe, the Crows showed them how they might circle the south end of the Range and cross over an open pass to the Seeds-kee-dee-Agie or Sage Hen River, now known as the Green. This was enlightening. But it was more easily said than done at that season.

The wind-whipped hillsides near the South Pass, over eight thousand feet in elevation, were bitter cold. It took the trappers over two weeks to make the trip. Clyman and Sublette, out on a hunt, nearly froze to death when they were obliged to spend a night on icy ground under one buffalo robe, with nothing for fuel but the "small and scarce" sage brush. Even in the woods, the blizzards blew their fires away. Provisions played out. An occasional beaver, buffalo, antelope, or mountain sheep gave but temporary relief. They were hungry enough to "eat large slices raw." For lack of water they melted snow, and the horses ate snow until Little Sandy River on the Pacific side of South Pass was reached. Here they found the stream seemingly "froze to the bottom." They had cut down through the ice with tomahawks until they could reach no farther. Clyman then pulled out one of his pistols and fired into the hole. "Up came the water plentiful for man and horse."

The company divided on Big Sandy. Smith and "six or seven men" went south along the Green to trap. The rest worked the upper branches of that stream. Indians stole their horses, but they continued trapping on foot until the middle of June. Then, burying their furs, traps, and saddles, they started off for the appointed rendezvous on Sweetwater. That same day they came "face to face with five or six Indians mounted" on some of the stolen horses. They returned with the Indians to the village, recovered all their stolen property, dug up the cache, loaded their supplies and made their way back across the Divide and down to the Sweetwater. Still "no sight of Smith or his party." Fitzpatrick and Clyman followed downstream some fifteen miles and judged it to be unnavigable. Clyman continued eastward alone to find "some navigable point below where I would be found waiting my comrades who would not be more than three or four days in the rear." Clyman walked slowly down to the junction of the North Platte and found himself endangered by a party of Indians. In the maneuvers of escaping his "disagreeable neighbors" he barely missed a meeting with Jed Smith who had come down to look for him. Smith found Clyman's camp site, with Indian sign all about it. Convinced that Jim Clyman had been rubbed out, Smith sorrowfully returned upstream.

Clyman, of course, knew nothing of Smith's proximity, and he also didn't realize that Fitzpatrick was only one day behind him in a bullboat loaded with furs, a cargo that was doomed to capsize in the boiling rapids at Devils Gate. So poor Clyman, confused and distracted, determined to walk to civilization, not knowing for sure whether he was on the Platte or the Arkansas, and seriously misjudging the immense distance to the Missouri.

He had his gun and "plenty of powder but only eleven bullets." He thought this would not be enough to carry him back if he spent any more time awaiting or searching for his lost companions. So he started walking down the sandy banks of the Platte. Near the remains of an Indian camp he found a bullboat lodged on a sand bar. Correctly he assumed that white men had been in the vicinity and he had some "fient hope" of meeting them. He didn't know that Hugh Glass had barely missed being killed at this place and that two of Glass's comrades lay dead nearby, victims of the treacherous Rees.

He saw a band of wild horses, shot a buffalo, made a halter of the hide and tried to crease the stallion leading the herd. This was a failure. He became so unbearably lonely that he decided to risk a visit to a Pawnee settlement. The Pawnees robbed him of his blankets, ammunition, firesteel and flint and finally barbered him with a dull butcher knife. They kept his hair as a memento: "I bearly saved my scalp, but lost my hair," said Clyman.

From then on he had but little to eat – some parched corn the Pawnees had given him and the carcasses of two fighting badgers that he clubbed to death with old bones picked up on the prairie. This scanty supply kept him alive until he came in sight of the flag flying above Fort Atkinson. Thereupon he fell into a faint from weakness and fatigue, after his lone journey of 700 miles.

Ten days later Fitzpatrick and Branch arrived "in a more pitible state if possible" than Clyman himself. A letter was posted to Ashley apprising him of the rich trapping waters of the Upper Green River and the new access route by way of the forgotten and now rediscovered South Pass. The main gateway to the West had at last been opened.

Ashley lost no time in reaching Fort Atkinson. There he got together an outfit – twenty-five men, fifty horses and a wagon. Early in November, 1824, he started for the mountain trapping areas. Tom Fitzpatrick, Zacharias Ham, Jim Beckwourth and James Clyman were with him. The expedition, almost disastrous, achieved success only after bitter struggles with cold and starvation. They went by way of the Loup Pawnee villages, the Forks of the Platte, up the South Platte and the Cache la Poudre to the Laramie Plains and on to Green River.

Here Ashley split his party for the spring trapping. Clyman and Ham were sent northward toward the headwaters of the Green. Fitzpatrick went into the Uintas, and Ashley vainly attempted to navigate the river southward through the treacherous gorges and rapids.

Clyman was instructed to join Jed Smith and John H. Weber. His party of five had good luck until one night, on what is now La Barge Creek, they were attacked by Indians and La Barge was killed while he was standing guard. A shot barely missed Clyman in his bed. Clyman then decided to join Fitzpatrick, and that summer (1825) they all finally met at rendezvous on Henry's Fork of the Green. Here Clyman sold his furs to Ashley, one hundred skins weighing 166 pounds.

William Sublette was at this first rendezvous. Evidently Clyman decided to join Sublette's company the next spring. They went over to Salt Lake, made skin boats, and Clyman with three companions paddled around the Great Salt Lake. His companions may have been Louis Vasquez, Black Harris and Henry Fraeb. The idea of this voyage was evidently to search for beaver, and it was determined that the lake had no outlet and of course no beaver.

Sublette's party, including David Jackson, Robert Campbell, Jim Bridger, Daniel T. Potts and probably Jim Clyman, made a trip to the Yellowstone in the fall of 1826. This was the effective discovery of what is now Yellowstone Park. Potts' letter, published in a Philadelphia newspaper, made that region known more surely than Colter's stories. And from then on it was familiar to the trappers through Bridger's tales and by later visits.

In the summer of 1827, Clyman, evidently still with Sublette's party on Green River, seems to have been near-victim in another hairbreadth escape from Indians. In this encounter it is possible that the Iroquois, Pierre Tivanitagon, was killed, but the episode is incompletely documented.

It is known that Clyman left the mountains in the late summer of 1827 as pilot to a party returning to the settlements with furs. They reached St. Louis in October. Clyman sold 278 pounds of beaver to Wilson P. Hunt for $1,257. He took the money and bought land near Danville, Illinois, where he placed his brothers to farm. Clyman himself, still allergic to farming, entered into business at Danville, in partnership with Dan Beckwith, in a primitive log cabin store.

Then came Black Hawk's uprising. Clyman volunteered. He found himself in Jacob M. Early's Company, along with a young man named Abraham Lincoln. After service of less than a month, failing to catch up with the fleeing Redskins, Clyman joined Major Henry Dodge's famous battalion of Mounted Rangers. Black Hawk was captured. The troops moved to Rock Island where Lt. Clyman was appointed assistant commissary of subsistence (quartermaster) for Jesse B. Brown's Company. He joined the First Dragoons the next year, while the Winnebagoes were being removed from their ancestral Wisconsin home. His resignation was accepted on May 31, 1834. He then returned to his long-neglected business, and was appointed Colonel of the Wisconsin Militia by Governor Dodge, two years later.

In the meantime he was subjected to another hairbreadth escape in the forests of Wisconsin. Clyman and Ellsworth Burnett had planned to visit Rock River to examine land. On the way Burnett was treacherously murdered by suspicious Indians, and Clyman had to run for his life while being fired upon with his own shotgun. He barely escaped, with a load of buckshot in his back and thigh, as well as a broken elbow from a shot fired from Burnett's gun. He barely managed to hide beneath a fallen tree while his pursuers stood upon that very log. And he finally made his way to the Cold Springs settlements, supporting his broken arm in his right hand during an agonizing two-day journey, wet and cold in the rain. Here his Rocky Mountain comrade, John Bowen, nursed him until he was able to return to Milwaukee to have the buckshot taken out. Near the scene of this disaster, a small town bears Clyman's name.

James Clyman and Hiram J. Ross built a sawmill in the spring and summer of 1836, on the Monomonee River in what is now Wauwatosa, just west of Milwaukee. At that time Clyman owned eighty acres which are now within that city. He had also taken up land at Green Bay. He was active in politics, belonged to the Whig party and still found time to continue his business at Danville. He also took out a contract for the placing of milestones on the state road from Vincennes, Indiana, to Chicago.

During his engagement at the Ross mill, in 1840, Clyman kept a diary and memorandum book which has been preserved. It contains some original philosophical speculations on such abstractions as the velocity of light and the cause of the drifted boulders scattered by glacial action, north of the mouth of the Ohio River.

He developed a chronic cough in the winter of 1843-4, which started him off again on his restless wanderings, in search of a cure. He found himself at Independence, Missouri, in the spring of 1844, just in time to join the emigrants leaving on the long trip to Oregon. He traveled to Oregon in Colonel Nathaniel Ford's detachment and in that of General Cornelius Gilliam, keeping an interesting diary, the best of the records of that year's expedition.

The guide of Clyman's company was Moses "Black"

Harris, the famous Mountain Man whose tall tales have become legends of the fur-trade days. The early spring was exceptionally rainy along the Missouri bottoms and the emigrants suffered delays and exposure.

[May 24:] It rained all night by day our teams ware moving to the river which we had been expecting [to] fall but which began to rise again we let down by cords over a steep rock bluff through mud knee deep an[d] in the rain pouring in torrents me[n] women and children dripping in mud and water over Shoe mouth deep and I thought I never saw more determined resolution even amongst men than most of the female part of our company exhibited The leaving of home of near an dear friend the war whoop and Scalping Knif The long dreary Journey the privations of a life in a Tent with all the horrors of flood and field and even the element seemed to combine to make us uncomfortable

[May 28:] after a very tidious & toilsome d[a]ys drive I arived at my mess — wet as water could make me and found them all sheltering themselves in the best way they could about the waggons they ware fortunate enough however to have furnished themselves with a fair supply of wood & now commenced the tug of war for the rain again renued its strength & fell in perfect sluces as though the windows of heaven had again been broken up and a second deluge had commenced intermingled with vived flashes of Lightning and deep growling thunder . . . and here let me say there was one young Lady which showed herself worthy of [the] bravest undaunted poieneer of the west for after having Kneaded he dough she watched and nursed the fire and held an umblella over the fire and her skillit with the utmost composure for near 2 hours and baked bread enough to give us a very plentiful supper.

[After several days of searching for horses stolen by the Kaws, Clyman finally] went 10 miles up the river to the village of the head chief a tall lean wrinkld faced Filthy looking man with a forehead indicating deceet Dissimilutoin and intriegue and more like a Beggarly scape gallows than a Chief but nodoubt these fine Qualities are higly prized by the Kaw nation . . . He talked with great energy assuring me that if he could See his rascally scamps with our horses he would immediately bring them to us. . . I however put but little confidence in his asseverations.

[Later, Clyman] arived at [the] village in the midst of a Tremendeous hail storm and found about 20 Drunken Indians in a dirt covered

lodge half knee deep in water Judge of my feeling A rapid hail
Storm out [side] A hog wallow within and all in unison the Thunder
Lightning & hail the schreems and yells within and my object to
recover stolen propiety being instantly known all eyes were directed on
me A loud angry Quarrel commenced between my Friends and
enemies and my situation was far from being envious for Knives ware
soon drawn and one Flourished over my head the indian that held it
was soon grappled & a half dozen ware as soon wallowing in the mud
[the horses were finally recovered.]

[June 22:] news from civilization . . . there has has been a
great Troubling & Striving of the eliments. the mountain having at
last brot forth J. K. Polk Capt. Tyler & the invincible Henry Clay as
candidates of the Presidency go it Clay Just Whigs enough in
camp to take the curse off.

[Aug. 16:] saw the notable rock Independence with the names of its
numerious visitors most of which are nearly obliterated by the weather
& ravages of time amongst which I observed the names of two of my
old friends the notable mountaneers Thos. Fitzpatrick & W. L. Sublette as likewise one of our noblest politicians Henry Clay coupled in
division with that of Martin Van Buren.

[Aug. 24: On the upper Sweetwater,] all roled out except ourselves
who remain to take care of Mr. Barnett whose prospects for living
seem a little better than yestarday allthough yet quite small every
preparation seemed dull & melancholly & many bid the sick man their
last farewell look a Spade was thrown out & left which looked
rather ominous The ravens came croaking around us and the Shaggey
wolf was seen peeping from the hills . . . [Late in the evening
of the 26th] he departed this life verry easy . . . & all his
troubles were in Silent death having nothing better we cut a bed of
green willows and laid him out on the cold ground & all of us seated
ourselves around our camp fire & listned to the hair beadth escapes of
Mr. Harris & other Mountaineers. [The headstone inscribed by
Clyman on Joseph Barnett's grave can still be seen on a lonely ranch
in Wyoming.]

[Oct. 8:] Reached Mr. Perkins missionary station in the fore noon
now occupid by Mr. Waller delivered to him a letter taken from the
office at West Port Mr. Waller apears to be a gentleman but I do
not recolect that he thanked me for the care & trouble of bringing the
letter but the reverend gentleman must be excused for my appearance
certainly did not show that I could appreceate any civilities not having
shaved for about 15 day or changed clothes for more than 30 and the

Reverend gentleman pricking himself verry much on outward appearances as I have since understood.

[In late October Clyman reached Fort Vancouver.] The present incumbent Doct. McLaughlin received me verry hospitably and intertained us in the most kind genteel and agreeable manner during our stay at the Fort giving us all the information desired on all subjects connected with the country but seemed anxious that greate Brittain might retain the north of the Columbia river saying that it was poor and of little use except the Fur and peltries that it yealded   this may or may not be the fact.

Clyman spent the winter of 1844-5 in Oregon traveling about freely and writing his observations for the benefit of Elijah White, who was leaving for Washington "in the hopes of obtaining the gubernatorial chair." White gave him a letter to be delivered to Thomas O. Larkin in California concerning the murder in California of Elijah Hedding, the son of the Wallawalla chieftain. One result of this incident was the tragic Whitman massacre.

In June, 1845, Clyman was elected Captain of a company of emigrants bound for California over the hazardous Siskiyou route. They followed directions given by Joel P. Walker, who had brought his family into California over this trail. One of the members of Clyman's party was the wheelwright James Wilson Marshall, who was to discover gold at Coloma less than three years later.

Clyman found California in "a verry unsettled state," owing to the rebellion of the previous winter and the dissatisfaction of some of the Yankee emigrants. He visited William Knight, John Wolfskill, William Gordon, William Hargrave, and the hunting camp or cabin of Benjamin Kelsey, who with his teen-age wife Nancy and their baby had come to California over the Sierra in 1841.

At Monterey, Clyman spoke with Dr. John Townsend, an emigrant of 1844.

[He] found the Dr. a good feeling man much attached to his own oppinions as likiwise to the climate and country of California   his

[wife] a pleasant lady does not enter into all of her husbands chimerical speculations.

[On August 2 and 3 Clyman encountered] the far famed and redoubtable Capt [Isaac] Graham the hero of Farnhams travels in california and in fact the hero of six or seven revolutions in this province and the chivalrous captain has again during the last winter passed through the ordeal of one more revolution and again been a prisoner in the hands of his old Enimy Colonel Castro the Eex governor and has once more returned to his peacable domicil to his heards and his sawmill surrounded by impassable mountains about Eight miles from the Landing of Santa Cruz and if report be correct the hardy vetrian is fast softning down and he is about to cast away the deathly rifle and the unerring tornahawk for the soft smile of a female companion to nurrish him in his old age

Clyman returned to George Yount's ranch in Napa Valley, by way of San Jose and Ignacio Martinez' ferry across Carquinez Straits, "completely satasfied with travelling through California for in 28 days travel mostly through the spanish settlements we never found one grain of food for our animals and only three places where we slept in houses and those three owned by foreigners." He continues with extensive descriptions of the country and grizzly bear hunting in the vicinity of the Kelsey camp.

[Jan. 12, 1846:] Heard that Mr. Freemont had arived at suitors Fort and still more recently that Mr. Hastings and Party had likewise arived Both from the U States But no information has yet arived of the Politicks of the states in fact information of all Kinds Travels slow and is verry uncertain when it has arived you know nothing certain unless you see it yourself.

On January 21, Clyman enjoyed a visit from Isaac A. Flint of Wisconsin and feeling a "great desire to see Milwaukee" again, he wrote to Frémont offering him a company of American emigrants for the return journey. This offer was refused, in a letter that Frémont seems to have written to Clyman in March or April.

On March 21 Clyman heard that Frémont had

raised an american flag at his camp neare the Mision of St. Johns, and
that he was caled on to apeare before some of the so caled Legal authorities whice he declined to do And this cercumstance alarmed all of
the Californians and caused General Castro to rais 400 men which
report says are now under arms at Monteray no report However can
be relied on as but few men in this country can write you may form
some Idea of what reports are carried verbally from one to two hundred miles by an ignorant supersticious people

On April 16, 1846, Clyman met Lansford W. Hastings at
Johnson's ranch on Bear River, a tributary of the Feather
River. Preparations had now been made for the return overland trip with Hastings, Hudspeth and a small party. One
of the members, Owen Sumner Sr., and his family had "been
to Oregon from thence to California and still being dis-
satisfied is now returning to the states again after having
[spent] nearly five years in Traveling from place to place
as Likewise a small fortune."

After some difficulty owing to the early season and the
snow in the mountains, old Caleb Greenwood, the guide,
conducted the party across Nevada and out onto the treacherous Hastings' Cutoff, which none of the party had hitherto
seen. This was the route advocated in Hastings' book,
printed the previous year, and Hastings was planning to
direct emigrants of '46 back over this most difficult trail
which he now was investigating for the first time.

Clyman did not succumb to Hastings' propaganda. When
he met the emigrant trains at Laramie he tried his best to
warn the people of the dangers of the Cutoff and the delays
to be expected in crossing the Wasatch Mountains. He did
succeed in diverting some to the regular route by way of
Fort Hall, but the Donners and Reeds and others were not
to be dissuaded and went on to their tragic fate in the Sierra
that winter.

Clyman returned to Wisconsin and spent the winter with
his old comrade, John Bowen, at Wauwatosa. He evidently

tried to interest some of his friends in the purchase of land in California, and early in 1848 made arrangements to return west. His party of that year, of which he was the Captain on the latter part of the way, consisted largely of farmers from Indiana and Michigan. They were seeking new land, as they had not yet heard of the gold discovery. This overwhelming news reached them in present-day Nevada, where they met returning members of the Mormon Battalion.

Clyman maintained that this 1848 trip was without accident or incident. His memory may have been clouded by the presence in that train of the girl whom he married in California: Hannah McCombs, the daughter of Lambert and Hannah McCombs of Indiana. They settled on a farm near Napa, moved to Sonoma County for two years, and returned to develop the Napa ranch. They had five children, four of whom died in infancy of scarlet fever. Their surviving daughter, Lydia, married the Rev. Beverly Lamar Tallman, and they in turn raised seven children on the Clyman farm. This passed out of the family only a few years ago.

James Clyman died at Napa on December 27, 1881, in his ninetieth year. His headstone stands in the Tulocay Cemetery at Napa. He was one of the last of the notable frontiersmen who led their independent lives in the vanguard of western expansion.[2]

---

[2] Early sketches of Clyman appear in some of the Wisconsin and the Napa County, Calif., local histories. Reference also appear in H. H. Bancroft's *History of California*. An extensive account, with citation of sources, may be found in "James Clyman, American Frontiersman," by the present writer, published serially in the *Calif. Hist. Soc. Quarterly,* 1925-27, and twice reprinted, with some amplification: by the Society in 1928, and at the Champoeg Press, Portland, Oregon, in 1960. The present sketch is largely summarized from that biography, wherein sources are fully given.

James P. Beckwourth

by DELMONT R. OSWALD
Brigham Young University

Of the fur trappers and traders of the American frontier who played a significant role in the exploration of the trans-Mississippi west, perhaps one of the most interesting was James Pierson Beckwourth. Shrouded in a cloak of historic controversy, primarily of his own creation, this adventurous mulatto emerges as one of the most enigmatic characters of the fur trapping era.

Always searching for some form of renown, Beckwourth gave a detailed story of his life and adventures which was published in 1856. This work provided material for several books on his life, but controversy has arisen over its authenticity. It did succeed in gaining him the ignominious title, "Gaudy Liar." However, time and new sources have begun to come to his rescue and prove many of his assertions to be based on truth.

Jim was born of a mixed union on April 26, 1798, in Fredricksburg, Virginia,[1] with the surname "Beckwith;" not the better known "Beckwourth" by which he ultimately became noted. His father, Sir Jennings Beckwith, was a native of Richmond County,[2] and according to most accounts worked as an overseer on one of the plantations in the area. Reliable sources indicate that his mother, known

---

[1] T. D. Bonner, *Life and Adventures of James P. Beckwourth* (New York, 1856), 13. Hereafter cited as Bonner's *Beckwourth.*

[2] Paul Edmond Beckwith, *The Beckwiths* (Albany, 1891), 55-57. The title of "Sir" was inherited from Jennings Beckwith's great-grandfather, who was created a baronet by Charles II of England in 1681. All such titles were officially given up in America after the American Revolution, but usage of the word often stayed on.

only as Miss Kill, was probably a slave.[3] This would account for Jim's dark, swarthy appearance and broad facial features.

In 1810 young Beckwith's father moved the family west to the recently acquired Louisiana Territory, where they settled on some land twelve miles east of St. Charles, Missouri, at what was called "The Point."[4] Here, bordered on the south by the Missouri River and on the north by the Mississippi, Jim found himself at the crossroads of the westward movement.

The Louisiana Territory was still a part of the untamed frontier in 1810, and Indian depredations on the settlements were common occurrences. Scenes of violence, death, and pillage were not strange to him and helped to cast the mold for what he was to become.

At the age of fourteen, Jim was apprenticed to George Casner and John L. Sutton at their blacksmith shop in St. Louis.[5] Here he spent the next five years, until trouble with his employers forced him to seek employment elsewhere. He hired out as a hunter and then worked in the Galena lead mines until the fall of 1824 when he responded to William H. Ashley's call for men to join a fur trapping expedition to the Rocky Mountains.[6]

It was a rash young man that joined Ashley's third expedition, especially so since he had heard of the disastrous results of two previous ventures. Undaunted, Jim contracted with Ashley to be an engagé, serving as a horse buyer while he waited for his employer to receive word of conditions in the

---

[3] *Ibid.*, 57. See also James Haley White, "St. Louis and Its Men Fifty Years Ago," unfinished manuscript in St. Louis History Papers, Missouri Historical Society, p. 3, and Colonel Henry Inman, *The Old Santa Fe Trail* (Topeka, 1916), 337.

[4] Deed Record B, Recorder of Deeds Office, St. Charles County, St. Charles, Missouri, pp. 104-108.

[5] Lewis H. Garrard, *Wah-To-Yah and the Taos Trail*, Ralph P. Bieber ed. (Glendale, 1938), 310.

[6] Delmont R. Oswald, "James Pierson Beckwourth, 1798-1866" (Unpublished M.A. thesis, Brigham Young University, 1967), p. 21.

mountains and complete an unsuccessful campaign for governor of Missouri. For these reasons the expedition did not
leave St. Louis until September 24, 1824, a very late date to
begin an overland journey to the Rockies. Attempting to
make up for lost time, Ashley mounted his party of some
two dozen men on the horses Jim had acquired and moved
north to Fort Atkinson where they awaited the arrival of
Thomas Fitzpatrick, who was returning from recovering
some furs cached on the North Platte.

All preparations being finally completed, the expedition
left Fort Atkinson November 3, with twenty-five men, fifty
pack horses and a wagon – the first vehicle to travel north of
the Santa Fe Trail.[7] Due to the lateness of the season, the
party moved as quickly as possible, Jim and the other raw
recruits learning their jobs as they went. Hoping to purchase supplies and horses from the Grand Pawnee Indians,
the expedition followed the Indian traces up the Platte
River Valley toward their villages. Snow began to fall and
hunger was already a threat because of the lack of game
along the way. Finding the villages deserted, morale dropped to an extreme low. Jim said their food supply consisted
only of a daily ration of gruel consisting of one-half pint of
flour mixed with water, an occasional duck or goose shared
by the entire group, and the bodies of the horses that died.
Forcing their way through the drifts, the men continued up
the Platte to the confluence of its two forks where they met
some friendly Loup Pawnees who were willing to offer aid.
After taking only a brief rest, the expedition then continued
up the South Platte River. Encountering deep snow drifts,
the wagon had to be abandoned.

On January 20, 1825, Jim caught his first glimpse of the
Rocky Mountains. Soon the party reached the site of
Greeley, Colorado, and rested while they trapped the

---

[7] Donald McKay Frost, *Notes on General Ashley, the Overland Trail and South
Pass* (Barre, Massachusetts, 1960), 41.

streams in the area. Here Jim gained his first experience in setting beaver traps in ice covered streams. After two weeks, Ashley led the men northwest to the Laramie Plains, north of the Medicine Bow Range, forded the North Platte River, and proceeded to cross the Continental Divide by going through the Great Divide Basin. Enroute seventeen horses were stolen by Crow Indians. With the rest of the men, Jim cursed the natives vociferously, not realizing that this aboriginal practice would soon become a part of his way of life. On April 19 the party struck the Green River about fifteen miles north of its confluence with the Big Sandy.[8] Here Ashley divided the party into four separate groups which were to trap in different directions and then rendezvous at a point he would designate farther down Green River.

Jim was one of the party of six under James Clyman. This group moved up the Green and began to trap successfully on a stream known as Horse Creek. Soon after, they were joined by a party of young Indian braves who pretended to be very friendly. These visitors traveled with the trappers for three or four days, then suddenly, at night, attacked their hosts. Thanks to their lone, luckless guard La Barge, who was killed, Jim and the others were warned and managed to escape.[9] With little debate, the entire party agreed to abandon the hunt and attempt to join one of the other trapping parties. They returned down the Green, soon meeting a party of Ashley men and proceeded to the spot marked for the rendezvous.

The rendezvous of 1825 was held on Henry's Fork some miles above its junction with the Green. Here on July 1st, Jim experienced his first trade fair and all the excitement which attended it. He could not have realized much of a

---

[8] "The Diary of William H. Ashley" as printed in Dale L. Morgan, *West of William H. Ashley* (Denver, 1964), 106.

[9] Bonner's *Beckwourth*, 64-65, and Charles L. Camp, ed., *James Clyman, Frontiersman* (Portland, 1960), 38.

profit at the fair for his share of the hunt; only 166 pelts had been collected by Clyman's entire party,[10] and most of the pay was in trade goods. However, seeing the large amount of goods acquired by such veterans as Jedediah Smith and J. H. Weber, who had been out for two years, he decided to fulfill his contract by going back to St. Louis where he could arrange his affairs so that he could return the next year. He was therefore included in the party to help transport the nearly 9,000 furs back east.

The return journey was relatively easy compared to the initial trip out. The party moved east over South Pass and descended Wind River to the Big Horn. Here Ashley raised a cache of forty packs of fur.[11] Near present Thermopolis, Wyoming, they killed enough buffalo to provide skins to build bullboats for all the furs and men going to St. Louis. The rest of the men returned to the valley of the Green for another winter's hunt.

At the mouth of the Yellowstone River Ashley and his men were fortunate in meeting the government expedition under General Henry Atkinson, and were able to obtain passage for men and furs on the expedition's boats. Thus Jim and the others were able to sail down stream protected by soldiers and with little to do except hunt and provide meat for the troops.

Upon reaching Council Bluffs on September 19th, Jim felt he could properly be called a Mountain Man. He had been one of the first trappers to make a winter expedition from St. Louis to the Green River region, and was one of the first Americans to explore the mountains of northern Colorado, to pass through the Great Divide Basin, and to cross most of southern Wyoming.

[10] Morgan, *West of Ashley*, 126.

[11] There is controversy over whose cache this was. See Oswald, "James Pierson Beckwourth. . . ," 37, footnote 48, and Hafen, *Mountain Men and the Fur Trade*, I, pp. 78-79.

The visit with Jim's family and friends was a short one, for preparations to return to the mountains began immediately and he had enlisted again – this time as a free trapper. Under the direction of Jedediah Smith the party left St. Louis on October 30th. Once again it was a late start, and again the men had to face extreme cold and deprivation. Following the south bank of the Missouri, they moved to the Kansas River and up it to the Republican. Here, due to food shortage and severe weather, they decided to make a winter camp. Over one third of the pack mules had died and there were not enough left to carry the trade goods. Smith then decided that Jim and Moses Harris should be sent to the Republican Pawnee Villages for horses. If none were available, they were to return to St. Louis and inform Ashley that the expedition was stranded. Jim, cocky and young, welcomed the assignment; he considered it a test to see if he could hold his own with an experienced veteran. In his own account of the ensuing trip, he places himself in the position of the hero, but facts tend to prove otherwise.[12]

The two men found no Indians at the Republican Villages, so, traveling on foot, they returned to the Missouri and started back to St. Louis to seek Ashley's help. It was an extremely strenuous trip and both men had to rest when they reached the post of Curtis and Ely at the mouth of the Kansas River. Jim then went to the post of F. G. Chouteau and stayed the winter packing furs while Harris continued on to St. Louis.[13]

By March 8, 1826, Ashley had a relief party under way. Picking up Jim on the way, he soon reached Smith's party near the Grand Island of the Platte. With the arrival of the relief party and the extra horses, the expedition was able to move to a point where game could be found. They proceeded up the North Platte, along the Sweetwater, crossed

---

[12] Oswald, "James Pierson Beckwourth. . . ," 47-49.

[13] Morgan, *West of Ashley,* 144.

South Pass and reached Green River. Then moving west-ward to Bear River, they pushed on and reached Willow (Cache) Valley in late May or early June. Here Jim witnessed the second rendezvous, a bigger and better one than that of the year before. The event of major importance was the selling of the company by Ashley to Smith, William Sublette and David Jackson.

At the end of the rendezvous, the three new owners each took a party and went in search of new fur grounds, Jim being with William Sublette's group. They first moved north to the Snake River, followed it to its forks, and then turned toward the Teton Mountains. They trapped the headwaters of both the Columbia and the Missouri and were the first white men to enter the Yellowstone Park area.[14]

Returning to the Willow (Cache) Valley area for the winter, the party was set upon by Blackfeet who succeeded in running off some of their horses. Jim claims that he and a Swiss trapper named Alexander attempted to recover them and in so doing were forced to run for their lives. His account, which helped to build his reputation as the "Gaudy Liar," is as follows:

> They soon discovered us, and, from their not making immediate pursuit, I inferred that they mistook us for two of their own party. However, they soon gave chase. They being also on foot, I said to my companion, "Now we have as good a chance of escaping as they have of overtaking us."
>
> The Swiss (named Alexander) said, "It is of no use for me to try to get away; I can not run; save yourself and never mind me."
>
> "No," I replied, "I will not leave you; run as fast as you can until you reach the creek; there you can secrete yourself, for they will pursue me."
>
> He followed my advice and saved himself. I crossed the stream, and when I again appeared in sight of the Indians I was on the summit of a small hill two miles in advance. Giving a general yell, they came in

---

[14] *Ibid.,* 162-63.

pursuit of me. On I ran, not daring to indulge the hope that they would give up the chase, for some of the Indians are great runners and would rather die than incur the ridicule of their brethren. On, on we tore; I to save my scalp, and my pursuers to win it. At length I reached the Buttes, where I had expected to find the camp, but, to my inconceivable horror and dismay, my comrades were not there. They had found no water on their route, and had proceeded to the river, forty-five miles distant.

My feelings at this disappointment transcended expression. . . The Indians were close at my heels; their bullets were whizzing past me; their yells sounded painfully in my ears; and I could almost feel the knife making a circuit round my skull. On I bounded, however, following the road which our whole company had made. . . My companions perceived me a mile from the camp, as well as my pursuers; and, mounting their horses to meet me, soon turned the tables on my pursuers. . . According to the closest calculation, I ran that day ninety-five miles.[15]

Upon reaching Willow Valley again, Jim and the others set to work constructing rough cabins in which to await spring and the renewal of the hunt, for winter had already set in. When it came, Jim and some others began constructing caches to hold their furs. One such cache caved in and buried a Canadian who had been inside digging. Thinking he was already dead, they merely left him and proceeded to dig another near by. As a result of this incident and the fact that there were other caches dug in the area, the trappers changed the name of the place to Cache Valley. Jim seems to have been the first to use the new name.[16] The death of the Canadian proved to be a windfall for Jim, who claimed the man's Indian wife. Now, like many other trappers, he had someone to cook and sew for him, make his bed, and attend to other trifling duties.

Jim spent the spring hunt in the party of Thomas Fitzpatrick, trapping along the Portneuf and Bear rivers, but returning to Bear Lake for the rendezvous of 1827. Here

---

[15] Bonner's *Beckwourth*, 123-24.
[16] Cecil Alter, *Jim Bridger* (Norman, 1962), 83.

as the trappers and Indians gathered, he, Sublette and others participated in a battle on the side of the friendly Snake Indians against the attacking Blackfeet, and distinguished themselves in a pitched battle.

After the rendezvous of 1827, Jim says:

> We spent the summer months at our leisure, trading with the Indians, hunting, sporting, and preparing for the fall harvest of beaver. We made acquaintance with several of the Black Feet, who came to the post to trade. One of their chiefs invited Mr. Sublet to establish a branch post in their country, telling him that they had many people and horses, and plenty of beaver, and if his goods were to be obtained, they would trade considerably; his being so far off prevented his people coming to Mr. Sublett's camp.
>
> The Indian appeared sincere, and there being a prospect of opening a profitable trade, Sublet proposed to establish a post among the Black Feet. . .[17]

Once again Jim went with the party of Sublette into the upper Snake River country. He claims that there he and two others separated from the main party and set up trade with the aforementioned Blackfeet along the Beaverhead River, a branch of the Missouri. Some historians question this statement, for the Blackfeet were always considered too treacherous to trade with. Jim's assertion, however, may well be true, for Ashley states in a letter to Thomas H. Benton: "These people (the Blackfeet) had always, until a short time previous to committing the outrages herein mentioned, been considered enemies to our traders; but about that time some of them manifested a friendly disposition, invited a friendly intercourse and trade, and did actually dispose of a portion of their furs to Messrs. Smith, Jackson, and Sublette."[18]

After twenty days of trading, Jim's group rejoined Sublette's and together they prepared to winter on the Snake.

[17] Bonner's *Beckwourth,* 113.

[18] Letter of William H. Ashley to Thomas H. Benton, St. Louis, January 20, 1829, as published in Morgan, *West of Ashley,* 186-188.

Spring of 1828 found them in the Salmon River-Birch Creek area of Idaho, where they were attacked and one of their number named Coty was killed by the Blackfeet. This attack was only one of many to take place during the ensuing year. Without apparent provocation, the Blackfeet had commenced hostilities with redoubled effort and continually attempted to drive the Americans out of their territory. Proceeding down Birch Creek, the whites reached the Snake and continued back to Bear Lake for the rendezvous.

Soon after their arrival, they received word that Robert Campbell's party was in the area. Jim and two friends rode out to met them. No sooner had they met however, than they were attacked by a large group of Blackfeet and chased to a small clump of willows where they tried to make a stand. After fighting nearly five hours, the trappers found their ammunition dangerously low. Jim and a fellow trapper named Calhoun volunteered to make a run for help on horseback. Taking the two best horses, they charged straight through the shooting Blackfeet and headed for the camp at the rendezvous. Returning with the necessary help, they found the Blackfeet gone and Campbell's party quite safe.

With the termination of the rendezvous of 1828, Jim entered the trapping fields for the last time as a member of a party of Smith, Jackson, and Sublette. This time he was with Robert Campbell and trapped in the Powder River area of Wyoming. It was here that he first became interested in and involved with the Crow Indians. They were peaceful with the trappers and, because of his dark skin, Jim found association particularly easy. Determining that he would make more money trading and trapping with the natives than he had with his fellow trappers, he decided to join them. He says:

 . . . I said to myself, "I can trap in their streams unmolested and derive more profit under their protection than if among my own men, exposed incessantly to assasination and alarm." I therefore resolved to abide with them, to guard my secret, to do my best in their company, and in assisting them to subdue their enemies.[19]

In January or February of 1829, Jim signed a promissory note for the amount he owed Smith, Jackson, and Sublette,[20] and leaving his white friends began a new life with the savages.

It was a commonly accepted practice of the different Indian tribes to adopt white men and even confer upon them chieftainships. They recognized the white man's power in warfare, and if they found one who could enter easily into their way of life, they would accept him and honor him with a measure of authority. Jim was such a man, and he claims to have become a chief in the tribe within a year after he joined it. Surprisingly enough, he records in his own account that he earned the chieftaincy by proving himself as any member of the tribe would have had to do and not by the outrageous means circulated in myths about him.[21] The title "chief" did not necessarily mean the one leader of the tribe among the Crow; any man achieving a war honor of each kind became a chief, although not necessarily the head chief.

The first years with the Indians were spent by Jim in learning the Crow language, getting used to their customs and habits, and, as he stated, participating in their war parties. A typical example of his numerous accounts of such activity is as follows:

> After fêting for about ten days among my new neighbors, I joined a small war party of about forty men, embodied for the ostensible

---

[19] Bonner's *Beckwourth,* 101-106.

[20] I.O.U. of James P. Beckwith to Smith, Jackson and Sublette dated January or February 6, 1829, Sublette Papers, Missouri Historical Society, St. Louis, Missouri.

[21] Oswald, "James Pierson Beckwourth. . . ," 70. For an explanation of the Crow title of "chief" see Edward S. Curtis, *North American Indian* (Cambridge, 1908), IV, pp. 9, 177.

purpose of capturing horses, but actually to kill their enemies. After advancing for three days, we fell in with a party of eleven of the Blood Indians, a band of the Black Foot tribe, immemorial enemies of the Crows. Our chief ordered a charge upon them. I advanced directly upon their lines, and had struck down my man before the others came up. The others, curveted aside in Indian fashion, thus losing the effect of a first onset. I corrected this warlike custom. On this occasion, seeing me engage hand to hand with the enemy's whole force, they immediately came to my assistance, and the opposing party were quickly dispatched. I despoiled my victim of his gun, lance, war-club, bow, and quiver of arrows. Now I was the greatest man in the party, for I had killed the first warrior. We painted our faces black, and rode back to the village bearing eleven scalps.[22]

One can easily see that with no fear of anyone disputing his stories, he went to great lengths to stress his personal bravery. How much is true and how much is fable will probably never be known; if properly gleaned, however, his accounts do produce some good general information concerning Crow Indian life.[23]

Sometime before 1833, Jim was approached by Kenneth McKenzie, head of the American Fur Company, and hired to act as an agent among the Crows. He was to use his influence to bring the Indians to one of the three company posts to trade. He also probably helped in the layout and construction of Fort Cass.

Jim says he had several wives and sweethearts selected from among the fairest of the Crow Indian maidens while he was a part of the tribe. Of these, he discusses only two in detail. One was a very virtuous woman he refers to as his "Little Wife," and the other was a female warrior known as "Pine Leaf."[24] There were children born from his connubial unions, although very little is known of them. Only the names of two have been recorded. Edwin Sabin says Jim

[22] Bonner's *Beckwourth,* 153-54.
[23] Robert H. Lowie, *The Crow Indians* (New York, 1935), 335.
[24] Bonner's *Beckwourth,* 170, 202.

". . . had a boy named Kit, after Carson; another called 'Panther,' remembered by citizens of early Denver."[25] Jim himself mentions only one son, named "Black Panther" or "Little Jim," born to him and his "Little Wife" in 1832 or 1833.[26] As was the custom with most of the half-breed children of the day, they were left with their Indian mothers when the father left the tribe.

Competition between the American Fur Company and Ashley's successors reached an all time high during the years 1833-34. It was only logical that Jim would become entangled in it, which indeed he did. Thomas Fitzpatrick, bringing a trading party into Crow territory, found himself suddenly held up and robbed by a group of young warriors who completely pillaged his camp. The blame for organizing such action was placed on Jim, and probably rightly so. He denied it, but if he was only enforcing his orders from McKenzie, he still made a strong enemy of an old friend.

Jim said that although an Indian could never become a white man, the white man could easily join in the life of the Indian. This is true in his own case if one can believe that he participated in even a third of the Indian warfare that he claims. Some historians, however, credit many of his adventures to Edward Rose.[27] His own account shows him to have been as bloodthirsty and to have killed as many or more Indians than any other member of the tribe with whom he lived. In his own defense he says:

> Many of my readers will doubtless wonder how a man who had been reared in civilized life could ever participate in such scenes of carnage and rapine. I have already related that I was brought up

[25] Edwin L. Sabin, *Kit Carson Days, 1809-1868* (New York, 1935), I, pp. 150-51. One questions if Beckwourth had even met Kit Carson by the 1830's. Beckwourth makes no mention of a son named "Kit."

[26] Bonner's *Beckwourth*, 247.

[27] Compare Zenas Leonard, *Adventures of Zenas Leonard, Fur Trader and Trapper, 1831-1836*, W. F. Wagner, ed. (Cleveland, 1904), 268-70, and Camp, *James Clyman, Frontiersman*, 33-34, 311-12.

where similar outrages were committed upon the defenseless inhabitants of the new settlements. . . I have seen the path of the trappers dyed with their blood, drawn from their hearts by the ambushed savage, who never knew mercy, but remorsely butchered all who came in his way. Such is Indian nature. When I fought with the Crow nation, I fought in their behalf against the most relentless enemies of the white man. If I chose to become an Indian while living among them, it concerned no person but myself; and by doing so, I saved more life and property for the white man than a whole regiment of United States regulars could have done in the same time.[28]

Sometime in the summer of 1835, Jim happened to meet with an old acquaintance from his Rocky Mountain Fur Company days, Thomas Smith, better known as "Peg-leg" Smith. Together they decided to make a joint trip to California in order to trade their furs for money and horses. They could, in turn then, make more money trading the horses to United States merchants. As a safety measure, it was decided to include Smith's friend Walkara, chief of a renegade band of Ute Indians who dealt in Indian slavery, with sixty of his warriors and four other American acquaintances. Leaving from Sanpete Valley (Utah) the expedition followed the Old Spanish Trail to Los Angeles.

The furs and Indian slaves undoubtedly sold rapidly after their arrival, but horses, he claimed, were not as easily obtained. The Spaniards drove a hard bargain, and the returns in horseflesh were small. Jim and Peg-leg proceeded to enjoy the comforts of civilized life, but vigorous Walkara decided to take matters into his own hands. Under the cover of darkness, he and his warriors rounded up nearly six hundred head of the ranchers' best horses and drove them quickly into the desert and toward Ute country. The two leaders of the expedition had no choice but to run with them or stand responsible to the ranchers. Thus they became branded as thieves.

---

[28] Bonner's *Beckwourth,* 232-33.

Jim stayed the winter in Salt Lake Valley and then with Smith drove his share of the horses to Bent and St. Vrain's Fort on the South Platte where they sold them. He then returned to the Crow tribe for a short time, but wander lust was in his blood. In the summer of 1836 he set out for St. Louis promising his adopted people that he would soon return.

Jim spent very little time visiting in St. Louis for his family had long since scattered. But he did make the acquaintance of General Edmund P. Gaines who was recruiting a company of Missouri volunteers to fight the Seminole Indians in Florida. Looking for a change of scenery and a chance for "renown," Jim decided to join. He enlisted for a three month period and landed with the other volunteers at Tampa Bay in the fall of 1836. He says he was immediately assigned the dangerous job of carrying dispatches from the coast to the interior.[29] Jim must have decided to re-enlist after serving his three months, for he says he served in the Battle of Lake Okeechobee under Colonel Zachary Taylor at Christmas in 1837. However, as the war continued to drag on with no end in sight, the inactivity began to wear upon Jim's adventurous spirit. Asking to be relieved of his duties, he decided to return to St. Louis the following spring.

Back in St. Louis, Jim again joined forces with an old friend from the trapping days – Louis Vasquez. Vasquez had quit the Rocky Mountain Fur Company and was now in a joint trading venture with Andrew W. Sublette. Knowing Jim's abilities and experience with the Indians, Vasquez immediately offered Jim a position with the company as a trader with the Cheyennes on the upper reaches of the

---

[29] How much truth there is in Beckwourth's account of serving in the Seminole War is questionable. We have found no proof except his own word that he participated in it. His accurate knowledge of the men involved, the geography and the fighting conditions, however, suggest that he was there and there is no evidence of his being somewhere else during this time. See Oswald, "James Pierson Beckwourth. . . ," 87-93.

Arkansas and South Platte rivers. Happy to go back to the mountains, Jim accepted. He traveled with an ox-drawn supply caravan along the Santa Fe Trail and soon found himself at Fort Vasquez in charge of trading operations. His was an important responsibility; he was not only competing with such accomplished traders as the Bent brothers, but also was faced with helping his employers pay off a heavy debt. This he attempted to do by being fair in his dealings with the Indians in order to gain their trade.

In the summer of 1839 Jim again fell in with his notorious cronies Peg-leg Smith and Walkara. Plans were soon set for another expedition into California. Dropping all pretentions of trading, they drew up an intricate set of plans for one of the biggest horse raids ever attempted. It was decided that Jim, who was not known in California, should go ahead as an advance agent and spy to find where the best horse herds were located and how they were guarded.[30] Smith and Walkara, with about 150 warriors, were to follow in the spring using his information to do the actual stealing.

Upon his arrival in California, Jim used the alibi that he was a trapper from New Mexico checking out the possible profits in hunting sea otter along the coast. This gave him near-perfect freedom to move about the area as he pleased, and for several weeks he explored the country and the ranches from Mission San Luis Obispo to Santa Barbara, mentally taking notes of everything that he saw. Everything was ready when Smith and Walkara arrived. It took only three days of surprise attacks to sack the entire Santa Ana Valley and run off nearly five thousand head of the best horses. They hurried over Cajon Pass and into the desert where they evaded the Spanish pursuers. Then they proceeded to Bridger's Fort and Bent's Fort and traded the horses for a good profit.

---

[30] Major Howard Bell, *Reminiscences of a Ranger* (Santa Barbara, California, 1927), 290.

With his return to New Mexico, Jim found that Vasquez and Sublette had decided to sell out. He then hired on with Bent and St. Vrain for a time, but having money and goods of his own, he decided to try trading independently.

At Taos Jim met a friend named Lee (possibly Stephen Louis Lee) with whom he formed a partnership to trade with the Cheyennes. After making a fair profit in the winter's trade, he married a young Spanish girl from Santa Fe named Luisa Sandoval. Taking her with him, he moved back to the South Platte country to trade.

At the camp of Jean Baptiste Charbonneau, the newly-weds met Fremont and his guide Kit Carson who were on their way to the Rockies in 1842. They then moved to the Arkansas River near the mouth of Fountain Creek where he and several other independent traders erected a fort which they called "Pueblo." Jim opened a small trading house and continued to conduct his business among the Indians as well as with the families that settled at the fort. There was not much profit in this venture, probably because of his inability to meet the competition of Bent's Fort. Whatever the cause, he decided to try another horse stealing expedition into California.

Leaving his wife at Pueblo, Jim departed for California with Jim Waters and thirteen others disguising his intentions by appearing as a trader. Once there, with the large amount of whiskey and other goods he brought, he enjoyed an extensive trade for nearly a year, at the same time taking note of the horse herds. While trading, he was asked with several other Americans to join the rebel forces of José Castro and Juan Bautista Alvarado against Governor Micheltorena in the California Revolution. Always ready for excitement and willing to fight on the side that would best enhance his trade, he readily agreed.

The two armies met in the San Fernando Valley for the Battle of Cahuenga Pass on February 20, 1845. As fighting

commenced, Jim and the other Americans in his unit suddenly found themselves shooting at former American friends
fighting for the other side. When a lull developed in the
fighting they debated across the battle lines about what to
do. Finally it was decided the Californians should fight
their own war, so the Americans of both sides withdrew and
together watched as Micheltorena was defeated.

Jim and Waters continued trading, under the grace of the
new Governor Castro, throughout most of the summer of
1845. Political unrest, however, was making the position of
any American there unstable – especially when rumors of
the "Bear Flag Republic" began to reach Los Angeles.
Deciding it was time to leave, they joined with four other
Americans and made plans for collecting the horses they
had been spotting for the past two years. Of the 1800 they
gathered, they were able to escape with nearly 1000, once
again in safety.[31]

Upon Jim's return to Pueblo he was greeted with what to
some would be very shocking news. He found his wife had
remarried while he was gone, taking with her their daughter, Matilda. Jim grieved very little at the loss and busied
himself by buying a hotel and bar in Santa Fe. Waters was
a partner and agreed to manage the establishment.

War had been declared with Mexico by the United States
in April of 1846, and much to the relief of the Americans
in the Southwest, General Stephen W. Kearny and his army
arrived to take control. Jim says that General Kearny asked
him to serve as a dispatch carrier between Santa Fe and
Fort Leavenworth and that he made his home at his hotel
in Santa Fe between trips.

On January 20, 1847, word arrived that the Mexicans had

---

[31] LeRoy Hafen questions whether Beckwourth or Joseph Walker led this group
of thieves. It is possible that Beckwourth and Waters joined Walker's band, whose
activities were of the same character and period. See LeRoy and Ann W. Hafen,
Old Spanish Trail, Santa Fe to Los Angeles (Glendale, 1954), 190, 245-47.

massacred all the Americans at Taos and were advancing toward Santa Fe. Colonel Sterling Price immediately organized his troops, calling on Ceran St. Vrain to recruit the local Mountain Men and merchants into a company of volunteers. Most of them, including Jim, signed up with a grim determination for retribution. Under Price's direction, the enemy were surprised and routed and Taos was reclaimed.

Hearing rumors of gold in California, Jim sold his holdings in Santa Fe and decided to go to the new eldorado. This time he traveled as part of a protective escort for Orville C. Pratt, a young military lawyer traveling to Los Angeles. Once there, he says he was engaged to carry dispatches in the service of the commissariat at Monterey. While thus employed, he discovered the massacre of the Reed family and their servants at Mission St. Miguel and gained a first hand knowledge of what vigilante law was to become by witnessing the culprits' capture and execution without trial or hearing.

Next Jim decided to try trading with the numerous miners that had flocked into California. Investing in some goods, he traveled to the gold camps of the Sonora area, but was only mildly successful.

The winter of 1849-50 he spent at his friend Charbonneau's hotel at Murderer's Bar. He then moved to El Dorado Canyon where he decided to have his memoirs written and published. Not being able to write, he asked an acquaintance named Philip Stoner to take down his story.[32] This was done in part, but for some reason the two parted, and the manuscript remained to be finished later.

Searching for gold in 1851, Jim chanced to explore the Sierras between the middle fork of the Feather River and

---

[32] Boutwell Dunlap, "Some Facts Concerning Leland Stanford and His Contemporaries in Placer County," *California Historical Society Quarterly* (October, 1923), II, pp. 204-205.

the Truckee River. He decided that the geography would allow construction of an excellent wagon road for emigrants into northern California. Enlisting the aid of the people of Bidwell's Bar and Marysville to raise money for the project, he set out to find some emigrants he hoped to persuade to try his new route. Reaching the Truckee Meadows, he intercepted a small wagon train which finally agreed to try his route. In this train was a ten year old girl, the niece of Joseph Smith, who was to be Ina Coolbrith, a friend of Bret Harte and Mark Twain and poet laureate of California. She recalled that as Jim led the wagon train over the pass which was to bear his name, he set her in front of him on his horse, making her one of the first to cross the Sierras on this route.[33]

This wagon train reached Marysville about August 31, 1851, but the celebration and glory Jim expected to receive for his success was not in evidence, for on this same night the town burned to the ground. His dream of opening a new wagon route still unshattered, Jim decided to wait out the winter at Indian Bar until spring when he could meet the new influx of wagon trains and introduce them to his pass.

While at Indian Bar, Jim made friends with an itinerant justice of the peace named Thomas Daniel Bonner.[34] Finding that Bonner had been a newspaperman before the gold rush and was always open to a money-making proposition, Jim asked him to write his memoirs while he dictated them to him. Bonner accepted the proposal, and the dream of gaining "renown" began to approach reality.

In the spring of 1852 Jim took up a land claim in a valley on the route from Beckwith Pass and built a combined hotel and store to cater to the emigrants. The town and valley were to bear his name. The next year Jim moved to his ranch located at the lower end of the valley and there in a

---

[33] George Wharton James, *Heroes of California* (Boston, 1910), 111-12.
[34] Oswald, "James Pierson Beckwourth. . . ," 130.

log cabin with Bonner he concentrated on retelling his past.
That there were many variations from the truth in this work
cannot be denied, and even Jim's name changed spellings.
As was mentioned previously, his name was legally Beckwith; in print, however, it now became "Beckwourth."
Whether this was done because he felt "Beckwourth" to be
more distinguished or because he was ashamed of his ancestry is not known, but "Beckwourth" became the title by
which he was recognized from this point on. In 1856 the
work was published, and Jim's best attempt at gaining
"renown" became a reality.

The last two years of Jim's stay in California are a
mystery, for there seems to be no record of his activities. It
is said by some that his dealings were closely watched by
the vigilantes, but for what reason is still a question. Whatever his reasons for leaving, he is next found in his old
home city of St. Louis.

Having been away from home for twenty-two years, Jim
found many changes, most of which made him feel like a
stranger, so he went to visit his old friend and former employer, Louis Vasquez. Again he was hired by his friend,
but this time to work as a storekeeper in Denver.

With little effort Jim easily established himself as a citizen of Denver and made many friends, especially among
the Indians that traded at the store. Because of his nature
and ability to understand them, their respect for him grew
and he soon found himself acting as a mediator between
them and the white people of Denver. So respected was his
work that it was even suggested that he be appointed Indian
agent for the territory, but such an appointment was never
made.

Although he was sixty-two years of age, Jim was still alert
and active. He married Elizabeth Lettbetter on June 21,
1860. In addition to managing the store, he took on the
responsibility of a company farm south of Denver. Here he

and his wife, whom he referred to as "Lady Beckwourth," set up housekeeping and entertained some of the influential men in the territory.

In 1861 when Vasquez terminated his holdings in Denver, Jim bought some farm land of his own on which he built a home and saloon. Farming and saloon keeping seemed to be too calm a life for him and he looked for other work. In 1862 he served as guide for E. L. Berthoud and for the Colorado Second Infantry. He then returned to the farm but became involved in two separate law cases. In the first he was accused of taking government property from a nearby fort, and the second was for shooting an intruder named William Payne. Charges were dropped by the government in the first case and he was acquitted in the second on the grounds of self defense.

The year 1864 was a trying one for Jim. An infant daughter died and his wife separated from him, taking their remaining son. Shortly after, he took an Indian common-law wife whom he called Sue, and she lived with him as a devoted mate. He continued to run the ranch, do some placer mining, and also trap beaver.

In November of 1864 Jim was hired as a guide for the Third Regiment of Colorado Volunteer Cavalry under Colonel J. M. Chivington. He led the troops to the Cheyenne camp at Sand Creek, where the notorious Sand Creek Massacre took place. He says the atrocities he witnessed there revolted him.[35] Returning to Denver, he made an unauthorized reconnaissance by himself to the remnants of the Cheyenne tribe. At their village he tried to talk peace but the Indians would not listen.

After returning to his farm, he spent much time trapping,

---

[35] Beckwourth's testimony before a military commission investigating the Sand Creek Massacre was published in the "Report of the Secretary of War," 39th Congress, 2d Session, *Senate Executive Document No. 26,* pp. 68-76.

accompanied by Sue. In the spring of 1866 he abandoned his holdings and went on a trapping expedition with four other trappers to his old haunts on the upper Green River. Fate was against the party; three were killed by the Blackfeet, and one drowned. Only Jim managed to survive and make his way back to Denver.

Desiring to return to the places of his youth, Jim sent Sue back to her people and returned again to Wyoming territory. He found employment as a scout and messenger at Fort Laramie, but with trouble brewing between the whites and the Crow Indians he was hired as a guide and interpreter by Colonel Henry B. Carrington. Hearing that Jim was at Fort C. F. Smith, the Crows agreed to open lines of communication if he would be the intermediary and would come back to their village. Carrington agreed to send him and offered a detachment of soldiers as escort, but Jim declined. He desired only one companion, so James W. Thompson of the 27th Infantry was assigned to accompany him.

Jim never returned from this journey, but before his death he did extract the promise of his friends, the Crows, to send warriors to help the white man fight the Sioux. The Crow village itself moved to Fort C. F. Smith and remained friendly to the whites. Concerning his death, there is a romantic account that Jim was poisoned by the Crow so that his spirit would remain with them.[36] A more sober and perhaps a more accurate account is that related by Thompson to Lt. George M. Templeton at Fort C. F. Smith. Templeton reports:

> Thompson says that he, Jim, complained of being sick on the same evening that he left here, and soon after commenced bleeding at the nose. On his arrival at the village he and Thompson were taken into

[36] LeRoy R. Hafen, "The Last Years of James P. Beckwourth," *Colorado Magazine,* v (1928), 135, quoting W. N. Byers.

the lodge of "The Iron Bull" and were his guests while they remained. There Beckwith died and was burried by his host.[37]

Thus, buried as a Crow Indian on a platform in a tree, James P. Beckwourth ended a long and eventful life. Perhaps the best eulogy for him would be the words of the noted historian Hubert Howe Bancroft:

> Beckwourth was by no means a bad man, though he had his faults, the greatest of which was being born too late. He should have swam the Scamander after Grecian horses, captured Ajax when calling for light, or scalped Achilles in his tent. Then had not been denied him the honor of dying like a Roman on his shield, in the lightening of lances, or a storm of Blackfoot braves.[38]

---

[37] There are several accounts given concerning Beckwourth's death. Perhaps the most accurate is that found in the *Templeton Diaries* as published in Nolie Mumey, *James Pierson Beckwourth, 1856-1866* (Denver, 1957), 171-74.

[38] *Works of Hubert Howe Bancroft* (San Francisco, 1886), XXVIII, p. 449.

The Ermatinger Brothers
Edward and Francis

by HARRIET D. MUNNICK
West Linn, Oregon

The Ermatinger name in the fur trade dates from the cession of Canada to Great Britain at the close of the French and Indian War, when a Swiss merchant, Lawrence Ermatinger, came from Europe to set up an outfitting business in Montreal. His account books and letters give an excellent record of the trade carried on by the independents before their absorption into the North West Company. In 1769 Ermatinger fitted out two canoes for the Great Lakes region; six years later he sent out six, manned by thirty-eight men, with a cargo of 600 gallons of beverages (rum and wine), 2000 pounds of gunpowder, 3600 pounds of ball and shot, 80 rifles, 85 bales of dry goods, 5500 pounds of tobacco, 15 cases of ironwork and ten cases of brass kettles. Little allowance for freeboard must have remained.[1]

Of the recorded sons born to Lawrence Ermatinger and Jemima Oakes, Frederick William remained in Montreal where he served as postmaster and sheriff, Charles Oakes became an independent trader like his father, established at Sault Ste. Marie, while Lawrence Edward, the eldest, went into the British Army commissariat. He married an Italian while stationed overseas; his son Edward was born in February 1797, on the island of Elba, and a second son, Francis, in 1798 in Portugal. His wife died shortly and his two sons were sent to England to be reared and educated.[2]

---

[1] Harold A. Innes, *The Fur Trade in Canada* (New Haven, Conn., 1962), 193.

[2] "Edward Ermatinger's York Factory Express Journal . . . 1827-28, with Introduction by Judge C. O. Ermatinger and James White," in Royal Society of Canada, *Transactions, Third Section,* vol. VI (Ottawa, 1912), 67.

In 1818 both sons were put into the service of the Hudson's Bay Company by their father, no doubt at the suggestion of the family traders in Canada. Terms of enlistment were for five years, with wages as clerks starting at twenty pounds per year, progressing to fifty pounds by the end of the period. The lads sailed from Gravesend on May 18 and reached York Factory on Hudson Bay on August 11. Within a few weeks the brothers, who had been close companions throughout boyhood and were to be reunited in old age, were separated for the first time. Edward was sent to Island Lake in the York District, about a hundred miles east of northern Lake Winnipeg, Francis to the Severn District still farther to the east, lying under the curve of Hudson Bay.

Edward remained at Island Lake four years until being transferred to Beaver Creek Post in the Upper Red River District. Francis kept on in the Severn District, part of the time being in charge of the Trout Lake Post, although still very young. The brothers may have met occasionally when the Express came down to York Factory; they were definitely reunited when in 1825 both were dispatched to the Columbia Department with headquarters at Fort Vancouver.

Though close to one another in age and affection, the two were greatly different in temperament. Edward was studious, having a good knowledge of Latin, French, and Italian, according to his son, "besides acquiring those habits of neatness and precision, both in caligraphy and expression, which his journals disclose."[3] His proficiency on the flute and violin helped him adjust to "the loneliness of the life, the absence of amusements, especially in the evenings of the protracted winters spent in remote outposts." His superior at Red River, Chief Factor John McDonald, wrote of him,

An accountant, a young Gentleman of Strict morals, mild disposition, unassuming manners, willing to make himself useful, acquainted

[3] *Ibid.*, 68.

with the trade of the Low country; where he had not sufficient field to shew his talents as a trader, yet he possesses every qualification necessary to become one, having passed the winter with myself I have every cause to be satisfied with his conduct.[4]

Governor Simpson's evaluation of his brother Francis was far less glowing. Although Simpson had an acid disposition, he was unsurpassed as a manager and issue cannot be taken lightly with his summary:

> A stout active boisterous fellow who is a tolerable clerk and trader and qualified to be useful where bustle and activity without any great exercise of judgment are necessary.[5]

To his fellow employees Francis was "Frank" or sometimes "Bardolph" by reason of his tippling, a merry companion who put valor above discretion, a teller of tales, a jokester. "Frank does nothing but bow-wow-wow!" Chief Factor McLoughlin is said to have exclaimed in exasperation, or it may be, in a light dismissal of Ermatinger's drolleries. Clerk George Roberts related with half-concealed relish the wag's treatment of the sanctimonious missionary William Gray:

> I remember Ermatinger was particularly kind to him, at the same time had fun of him. I heard "E" say, "Mr. Gray and I were partaking of Brandy and water together" – Gray's confusion – "E's" saying, "I beg pardon, Mr. G., I was drinking the brandy and you the water. . ."[6]

Edward remained until 1828 as personal clerk to McLoughlin and although his clerkship lasted but three years a warm relationship grew up between the two. Over the years his former chief wrote Edward about the progress and changes taking place in the West or about the affairs of

---

[4] E. E. Rich, ed., *Colin Robertson's Letters* (Hudson's Bay Record Society, vol. II), 211.

[5] Burt Brown Barker, ed., *Letters of Dr. John McLoughlin* (Portland, Ore., 1948), 306.

[6] George B. Roberts, "Letters to Mrs. F. F. Victor," in *Oregon Historical Quarterly,* LXIII (1926), 211.

brother Francis, who was perhaps dilatory in writing to his brother Edward in Canada.

In the meantime Francis was in the field on various expeditions, one of which was under Alexander McLeod to Puget Sound to avenge the killing of several Hudson's Bay Company men by the Clallam Indians. In his journal, which he may have intended to be private, he wrote brashly about the leadership of McLeod, which he considered to have been indecisive. His words somehow came to Governor Simpson's knowledge. Simpson demanded an explanation from Ermatinger's immediate chief, McLoughlin, who tried to calm the waters while shielding Ermatinger, with whom he was inclined to agree. The latter appeared to ignore his chief's orders to "send me a copy of that journal at once," and finally was told, "If you think you cannot give me a Copy of your journal . . . it is necessary for you to go to York Factory."[7] As Ermatinger did not go, it is presumed he produced the journal.

The year 1828 saw him in charge of Fort Kamloops on the Thompson River in British Columbia. Governor Simpson passed through the post on his second western tour of inspection, accompanied by much blowing of trumpets and beating of drums. He noted that there were but four men at the fort besides Clerks Ermatinger and Dears, "and six men gone to the Fraser River for salmon." Malcolm McLeod, whose father had held the post previously, wrote, "I remember the old compact and well-palisaded Fort and the stockade a little distance off, large enough for three or four hundred horses, for the horse brigade for transport of 'goods in' and return of 'goods out' for the district and for New Caledonia generally numbered 250 horses."[8]

At this remote post Ermatinger fell easily into the custom

---

[7] Barker, *op. cit.*, 65, 103.

[8] E. E. Rich, ed., *Simpson's 1828 Journey to the Columbia* (Hudson's Bay Record Society, vol. x), "McLeod's Reminiscences," p. xxx.

of the trade by taking a native wife, one who subsequently gave him a retarded son and no little marital trouble. When she presently eloped with an Indian, Ermatinger retaliated in the established native fashion by sending his interpreter Lolo to brand the man by cutting off his ear, or at least the tip of it. ". . . and though in the civilized world such an act will appear harsh and on that account it would be preferable that he had resorted to some other mode of punishment," wrote his chief, again explaining the impetuous Ermatinger to Governor Simpson, "Still, if the Indian had not been punished it would have lowered the Whites in their Estimation as among themselves they never allow such an offense to go unpunished. However, to prevent any further difficulty on this subject I kept Mr. Ermatinger here (Fort Vancouver) and appointed Mr. (John) Clark at Thompson River. . ."[9] He then arranged to have Ermatinger's little son brought down by Samuel Black's next brigade to Fort Vancouver where he could be cared for and, in time, sent to school.

In the autumn of 1830 an illness of epidemic proportions spread across the country. In addition to managing the affairs of the Department, Chief Factor McLoughlin now had to double as doctor, as the fort physician Kennedy was "ill of the fever." Instead of fleeing the infection, the Indians camped closely around the stockade, saying that if they died, as seemed likely, they would be decently buried. Officers Birnie, Douglas and Ermatinger as well as the chief factor kept constantly employed from daybreak until eleven at night in tending the sick, who numbered seventy-five at one time during November. However, no great number of deaths, aside from Indians, seems to have resulted.

By the following spring his chief considered conditions quiet enough for Ermatinger to return to the outlying

---

[9] E. E. Rich, ed., *McLoughlin's Fort Vancouver Letters, 1825-1846, Second Series* (Hudson's Bay Record Society, vol. VI), 227.

country and he sent him to take charge of Fort Colville on the upper Columbia. Here he remained through the winter, and here Governor Simpson wrote his unflattering report. Later in the spring Ermatinger was sent to the Snake River country with a small party to trade for furs with the American trappers now penerating the Rocky Mountains and western plateaus.

During the six years from 1832 to 1838 Francis Ermatinger was constantly coming and going on the trails to the mountain rendezvous and as far to the south as California, meeting all comers and keeping an ear out for all that was going on in the fur trade. Scarcely any traveler who left a written record failed to mention him, be the traveler a competitor, emigrant or missionary. Many of them fell in with the trader's brigade and traveled with it for the sake of safety; some of these, like Nathaniel Wyeth or Jason Lee, were returning to the East on business, some were scouting the country with an eye to entering the fur trade, some, like David Douglas and John Townsend, were scientists investigating the flora and fauna of the region, and still others were missionaries, both Catholic and Protestant, bent on converting the natives. All, with the possible exception of Captain Bonneville, who was actually spying out the fur trade under the guise of a military expedition, spoke warmly of the help they had got from Ermatinger in all circumstances.

A photograph of him and a girl, her arm about his neck, seems to betoken an affection for children that is borne out in other recorded fragments.[10] Robert Newell, an Ameri-

---

[10] The child has been variously listed as Ermatinger's niece or granddaughter, but has since been identified as his daughter, Marie Frances, only child of Francis Ermatinger and Catherine Sinclair. The sharp-eyed and sharp-tongued Letitia Hargraves wrote in 1850 that although Ermatinger had grown harsh toward his wife, he was devoted to "the Baby," who was at this time seven years old. Margaret A. MacLeod, ed., *Letters of Letitia Hargraves* (Champlain Society, vol. 28, 1947), 254. Frances grew up to marry a Company clerk of St. Thomas, John Crawford. She was the mother of three daughters and one son.

can "Mountain Man" who had become a close friend of the British trader, gave the name "Francis Ermatinger" to his first son, born on the trail to Newell and his Nez Perce wife Kitty. Shortly after the birth of Alice Clarissa Whitman in 1837, Ermatinger and Pierre Pambrun called politely at Waiilatpu Mission, perhaps to congratulate the parents on the event and to enjoy the sight of a golden-haired white infant in a land of dark little papooses, although her mother complained with some resentment about the presence of several extra men to be fed when they talked only about the plowing to be done.[11]

Many years later Ranald McDonald recalled "the kindly Frank Ermatinger" at Fort Kamloops: "He would sometimes give me a cake – then a great rarity – for our allowance of flour was two sacks brought from London by way of Cape Horn, then transported to the interior – tea and sugar in limited proportions. I must not forget, to us children, that great luxury – a few cakes of gingerbread – how Mr. Ermatinger would say, 'I won't tell.' "[12]

But of his own little son, born during the same era at Fort Kamloops and sent down to Fort Vancouver after the desertion of his mother, Ermatinger may have had little joy, in view of the report his guardian, Dr. McLoughlin, gave of him to Edward Ermatinger in Ontario:

Feb. 1, 1835 . . . I have not heard from your Brother since the month of June – though I expect news of him every Moment – you know he is in the flathead country – I am told he has a Clooch-I-man [squaw].

Feb. 1, 1835 Your brother is still in the Snake Country and doing every justice to his charge – and had a very narrow escape last summer of being killed by the Blackfeet. His son is here at a school I have established for the good of the native children in this quarter. But the boy had so much misery in his youth [the child was now seven years

11 *Oregon Historical Quarterly*, xxxviii (1937), 55.
12 William S. Lewis and N. Murakami, *Ranald McDonald* (Spokane, 1923), 24.

old] and has been so sickly that he makes but slow progress. He has also an infirmity – he is a little deaf, however, it is wearing off and I hope he will be cured of it.[13]

The same year, 1836, saw Ermatinger at French Camp (Stockton) with Michel Laframboise, who had charge of the annual brigade to California until it phased out. In addition to trapping and trading, the 1836 hunt was to negotiate terms with the increasingly restive Mexican government regarding the Hudson's Bay Company's presence in California. No better emissaries than the affable pair of Laframboise and Ermatinger could have been sent to arrange the matter of permits and duties, which, once agreed upon, were thereafter pretty much ignored by the traders. Following a hunt of "better than usual returns," Ermatinger was sent to Fort Hall, replacing Tom McKay, "to send runners from camp to camp during the winter in order to keep a check on American opposition."

He appears to have used other devices as well to further the company's interest, if there is any truth in an old story that the creek now called Finley's was formerly known as Course de Femmes from the "squaw foot races, with handsome prizes" he organized there to stimulate Flathead trade. Whatever his methods, he satisfied his superior, James Douglas, who wrote an excellent account of his management to the company in London.[14]

He remained at this post at the division of the trail until 1842. A general company policy directed him to divert settlers toward California whenever possible, rather than have

[13] The boy, Lawrence, named for his grandfather Ermatinger, was sent east in charge of the Rev. William H. Gray to be educated in the home of Edward Ermatinger. "He was the despair of his father, who finally said he could do nothing more for him. He left St. Thomas for Chicago and I believe nothing more is known of him." This is the recollection of local (St. Thomas, Ontario) historians.

[14] Douglas' recommendation specifically noted his "zeal, activity, implicit attention to orders and general management of a difficult charge." He was apparently willing to overlook several notable lapses in Ermatinger's "implicit attention to orders." See Rich, *McLoughlin's Fort Vancouver Letters,* appendix A, p. 226.

them continue to the Northwest, which the company hoped to hold for its own. Ermatinger's genial nature made him as oblivious of this directive as of the earlier Mexican restrictions, with the result that Fort Hall, standing on the inhospitable sagebrush plains of Idaho, came to be something of an oasis on the overland trail. Here exhausted travelers could receive a final impetus on their way to Fort Walla Walla and the equally hospitable Pierre Pambrun. Father Pierre deSmet, for instance, who had lost several mules and their loads in the river, had his goods replaced "for a sum truly inconsiderable." He wrote,

> Although a Protestant by birth, this noble Englishman gave us a most friendly reception. Not only did he repeatedly invite us to his table, and sell us at first cost, or one third of its value, in a country so remote, whatever we required; but he also added as pure gifts many articles which he believed would be particularly acceptable; he assured us that he would second our ministry among the populous nation of the Snakes, with whom he had frequent intercourse. So much zeal and generosity give him a claim to our esteem and gratitude. May heaven return him a hundredfold the benefits he has conferred on us.[15]

The Protestant missionaries also had their say, albeit in less flowery terms. Wrote Myra Eels, one of a reinforcement party for the Whitman Mission, on July 12, 1838:

> Mr. Ermatinger eats in our tent; loses the letters Mr. Lee sent to his wife by him.

And on July 29:

> About 10 o'clock Mr. Ermatinger comes to invite us to breakfast; says he just got up. After breakfast he comes again to invite us to have preaching at the Fort.[16]

The services were duly held and the missionaries left the next morning with a parting gift from their host of ten pounds of sugar.

---

[15] Pierre Jean DeSmet, *Letters and Sketches . . . of the Rocky Mountains,* in R. G. Thwaites, ed., *Early Western Travels,* XXVII (Cleveland, 1906), 235.

[16] Quoted in Clifford M. Drury, *First White Women over the Rockies* (Glendale, Calif., 1963), II, pp. 102, 109-10.

It is of some interest to note that the famous little printing press, first in the West, that was given by a mission in Hawaii for use at Waiilatpu and Lapwai was transported to the interior from Fort Vancouver by batteau and pack horse "in charge of Frank Ermatinger" in 1839.

During his term at Fort Hall, Ermatinger made one, possibly two more trips to California. "The party under Ermatinger made poorly out," wrote the chief factor, "but still, as by letting the men hunt in the vicinity they would be tampered with by our opponents (John Sutter et al) I sent them back to hunt in the Bay of San Francisco under the charge of Mr. Laframboise and it is probable they will remain two years. Mr. Ermatinger brought some cattle with the party, and before I knew anything about it, sold them, but as this is irregular I wrote him on the subject and he in consequence placed them at the disposal of the Company. All who are employed in the service ought to know that the whole of their time and talent is due the Company and that they are bound to devote their energies exclusively to its interests." [17]

The California fur traffic was by this time "worthless," Ermatinger insisted, and he refused to go south again. He was sent instead to Kamloops to investigate the murder of his fellow trader, Samuel Black, in 1841, and in 1842 was replaced at Fort Hall by Richard Grant.

In the same year he was promoted to chief trader, an advance in both rank and pay. He also married a charming young wife twenty-six years his junior. She was Catherine (always called Kate), daughter of Chief Factor William Sinclair, Jr., of Red River. She had been educated in the academy at Fort Garry (Winnepeg) and had come to visit her grandmother, Madame McLoughlin, with the brigade of Chief Factor McLoughlin on his return journey from Europe in 1840. Ermatinger and Catherine apparently slip-

---

[17] Rich, *McLoughlin's Fort Vancouver Letters, op. cit.,* 81-82, 314-15.

ped away without fanfare to the house of James Birnie at Fort George to be married by the Protestant missionary Frost on Clatsop Plains.

> 1841   August 12   On the 9th I was very unexpectedly called upon to go to Fort George [Astoria] in order to administer the ordinance of Matrimony. On the 10th Mr. Francis Ermatinger and Miss Catherine Sinclair were married and after dinner of the same day they came down with us and continued here [mission of the Clatsops, near Warrenton] until this morning. Mr. Ermatinger is one of the Chief Traders of the Hudson's Bay Company, and Miss Sinclair is a daughter of a gentleman of the same service and a grand-daughter of John McLoughlin, Esqire. We had a very pleasant visit with them and hope their union may prove a blessing to them through life.[18]

The following June a record of their only known child appears in the St. James Catholic Church of Fort Vancouver:

> B. 94   Francis Marie Ermatinger, June 18, 1843
> Francis Marie Ermatinger, born the 3rd of the present month. Legitimate daughter of Francis Ermatinger, Esq., Chief Trader of the Hon. H.B.Co., and Dame Catherine Sinclair, residents of Vancouver. Godfather, John McLoughlin, Esq., Chief Factor Hon. H.B.Co., and godmother, Madame Marie Barclay. (signed) Maria Barclay, John McLoughlin, Francis Ermatinger, David McLoughlin, Dugald McTavish, Forbes Barclay.   ANT. LANGLOIS, priest.[19]

Until 1846 Ermatinger had charge of the Hudson's Bay store at the young town of Oregon City that was springing up at the falls of the Willamette. It was a position well suited to his gregarious nature. He identified with the growing American population as few of the company employees were able to do, even being elected treasurer of the Provisional Government and a member of the Pioneer Lyceum and Literary Club instituted by American immigrants "to discuss the whole round of literary and scientific pursuits."

Meanwhile, the breach between Governor Simpson and

[18] *Oregon Historical Quarterly*, XXXVI (1935), 338.
[19] Records of St. James Catholic Church, Fort Vancouver.

Chief Factor McLoughlin had progressively widened. "Ermatinger was rather too intimate with Dr. McLoughlin to be pleasant to Sir Geo.," wrote George Roberts. "He was at the head of the Company's business at Oregon City and was a general favorite, I think, with the Americans." As a consequence, apparently, of the feeling between his two superiors, Ermatinger, on his return from a visit to England in 1846, was met with an order to report at once to York Factory on Hudson Bay to take charge of the fur store there, leaving his young wife stranded in the West. She eventually rejoined him by way of some brigade "or any canoe at liberty."

One year at Fort York, followed by a stint in charge of the Athabaska District at Fort Chippewyan, two years' furlough, and a year or two in charge of Fort William on Lake Superior rounded out thirty-five years of service. He retired in 1853, still "full of jaw" and "rather loose in his assertions," in the opinion of the proper Englishman, Eden Colville, Governor of Rupert's Land.[20] He rejoined his brother Edward at St. Thomas, Ontario, where he died in 1858.

His widow Catherine never remarried. She returned to Red River to be near her parents and there died. The St. Johns Cemetery record, Winnipeg, carried the entry,

Diocese of Rupert's Land, November 11, 1876
This eleventh day of November, one thousand eight hundred and seventy six was buried by me Catherine Ermatinger of Winnipeg in the County of Selkirk, who died on the tenth day of November, aged fifty two years.   JOHN GRISDALE, Officiating Clergyman

While Francis Ermatinger was spending his years in the Columbia Department somewhat riotously, his brother Edward remained a sober clerk at Fort Vancouver, where he seems to have been a general favorite with his seniors and where he formed many lasting friendships. In 1827 and 1828, at least, he accompanied the Express brigade to Fort

---

[20] *Eden Colville's Letters, 1849-1852* (Hudson's Bay Record Society, vol. XIX), 175.

York as keeper of the official journal for certain legs of the
route. In addition to statistics of distances covered, supplies
and traveling conditions, his journal included highly read-
able incidents on the weary trail traversed by thousands of
un-named voyageurs year after year.

June 2, 1827   Mr. H [Harriot] goes off and kills 2 Bulls – a very
serious accident attends the evening's hunting. Mr. H. having wounded
two other Bulls goes off with a view of getting them accompanied by
Messrs. F. [Finan] McDonald and E.E. [Edward Ermatinger]. On
aproaching them they made off. Mr. H. pursued and overtook one,
followed by Mr. McD. – the former fired but did not bring the Bull
down. Mr. McD's rifle snapped, and while he was endeavoring to
distinguish his object in the dark of the night to have another shot, the
animal rushed toward him with the utmost impetuosity. Mr. McD. as
soon as he perceived him, which was not until he was very close, tried
to escape by running across a small plain to shelter himself in a small
hammock of woods, but before he reached it he became out of breath
and threw himself down trusting to fate. The first blow the animal
gave him he tossed him with great violence and gored the most fleshy
part of his thigh nearly to the bone. Mr. McD., after this, seized him
by the wool of the head and held him for some time, but the immense
power of the animal obliged him to quit his hold – on doing this, he
supposes, he dislocated his wrist. He remembers having received six
blows, one of which was so dreadful that his whole side is bruised
black and blue and some of his ribs appear to be broken – the last
furious butt made him call out, and what is strange the Bull at the
same instant fell down as if a ball had struck him. In this state they
both remained for above an hour while Mr. H. ran to the Boats at
least 2 miles distant for assistance, Mr. E. remaining near the spot to
point it out, for altho' these two gentlemen heard and saw as far as
the night permitted the whole of this distressing affair, they were unable to render immediate relief, lest in firing at the Bull they might kill
the man. A large armed party being collected were devising means of
extricating Mr. McD. from his painful situation, when one of the
men's guns went off in the air by accident. This caused the Bull to
rise. He looked at the party attentively for a moment and then galloped
off. Mr. McD., whom they found perfectly sensible altho' he had
fainted several times as he himself says, also states that the Bull
watched him the whole time they lay together and that he durst not
stir. . .   The ground around bore evident marks of this deplorable

catastrophe, being gored up in many places and covered with blood – a shot pouch which Mr. McD. wore at his left side, made of thick seal-skin covered with porcupine quills and stuffed with rags, &c., for wadding was found to be pierced thro' and thro' and must have saved his life, altho' he was not aware when this happened. He was conveyed upon blankets fastened upon poles upon the men's shoulders to the Boat and in order to reach Carlton as soon as possible, we drift down the river all night in hopes of finding Dr. Richardson at that place. His wounds were dressed as well as the means of the party permitted.[21]

Despite such accidents, which were part of the every-day life on the trail, the entire account indicated the solidarity of the crew's morale and a general sunniness on the part of the clerk Ermatinger. If the Express was delayed by illness, or one of the boats "broken against a rock," or the cargo wet, the "Pas d'ours" (snowshoes) traded from the Indians "too small and break often," the Express windbound on some bleak shore, still the following entries open "Fine day," "Fine day" for weeks at a stretch. The botanist, David Douglas, who was traveling east with the Express, shared the same easy outlook:

[They were crossing the Rockies, in April] We did not require snow-shoes here, as there was a fine hard solid crust, but in coming out of the water and trotting along on the hoar-frost, we found it intensely cold, and all our clothing that was wet, immediately became cased with ice; still no inconvenience of any consequence was sustained.[22]

Typical daily entries noted,

Saw the corpse of a woman on this portage, lying in a hole, close to the track, which had been made for some other purpose, entirely naked, left a prey to the crows.

Ouvrie . . . took their arrows away from them (horse thieves) which Ouvrie brought with him as spoils of war.

River becomes more rapidous as we ascend.

Lash the boats together and drive all night.

View of the mountains very grand.

---

[21] "Edward Ermatinger's York Factory Express Journal," *loc. cit.*, 87-88.
[22] *Ibid.*, 129.

At the end of the 1828 Express trip to Fort York, Edward Ermatinger resigned from the Hudson's Bay Company, having completed two five-year terms. He had come to feel that a career in the fur trade was not for him, saying "Nothing could induce me to spend the remainder of my life in a country where so much hardship and privation had to be endured, beyond the bounds of civilization." He went with an Express down to Lachine and two years later settled permanently at St. Thomas, Ontario.

The following year he married "the daughter of Hon. Zacceus Burnham of Coburg," who does not appear to rate a name of her own. He built a fine home, called Multnomah (now known as Oakton) in memory of his young days in the West, which perhaps looked rosier in retrospect than in participation. He became a merchant, a banker, and postmaster, a thoroughly solid citizen who represented Middlesex County in the Parliament of the United Provinces. His sons in due time carried on the substantial civic works of their father. A portrait of Edward appears herein at page 16.

His former companions of the fur trade wrote him faithfully over the years; John Work, for one, continued the correspondence until 1856, when Work was sixty-five years old, yet he had known the young Edward only three years, long before. And when John Tod, in the remote McLeod Lake post, enduring more "hardships and privation" than had ever been the lot of Edward, received his first letter from him, he replied fervently with, ". . . and though the reiterated cries of 'Mr. Tod! Mr. Tod!' resounded from various parts of the Fort, I lent a deaf ear to the whole . . . until I had finished Your Kind, interesting, & highly entertaining letter. . ." [23]

Work was inclined to ponderous advice:

Fort Vancouver   August 5, 1832   It gives me particular pleasure to hear that you are hearty and well and had at last fairly got under

---

[23] Rich, *Simpson's 1828 Journey,* 114n.

way in business with a good reason to entertain hopes of succeeding well. You will, no doubt, my friend, meet with some difficulties, and experiences, some vexing and untoward occurrences at the commencement, let me entreat you not to let these discourage you, persevere and there is no doubt prudence and assiduity will eventually command success. Heaven's grant that the time may soon come that your success may equal your most sanguine expectations. [Here follows an account of the current fur trade state of affairs, written with Work's characteristic grousing, and then a feeler about chances for his own success "in a middling and high scale" at St. Thomas and an inquiry about "farming – capital – society – manner of living and other particulars in your quarters."]

Most touching of all were the letters from Archibald McDonald, chief trader, and father of Ranald McDonald by a native woman. In common with most of the officers who had contracted such alliances lightly, the father was later faced with the problem of rearing his half-blood children, to whom they had become profoundly attached while still recognizing the peculiar disabilities inherent in a mixed heritage. Ranald, like most of the officers' children, had been sent to Red River to be educated, and although brilliant in his own way, made poor progress in a system against which he was in constant rebellion.

A note of sad urgency runs through McDonald's letters to his old friend Ermatinger: "My little Chinook," he wrote, "by 1838 I think he ought to be qualified enough to begin the world for himself. Will you then do me a favor to take him in hand?" [24]

This Ermatinger did, and for two years gave the lad a home and a continuing education at Multnomah. According to his guardian, Ranald made satisfactory progress but his head was too much filled with visionary schemes to augur well for the future. When he left the Ermatinger home to roam around the world, his despairing father wrote to

---

[24] Lewis and Murakami, *op. cit.,* 27.

Edward, "Here, for all I shall ever do for him again, he may just crawl through life as the Black Bear does, lick his paw. We are all most unfortunate parents." [25]

Edward's busy and successful life closed in 1876. The final years of his brother Francis's life had been spent at St. Thomas near his brother, who outlived him by eighteen years. They are said to lie "side by side" in the parish churchyard.

The St. Thomas *Times* of October 31, 1876, printed this obituary:

DEATH OF EDWARD ERMATINGER, ESQ.

The death of the venerable gentleman whose name stands at the head of this notice took place at his residence in this Town on Saturday evening last at 9 o'clock. Mr. Ermatinger lived to within a few months of his 80th birthday, and up to three weeks ago continued unusually active, both in mind and body, for one of his advanced age. About three weeks ago he suffered from a partial paralytic stroke, from which he never recovered and which brought on his death at the above mentioned hour. . . For a number of years past he felt himself incapacitated for business duties and devoted a greater portion of his time in preparation for his approaching entrance upon another world, to which he looked forward with pleasurable anticipation. Though suffering some physical pain at the last, his end was on the whole a peaceful and happy one. The funeral will take place this (Tuesday) afternoon at halfpast three from Oakton, his late residence, to the St. Thomas burial ground.

---

[25] *Ibid.,* 28. Despite his father's gloomy forebodings, Ranald proved capable of looking out for himself in highly unusual circumstances, and is generally credited with having paved the way to opening up Japan to world commerce.

John Gantt

by HARVEY L. CARTER
Colorado College, Colorado Springs

The last of fifteen children, John Gantt was born at Queen Anne, on the eastern shore of Maryland, in 1790. His father, Edward S. Gantt, was a man of some distinction. He was born in Loudoun County, Virginia, on May 25, 1742, and spent some time in England, where he was ordained a deacon of the Anglican Church at Oxford, on January 25, 1770, by the Bishop of Oxford and ordained a priest by the Bishop of London on February 2, 1770. Returning to the colonies, he married Ann Stoughton Sloss, of Hagerstown, Maryland. He was a doctor of both medicine and divinity and a Fellow of the Royal Society. He served five terms as Chaplain of the United States Senate, and upon the completion of this appointment, removed from Georgetown, D.C., to Louisville, Kentucky, in 1808.[1]

Nothing is known of John Gantt's early years but, since he was appointed from Kentucky to the Army of the United States as a second lieutenant, it is a reasonable presumption that he must have accompanied his family when the migration was made to that state. His appointment as second lieutenant of a rifle company was made on May 24, 1817, and he was promoted first lieutenant April 5, 1818. Three years later, on June 1, 1821, he was transferred to the infantry, where he attained a captaincy on February 28, 1823.[2]

---

[1] The Francis W. Cragin Papers, in The Pioneer Museum, Colorado Springs, Colorado, Notebook IV, p. 2. Cragin's information was obtained in an interview with Mrs. Judith M. Gallup, a grand niece of John Gantt, at Pueblo, Colorado, on July 24, 1908. Alice B. Maloney in "John Gantt, Borderer," in the *California Historical Society Quarterly* (March 1937), XVI, p. 48, gives the dates 1738-1832 for the elder Gantt and 1810 as the date for his westward migration. Since Cragin's information was precise and definite, it may be assumed that it is correct.

[2] Francis B. Heitman, *Historical Register and Dictionary of the Army, 1789-1903* (Washington, 1903), I, p. 444.

Of his twelve years as an army officer, enough is known that it can be said that he was regarded as an able and efficient man and that he was also well liked by his company. Although doubtless much of the time was spent at Jefferson Barracks near St. Louis, some of it was spent on active service at frontier forts and in Indian campaigns, notably Colonel Leavenworth's Arikara campaign of 1823. We know that Capt. Gantt was officer of the day at Fort Recovery when, on May 13, 1824, two keelboats of the Missouri Fur Company arrived there from the Upper Missouri with a cargo of furs. Charles Bent and other traders reported to Gantt on this occasion, as recorded by James Kennerly.[3] He also participated in the expedition up the Missouri River to the mouth of the Yellowstone, made in the summer of 1825 by General Henry Atkinson and Major Benjamin O'Fallon, Indian agent. Treaties were made with twelve tribes for the better protection of fur traders operating on the Missouri. Captain Gantt is mentioned as riding ahead to the mouth of the Yellowstone, August 14 to 17, 1825, and again on the return he was detailed to remain with the repair crew of one of the boats, "The Rackoon," with orders to bring her on to Council Bluffs when repaired.[4]

Gantt's army service on the frontier gave him an opportunity to learn a good bit about the fur trade from contact and observation. His army career was suddenly terminated on May 12, 1829, as a result of his having been found guilty by court-martial, March 19, 1829, on two of four counts, involving the falsification of pay accounts. The court recommended clemency, which was refused by President Jackson, despite a petition signed by other officers of the Sixth Regi-

---

[3] Dale Morgan, *The West of William H. Ashley* (Denver, 1963), 253.

[4] *Ibid.*, 130, 136, quoted from Henry Atkinson's Journal, 1825. See also "Journal of the Atkinson-O'Fallon Expedition" in *North Dakota Historical Society Quarterly*, IV, p. 15, where it was reported, on May 31, 1825, that "a very large black bear was shot by one of Capt. Gantt's men last evening. . ."

ment, on the ground that Captain Gantt had been tried and found guilty of a similar offence on March 26, 1828. The penalty of a year's suspension had been disallowed in the earlier case by General Winfield Scott. The court expressed its belief that Captain Gantt intended to redeem the accounts personally but had been slow in doing so.[5]

Some further light may be shed upon this affair by the fact that Lieutenant Colonel A. R. Woolley had been found guilty by court-martial shortly before Gantt's second trial, of "conduct unbecoming an officer and a gentleman towards Captain Gantt especially of procuring through a highly colored charge the court-martial of Captain Gantt" and also of punishing a private, Thomas Powell, by lashes.[6] This looks very much as if Woolley had brought the original charges against Gantt, that Gantt then got his revenge when Woolley was dismissed, but that new charges were then brought against Gantt, which produced his dismissal. However this may be, John Gantt now found himself out of the army and under the necessity of making a living for himself and wife, for he had married Virginia McClanahan in 1827, by whom he had one child who survived, N. Beale Gantt.[7] Nothing was more natural than that he should have turned to the fur trade, in which others had reaped fortunes in the past decade. Although dismissed from the army, he was still known as Captain Gantt and was so referred to for the rest of his life. Sometimes it was spelled Gant, or Gaunt, or Ghant, or even miscalled Grant, but it was always pref-

---

[5] *The Niles Register* (May 23, 1829), XXXVI, pp. 204-5.

[6] *Ibid.,* (July 11, 1829), XXXVI, pp. 325-6.

[7] Cragin Papers, Notebook IV, p. 2. N. Beale Gantt married Amanda Morgan, of Louisville, and resided there until his death in the 1890s. His widow is known to have been living in 1914 and to have had in her possession an oil portrait of John Gantt, done about 1829. Professor Cragin secured a photographic copy of this portrait but it has unfortunately disappeared from his collection. The portrait may possibly have been done by George Catlin. Efforts to locate it have, thus far, been unsuccessful.

aced by his military title. Perhaps it was not out of place, for in the fur trade he was the leader of nearly as many men as he might have commanded in the army.

During the year 1830 he matured his plans and formed a partnership with Jefferson Blackwell. A three-year license to trade for furs was issued to them on April 5, 1831. The license indicated several locations already exploited by Ashley and his successors as their intended destination but it is well known that the specification of locations was merely a form to be complied with. Also, it was taken for granted that the men would trap, as well as trade, for beaver.[8]

The route to the mountains followed by Gantt and Black-well and their sixty or seventy men was from St. Louis, which they left on April 24, 1831, up the Missouri to Fort Osage, where they purchased food supplies, and continued along the Kansas and Republican rivers. They ran out of food on the latter and, finding no game, Gantt gave orders to kill two horses for eating. They went north to the Platte River, which they crossed by bull boats constructed for that purpose, and continued up the North Platte, where they at last found plenty of buffalo. On August 27, 1831, they reached the mouth of the Laramie River. Here they decided to divide into three companies and begin trapping. One group under A. K. Stevens was to ascend the Laramie, another under Washburn was to trap the Timber Fork, and Captain Gantt himself would lead a group up the Sweet-water; meanwhile, on September 3, Blackwell and two others returned to St. Louis for supplies.[9] Here, too, they encountered Thomas Fitzpatrick and a few men on their

---

[8] Abstract of Licenses in the Indian Affairs File of the National Archives, Washington, D.C. Places mentioned are "Camp Defiance on the waters of a river supposed to be the Bonaventura; Horse Prairie on Clark's R. of the Columbia; mouth of Lewis Fork of the Columbia. . ."

[9] *The Adventures of Zenas Leonard,* ed. by John C. Ewers (Norman, 1959), 3-8.

way from Santa Fe to join the rest of the Rocky Mountain
Fur Company. Fitzpatrick was reticent about any information that might help this rival company to gather furs.[10]

The plan was for all three parties to return to the mouth
of the Laramie River to spend the winter. The Stevens
group, of which Zenas Leonard was a member, camped on
the Laramie until January 1832, tried to go to Santa Fe and
failed, and finally returned to the mouth of the Laramie
about the end of April. Here they encountered Fitzpatrick
with 115 men, who said that Gantt and Blackwell had become insolvent. The Stevens group then sold its furs to
Fitzpatrick and joined him, going eventually to the rendezvous at Pierre's Hole in June 1832.[11]

At this rendezvous W. A. Ferris reported that he had
learned from a party of trappers that they "saw Captain
Ghantt at the head of fifty or sixty men, on Green River;
he had procured horses from the Spaniards of New Mexico,
and had made his hunt on the sources of the Arkansas, and
tributaries of Green River, without molestation by the Indians."[12]

Another reference to this same activity is found in a letter
from Captain B. L. E. Bonneville to Major General Alexander McComb, headed Crow Country, Wind River, July
29, 1833, which says, "Gantt came up in 1831 with about 50
men mostly afoot done little, then retired to the headwaters
of the Arkansas where I understand he has opened a trade
with the Comanche, the Arapahoes & Shians."[13]

In February 1833, Zenas Leonard and others camped at
the mouth of the Laramie once more and found a letter in
Captain Gantt's hardwriting which told what had occurred.

[10] LeRoy R. Hafen and W. J. Ghent, *Broken Hand: The Life of Thomas Fitzpatrick, Chief of the Mountain Men* (Denver, 1931), 93-4.

[11] *The Adventures of Zenas Leonard,* 9-29.

[12] W. A. Ferris, *Life in the Rocky Mountains,* ed. by Paul C. Phillips (Denver,
1940), 150-151.   [13] Maloney, *op. cit.,* 49.

Gantt and Washburn had returned as agreed upon but did not find Stevens and his men. Since their horses had been stolen by Indians, Gantt had gone to Santa Fe and purchased more. On his return, he had encountered Washburn and had made the hunt already alluded to by Ferris and by Bonneville. Meanwhile, Gantt had learned that the Stevens group had gone over to Fitzpatrick. He had received supplies from his partner Blackwell and they had left the mouth of the Laramie in September 1832 to go to the Arkansas River, where they had decided to establish a post for the purpose of trading with the Arapaho Indians.[14]

A letter of Gantt's headed San Fernando de Taos, February 20, 1832, and addressed to the Governor of New Mexico, Santiago Abreu, gives some further indication of his past operations and even more indication of his future plans.[15] He says that he left his camp at the junction of the Snake and Bear rivers on December 25, 1831, and came to Taos for the purpose of buying mules. He specifies that he has twenty-two trappers on the North Platte, eleven on the South Platte, twenty-five on the Snake, five with him in Taos, and that he will be joined by forty more from St. Louis on the Arkansas in July. All this is by way of leading up to the fact that he proposes to establish a trading post on the Arkansas River at its junction with the Purgatoire and that he wishes to cultivate friendly relations with the government in New Mexico. He speaks with assurance concerning the probable establishment of a fort by the Army of the United States on the Arkansas in the near future and indicates that the garrison of such a fort would cooperate

---

[14] *The Adventures of Zenas Leonard,* 52-53.

[15] This letter is ms. 1832 in the Ritch Collection of the Huntington Library, San Marino, California. It is translated and quoted in full in Janet Lecompte, "Gantt's Fort and Bent's Picket Post" in *The Colorado Magazine* (Spring, 1964), XLI, pp. 113-4. Mrs. Lecompte's authoritative and closely reasoned article settles the question of the location of the forts along the Arkansas and also proves that Gantt, rather than William Bent, was first to trade with the Arapaho and Cheyenne tribes.

with the New Mexico authorities in policing the Indians along the border and would also expect to draw its supplies from Taos. Thus, he cleverly holds out the advantages of trade to the governor, while at the same time hinting that he would have the backing of his own government's military power.

Gantt now returned to the mouth of the Laramie, only to learn that the twenty-two men he expected to find there, under Stevens, had gone over to Fitzpartick. He left the letter there for them at this time (early April of 1832) which Leonard found in February 1833, as has been related already. Gantt now returned to the Arkansas and met Blackwell, who brought needed supplies. He then returned to the mountains where he trapped until September, 1832. Either in South (Old) Park or North (New) Park, he was joined by Kit Carson and three companions who had heard from Alexander Sinclair on the Green River, that "Captain Gaunt, who was an old mountaineer, well known to most of the whites present" was trapping there.[16] Constructing a few log cabins enclosed by a stockade, Gantt left his men on the Arkansas in September and went to Taos for two months. On his return they wintered in the new quarters, presumably at the mouth of the Purgatoire. They spent a comfortable winter, except for the fact that the Crow Indians stole their horses which Carson and others succeeded in recovering.[17]

In the spring, having cached three hundred pounds of beaver skins, they set out for the Laramie once more. On the South Platte, two men deserted and Gantt sent Carson and a companion after them. As had been suspected, these men had stolen the cache but Carson was unable to overtake them and he and his companion spent a month forted up at Gantt's

---

[16] Blanche Grant, ed., *Kit Carson's Own Story* (Taos, 1926), 21, says New Park. DeWitt C. Peters, *Kit Carson's Life and Adventures* (Hartford, 1874), 59, says South Park. It seems impossible to determine which is correct. Peters, p. 60, says they later trapped in North (New) Park. [17] Grant, *op. cit.*, 22-25.

Post until Blackwell arrived with fresh supplies. Shortly after this, four of Gantt's trappers came with the news that Gantt was in the Bayou Salade (South Park) and all six trappers went there to join him. However, they did so poorly that Carson and two others detached themselves and took up free trapping with some little success.[18]

Gantt's thoughts now turned to the possibilities of trade with the Indians at some fixed point on the Arkansas, which he had already begun in a small way. He had met with many losses and misfortunes in his trapping ventures and it was clear that beaver were becoming scarce and that there were too many competitive companies scouring the mountain streams.

Contemporary evidence indicates that Gantt began trade with both the Arapaho and Cheyenne tribes in the winter of 1832. Rufus Sage, writing in 1843, said, "About the year 1832, Capt. Grant succeeded in effecting a treaty with the Arapahos.   ." One of the items discussed was the possible return of Friday, the Arapaho boy, found by Fitzpatrick a year earlier.[19]

Writing in 1837, the Rev. Moses Merrill, a missionary among the Oto Indians, recorded that "the Shiennes, a tribe of Indians on the Platte River, were wholly averse to drinking whisky but five years ago – now (through the influence of a trader, Captain Gant, who by sweetening the whisky induced them to drink the intoxicating draught) they are a tribe of drunkards."[20]

Then Ferris, a contemporary trapper, also mentions "Capt. Ghant, whose firmness and liberality they (the Arapahos) have reason to remember long, has established

---

[18] *Ibid.*, 27.

[19] Rufus B. Sage, *Letters and Scenes in the Rocky Mountains,* ed. by LeRoy R. and Ann W. Hafen in *The Far West and the Rockies Series* (Glendale, 1956), V, p. 303.

[20] "Diary of Rev. Moses Merrill" in *Transactions and Reports of the Nebraska State Historical Society* (1892), IV, p. 181.

a post among them on the Arkansas, four days march from Taos. . ."[21]

Liberal Gantt may have been, but the 180 gallons of whiskey which he was authorized to have for trading purposes when he first went to the mountains, was to last for three years and, unless the supply was replenished in much greater quantity, it was not enough to make the Cheyennes into a tribe of topers.[22] Nevertheless, it is clear that Gantt was the first to trade with these two important tribes, although it is not clear which of Gantt's trading posts Ferris had in mind.

For Gantt built a second fort and trading post on the Arkansas in 1834, which he named Ft. Cass.[23] It was located on the north bank of the river, but near to it, about six miles below the mouth of the Fontaine Qui Bouille. It was built of adobe which was made by Guadalupe Avila and Dominguez Madrild, who were sent from Taos for that purpose by Jim Wilkes, a friend of Gantt's in that place. Construction was begun in May 1834, only three miles above a log trading post of William Bent's, known as Ft. William, which had probably been there less than a year.[24]

During that summer, William Bent and his men made an unprovoked attack on some Shoshone Indians encamped near Ft. Cass. Gantt and several of his men witnessed this fight, in which three Shoshones were killed and scalped, thirty-seven horses and all the camping equipment belong-

---

[21] Ferris, *op. cit.,* 312.

[22] Indian Affairs File, 1831, in the National Archives, Washington, D.C. Gantt and Blackwell were issued a permit for 180 gallons of whiskey for three years on April 10, 1831. By contrast, the American Fur Company's permits were for 2,666 gallons for a year and a half.

[23] See Lecompte, *op. cit.,* XLI, pp. 117-125. The location of this fort, and that of William Bent's Ft. William, is fully discussed and definitely established in this important article.

[24] F. W. Cragin Papers, Notebook II, pp. 35, 68-69, and Notebook X, p. 38. The location of Fort Cass was near present Baxter, Colorado, and that of Ft. William just east of present Devine, Colorado. Cragin's informant was Tom Autobees, son of Charlie Autobees, and nephew of Guadalupe Avila.

ing to eight lodges taken.[25] The importance of this episode has not been generally appreciated. It was the turning point in Bent's career and a fatal crisis for Gantt. By 1835 Bent was established in his adobe castle, to be known as Bent's Old Fort, and Gantt was out of the fur trade forever. The question may well be raised as to why Bent succeeded where Gantt failed.

It has generally been believed that Gantt and Blackwell became insolvent, but it is certain they were not insolvent when Tom Fitzpatrick started the rumor that they were, in 1832, because Blackwell brought supplies to the mountains and Gantt continued to trap and trade for two years after that. It is not even certain that they were insolvent in 1834, when they went out of business. William Bent had the backing of an established Santa Fe trading company but Gantt had the advantage of good will among the Cheyenne and Arapaho tribes. This good will was destroyed at one stroke, and gained for Bent Brothers and St. Vrain, when William Bent attacked the Shoshone interlopers in the shadow of Gantt's own fort and before his very eyes, on July 29, 1834. Bent by this act established himself as a stronger power than Gantt, in the eyes of the Indians of the region. As his trade fell off in the months that followed, this must have become so evident to Gantt that he saw it was hopeless to continue the competition with Bent. The fur trade was a cut throat business and Fitzpatrick by his crafty lie and Bent by his attack on Gantt's customers had both helped to ruin Gantt, who was too much of a gentleman for such a lawless business. But it was Bent who delivered the decisive blow.[26]

---

[25] Gantt may possibly have been the writer of the unsigned letter reporting this incident to the Indian agent, Major Cummings, at Ft. Leavenworth. This letter is reproduced in full in Lecompte, *op. cit.*, XLI, p. 121.

[26] David Lavender, *Bent's Fort* (Garden City, 1954), 151-2, considers this affair to be "the blackest mark on William Bent's record." It is a black mark from any

George Bird Grinnell tells us that among the Cheyennes, Gantt was known as "Bald Head," and Blackwell as "The Crane," because he was tall and thin. But "Little White Man," as the Indians called William Bent, had supplanted them in the trade, which they were the first to conceive and attempt.[27]

In the summer of 1835, Colonel Henry Dodge led a regiment of Dragoons to the front range of the Rocky Mountains for the purpose of conferring with the Indian chiefs of the high plains and establishing better relations with them. He left Ft. Leavenworth in May, and traveled up the South Platte with John Gantt, ex-army officer and ex-fur trader, as his guide. Gantt also did a good bit of the hunting, made a bull boat for crossing rivers, and had the task of finding and bringing in the chiefs for conferences.[28] The Dragoons passed from the South Platte to the Arkansas and, on August 1, 1835, were at an "old trading establishment formerly occupied by Capt. Gant," as reported by Hugh Evans who kept a diary of the expedition. Lemuel Ford, another diary-keeping member of the group, made a map

moral viewpoint and the same can be said of Fitzpatrick's lie about Gantt and Blackwell's financial position. But Fitzpatrick obtained twenty-two men and 120 beaver belonging to John Gantt; and Bent drove Gantt out of business at the cost of the lives of only three Snake Indians. The pragmatist will approve what the moralist will condemn. Gantt fought fairly; his rivals were less scrupulous and more successful.

[27] See George Bird Grinnell "Bent's Old Fort and its Builders," in *Kansas Historical Society Collections* (1919-22), XV, p. 18. But George Bent, William Bent's half-breed son, writing to Professor Cragin from Colony, Oklahoma, on September 23, 1905, said that Gantt was called "Tall Crane" and that Blackwell was called "Bald Head." He also said that "Tall Crane" had a child among the Cheyennes. In the absence of any known likeness of either Gantt or Blackwell, it is difficult to decide which name belonged to which partner or which one fathered the child.

[28] "Report on the Expedition of Dragoons under Colonel Henry Dodge," in *American State Papers, Military Affairs,* VI, pp. 130-146. See also Fred S. Perrine, editor, "Hugh Evans Journal of Colonel Henry Dodge's Expedition to the Rocky Mountains in 1835," in *Mississippi Valley Historical Review* (September 1927), XIV, pp. 192-214.

which shows the locations of both Fort Cass and Fort William, as already designated.[29]

Four years later, Sidney Smith, on the way to Oregon with T. J. Farnham, recorded in his journal, under date of July 15, 1839, "encampt on the fontinkaboya [Fontaine Qui Bouille] passed two forts that have been abandoned." [30] Gantt returned to Missouri after having guided Colonel Dodge for over 1600 miles.

The next that is heard of Gantt is that, along with William Stoner, he agreed to mine and sell coal from a mine in Missouri owned by William L. Sublette, another well known Mountain Man. How long this arrangement lasted and with what success it was pursued, is not known.[31]

While with the Dragoons, Gantt had made the acquaintance of Lancaster P. Lupton, an officer who was soon to follow Gantt's example and engage in the fur trade. Doubtless he was influenced by what he learned from Gantt. Also accompanying the Dragoons was George Catlin, the famous painter of Indians. A testimonial signed by Gantt and dated November 27, 1837, New York City, was used by Catlin in connection with his exhibit there.[32] Gantt's father had died in Louisville, on September 24, 1837, at the age of ninety-five. This event may have taken him there and he may have continued to New York and also to Washington, for we know that he served as Indian agent for the Pottawatomies at Council Bluffs during 1838 and 1839, and he may have procured the appointment on his trip to the East.[33]

From 1839 to 1843 nothing is known of Gantt's move-

[29] Louis Pelzer, editor, "Captain Ford's Journal of an Expedition to the Rocky Mountains" in *Mississippi Valley Historical Review* (March 1926), XII, pp. 550-579. The map is reproduced in LeCompte, *op. cit.*, XLI, pp. 122-123.

[30] LeRoy R. and Ann W. Hafen, editors, *To the Rockies and Oregon, 1839-1842* in *The Far West and the Rockies Series* (Glendale, 1955), III, p. 72.

[31] Sublette Papers, Missouri Historical Society, St. Louis, Mo.

[32] Maloney, *op. cit.*, XVI, p. 53.

[33] *House Document 103*, 25 Cong., 3 Sess. (Serial No. 346), p. 9.

ments but, in the latter year, he contracted to guide as far as Fort Hall 875 emigrants bound for Oregon, at a price of one dollar per person. This "Great Emigration" left its rendezvous, twelve miles west of Independence, Missouri, on May 22, 1843. They reached Independence Rock on July 26 and Fort Hall a month later. Gantt performed his duties well and is uniformly mentioned with approval in the various journals of the emigrants. James Nesmith refers to him as "our respected pilot" and Jesse Applegate later wrote: "The pilot (a borderer) who has spent his life on the verge of civilization and has been chosen to the post of leader from his knowledge of the savage and his experience in travel through the roadless wastes stands ready, in the midst of his pioneers and aids to lead the way.   .   ."[34]

Having fulfilled his contract, Gantt left Fort Hall on August 27, 1843, with a party, led by Joseph B. Chiles and Joseph Reddeford Walker, headed for California. This party divided, Walker taking the wagons over Walker Pass, while Chiles, with a few men on horseback went by a new route along the Feather River and eventually reached Sutter's Fort. Gantt accompanied the latter group.[35]

In 1844 and 1845, Gantt played an important part in California public affairs. He was elected captain of a company of one hundred mounted riflemen. This company was formed by Sutter, who expected to command it himself, for the purpose of aiding Governor Micheltorena against discontented groups who were in arms against him. However, Gantt's company of Americans found that there were many Americans aiding the rebels when they met them at Cahuenga Pass on February 21, 1845, and they refused to engage in battle with them. The result was the defeat and exile of

---

[34] See Jesse Applegate, "A Day with the Cow Column," in *Oregon Historical Society Quarterly,* I, p. 373; Peter H. Burnett, "Recollections and Opinions of an Old Pioneer" in *ibid.,* v, pp. 67-8; Maloney, *op. cit.,* 53-6.

[35] See W. J. Ghent, *The Road to Oregon* (New York, 1934), 72-77.

Governor Micheltorena by General Alvarado, with Gantt and his command taking no part. The outcome was not satisfactory to Sutter and John Bidwell but was highly so to Gantt's friend, Dr. John Marsh. Pio Pico was chosen governor and Gantt and Marsh contracted with him to recover horses from thieving Indians, although it is thought that they were never active in carrying out their contract.[36]

Two letters of Gantt's to John Marsh, in the spring and fall of 1845, are of interest. In the first, headed New Helvecia, March 11, he speaks of having had a rupture with John Bidwell over the Cahuenga Pass affair. He indicates that Sutter owes him money but that he will not take worn out horses in payment. He plans instead to go on a trapping expedition to the mountains and then to go south. In the second, headed Feather River, October 21, 1845, he says that he has just returned from a beaver hunt on the Trinity River, where the whole party was sick and did not put a trap in the water. He says further that he has been ague and fever proof for thirty years and that he has become almost mosquito proof.[37]

Nevertheless, it appears that Gantt took no part in the events of the Mexican War in California in 1846 because he was in very bad health at that time. Edwin Bryant found him very ill at Dr. Marsh's ranch in September, 1846. He wrote, "Capt. Gant, formerly of the U.S. Army, in very bad health, is residing here. He has crossed the Rocky Mountains eight times and, in various trapping excursions, has explored every river between the settlements of the United States and the Pacific Ocean."[38]

---

[36] Maloney, *op. cit.*, XVI, pp. 56-58; H. H. Bancroft, *History of California,* IV, pp. 516, 543.

[37] Alice B. Maloney, "Three Letters of John Gantt," in *California Historical Society Quarterly,* XX, pp. 148-150.

[38] Edwin Bryant, *What I Saw In California* (London, 1849), 247. Bryant was a newspaper man. The exaggeration, concerning the area trapped over, is probably his rather than Gantt's.

It seems probable that this was the beginning of the heart trouble which caused his death. He recovered sufficiently to go to the Napa Valley, where he formed a partnership known as Gantt and Hannah and projected the building of a saw mill. This was in 1847 and 1848. A letter of his to Dr. Marsh, headed Napa Valley, August 22, 1847, urges Marsh to get married and promises to introduce him to some ladies, if he will pay him a visit. It also contains some humorous references to the efforts being made by old Mountain Men Moses Carson and George Yount to find wives for themselves.[39]

John Bidwell recalled that Gantt attempted to do some gold panning near Bidwell's Bar in the fall of 1848 or the spring of 1849. If so, he soon gave it up and returned to the Napa Valley where, at the ranch of George Yount, he died on February 14, 1849. He was buried in the Yountsville cemetery.

John Gantt was one of the few men who made friends with the eccentric Harvard graduate, Dr. John Marsh. Apparently, Marsh recognized Gantt as a gentleman and an equal and they got along well.[40] Though Gantt was dishonorably discharged from the army, it seems clear that he was, by training and by nature, an honorable man and that he was unsuccessful in the fur trade, at least partly, because his competitors were less honorable and more unscrupulous than he was. His greatest claim to fame must be that he was the first to perceive the opportunity for a trading post on the Arkansas River, a project which was carried out successfully by his rival, William Bent.

---

[39] Maloney, *op. cit.*, XX, pp. 150-151.   [40] Maloney, *op. cit.*, XVI, pp. 58-59.

William W. Bent

by SAMUEL P. ARNOLD
Morrison, Colorado

South of Las Animas, Colorado, a tall stone monument rises from the grassy cover of the local cemetery. Larger than most of the other stones, it carries the name of William W. Bent, and that of his daughter, Mary. The peaceful stillness of the large trees and of the well-kept grounds gives an appropriate resting place for the man who played a major role in the early development of the West.

What sort of man was William Bent? In stature, slightly less than medium height. His dark hair and eyes with sun-bronzed skin belied his Anglo-Saxon origins. Some thought he came of a French-Canadian background[1] and his high cheek bones and wise eyes had an Indian look. Smallpox scars in his cheeks hardened his features. But his large jaw with a wide smile doubtless gave Indians and Mountain Men alike a feeling of openness and straight talk.

William first saw daylight on May 23, 1809. He was one of eleven children born to Judge Silas Bent in St. Louis. The judge resided in a large home with landscaped grounds, blooded horses, and a complement of servants. He had been appointed principal deputy surveyor of the Louisiana Territory in the summer of 1806 by Gallatin, Secretary of the Treasury. In 1807 he was appointed justice of the Court of Common Pleas, and later Supreme Court judge of the territory. As his position made him an important man to know, Judge Bent's friends and houseguests represented key

---

[1] Henry Inman, *Old Santa Fe Trail* (N.Y., 1897), states that the Bent brothers were French-Canadian hunters and trappers.

figures in the fur and merchandise trades. He was more readily accepted than most American newcomers by the French leaders in Missouri. Bernard Pratte and Auguste Chouteau, fur trade leaders, were among his acquaintances.

A family story has it that William Bent's grandfather, also named Silas, led one of three groups dressed as Indians, who emptied the tea into Boston Harbor in 1773.[2] This heritage, along with Grandfather Bent's long service throughout the Revolution (ending with a rank of lieutenant colonel), and his father's governmental position doubtless influenced William in building a strong loyalty for country – loyalty often sorely tested in later years.

Though for many years William Bent was to live in Indian tipis, log stockades, and other primitive circumstances, his early background of wealth and luxury reflected itself in his mode of life. St. Julian Medoc and other French wines were served at his Arkansas River fort.[3] Damask table cloths, crystal and silver graced his board, set with English blue feather-edged chinaware.[4] Photographs in later years show him in a handsomely-tailored formal suit. So all was not buckskin and raw buffalo liver.

When William was but a youngster, swarthy Spaniard Manuel Lisa ranged northwest from St. Louis, up the Missouri River with his Missouri Fur Company. Lisa's dream of a network of trade forts from the Missouri to the Pacific required the services of educated young men. Although William's older brother Charles is believed to have begun working for Lisa's firm in 1818, the only definitive record

[2] David Lavender, in his *Bent's Fort* (N.Y., 1954), 369, lists a letter from Silas Bent, brother of Charles and William and grandson of Revolutionary Silas, which states the family story.

[3] Recent excavations by the National Park Service have provided actual French bottles with Bent's Fort fur trade period provenience.

[4] Wine cask remains with spigots were found in the fort's cellar. English chinaware also included the "Boston Mail" series commemorating the first Cunard steamships.

naming him is dated 1824.[5] Following Lisa's death in 1820, Joshua Pilcher assumed the reins of the firm. In 1822, Astor's American Fur Company succeeded in lobbying through Congress the removal of the government posts which had competed with the limited number of trade license holders. The Superintendent of Indian Affairs was empowered to issue licenses without limit.

By 1825, fierce competition from the St. Louis French traders headed by Bernard Pratte put Pilcher's Missouri Fur Company in bankruptcy. Young Charles Bent, now with considerable experience as well as influential St. Louis connections, became a partner in a re-organized firm called Pilcher & Company. But it was too late. The tightening monopoly of Astor's American Fur Company, now strengthened by the absorption of Pratt, Chouteau and Kenneth McKenzie's fur companies, edged Pilcher & Company toward oblivion. It was finished off in 1827 by an abortive wintertime expedition up the Platte and to the Green River. Indians ran off their horses. Their trade goods had to be cached. Heavy blizzards and deep snows made difficult an escape to their shelter in the valley of the Green. No proof presently exists placing young William Bent with the group. Yet in later years his son George stated that William "was very young when he went up the Missouri with his brother." It would seem logical that the 1827 trip, when he was age 18, was his first major experience.[6]

On their return in the spring of 1828 from the Green, Charles and William found their father had died. The American Fur Company had consolidated its position still further, controlling virtually the entire fur trade on the Missouri.

Failing in an attempt to join the American Fur Company,

---

[5] E. B. Wesley (ed.), "Diary of James Kennerly," *Missouri Hist. Soc. Collections,* VI, p. 69; entry of May 13, 1824.

[6] American Fur Co. ledger, retail store, Western Department, July 7, 1828.

Charles and William put together a sum of money – possibly borrowed from friends and relatives, or inherited from Judge Bent's estate. It was invested in equipment and trade goods for a caravan to Santa Fe. Four years earlier, traders Wetmore and Storrs had effectively stimulated trade to the Northern Department of Mexico (New Mexico) by answers to a series of questions put forth by Missouri Senator Thomas Hart Benton. In reply to questions about trade, it had been stated that quite conservatively, a man might multiply his money by ten times in bringing American goods to Santa Fe and Chihuahua.[7] A rash of goods had quickly filled the vacuum.

Four years before, in the spring of 1825, young Ceran St. Vrain from Missouri had entered the trade. Coming to Taos, he found the village short on hard cash and long on Missouri merchandise. Entering into the beaver pelt trade, St. Vrain ranged over northern New Mexico, Colorado, and as far north as the Green where possibly in 1827 he had met Charles, and perhaps William Bent.[8] The Missouri-to-Santa Fe journey had been proving increasingly difficult. In 1828 Comanches had successfully attacked and decimated several large trains of wagons returning with silver and hides from New Mexico. Veteran trade merchants soon came to look upon the trip to Santa Fe as fraught with dangers. With their Missouri River experience behind them, the Bents must have "shone" among the others in the 1829 wagon train, for Charles was elected captain of the thirty-eight wagons and seventy-nine men.

On the trail there was one bright note. At Chouteau's Island, they recovered some thirty bags of silver deposited there the previous year by the Indian-attacked wagoneers.

---

[7] Augustus Storrs and Alphonso Wetmore, *Santa Fe Trail: First Reports, 1825* (Houston, 1960).

[8] A well-supported presumption of David Lavender's, based upon known facts that St. Vrain was on the Green, as were Charles and perhaps William, in 1827. See *Bent's Fort*, 73-79.

Shortly after the U.S. Army military guard halted its escort at the Arkansas River, the wagon train came under Indian attack. William, riding a mule some distance from the train, spotted the Indians. Whooping, they chased him as he rode back to warn the caravan. Another group of Indians attacked the advance guard. The Bents apparently saw that the attack would soon center on the wagons. They wheeled about and rode firing head-on into the attacking Indians. The bluff worked, giving time for the traders at the wagons to get organized and fire a small cannon at the attackers. As the Indians scattered for cover, Charles sent riders back for the troops. After a sleepless night, the troops arrived and the Indians vanished.

Thoroughly terrified, the wagon train was halted. Many wanted to return, or at least to stay with the U.S. troops on American soil. Charles Bent first attempted to convince them to go on. Failing this, he made a strong plea to the military to escort the train into Mexican territory. Major Riley, commanding, refused. The train moved onward toward Mexico. Almost immediately, they were joined by a group of more than a hundred Mexican buffalo hunters who appeared out of the sandhills. These men were even more terrified than Bent's wagoneers, for they brought news of some two thousand Indians on the warpath. For days as they edged their way toward Santa Fe, they suffered from alarms and fears of sudden attack. American Ewing Young in Taos heard through the grapevine that an American train was under attack. He gathered forty Mountain Men and set out to give relief. He met Indians and had to send back to Taos for reinforcements. Another fifty-five men joined him. They finally found the wagon train and escorted it in. Young Kit Carson was one of the rescuers.

Santa Fe's ruby-lipped, cigarillo-smoking senoritas entertained the wagoneers for about five weeks. Hardware, linens, woolens, glass, "quentoque juisque" (Kentucky whiskey)[9], Russell's Green River knives[10] from Massachusetts, Dupont powder and galena were exchanged for mules, furs, gold and silver. The trades were so good that Charles Bent and his companions had goods which in Missouri would bring as much as $200,000 – a healthy return from the desperate fringes of bankruptcy he had so lately experienced. They set out for home.

Twenty-year-old William, however, decided to stay in the area and not return that year. Instead he joined a group of independent trappers. One of these is believed to have been Charlie Autobees, a French-Canadian who later played a major role in bringing warning to Santa Fe of the Taos rebellion of 1847, when Charles Bent was murdered. The party worked its way north trapping and looking for parties of Indians with pelts.

Eventually they made winter camp.[11] Stories tell of a stockade being built on the Arkansas between present-day Pueblo and Canon City, Colorado. A group of Cheyennes paid a visit to the fort. They came in peace, viewed the trade items, and then left. Two of the warriors had lingered on for a time with the trappers. Suddenly from over a hill came a raiding party of Comanches looking for Cheyenne horses. William quickly hid the two Indians within the stockade. The Comanche leader, Bull Hump, spotted the fresh Cheyenne tracks and demanded to know where they were. In peril of his life if found to be lying, Bent nonethe-

---

[9] This phonetic spelling of American words in Spanish by customs officials in New Mexico was common. New Mexico state archivist, Myra Jenkins, found this whiskey reference in old customs papers.

[10] Green River knives were first produced by John Russell in 1834 on the banks of the Green River near Greenfield, Mass. They soon captured the Western market and were carried by such famous frontiersmen as Kit Carson and Uncle Dick Wootton. They are still in production today. They were highly copied by foreign manufacturers who sought to trade on the knife's fine reputation. See also G. F. Ruxton, *Life in the Far West,* ed. by L. R. Hafen (Norman, Okla., 1951), 189.

[11] G. B. Grinnell, *Bent's Old Fort and its Builders* (Topeka, Kas. St. Hist. Soc., 1923), 38. The exact location of the wintering site has not been determined. Current speculation includes a site on the Camp Carson military base.

less told the Comanche leader that all the Cheyennes had departed. Bull Hump left. In saving the two lives, William began his association with the Cheyennes, thus altering the course of his life.

Upon returning to Santa Fe that summer of 1830, William found that his brother Charles had been back and forth to Missouri, and was again planning a fall trip. In spite of the trail dangers, profits were exceptional. But William liked the wilderness and this new life of the Mountain Man. He may have served his older brother by learning firsthand the best beaver and hunting areas, and the trails and temper of the various Indian tribes. Without any doubt, William liked the rough and ready life. In later years, despite considerable wealth, he would spent weeks in Indian camp in his own tipi. As a young man in Missouri, he had already learned passable French, Sioux and universal Indian sign language. Now in the West he learned the archaic 18th Century Spanish tongue spoken so purely in Santa Fe. From French-Canadians like Charlie Autobees he doubtless received a liberal education in the different brand of bastardized French used by those hardy northwoodsmen.

In the fall of 1830 William joined up with Robert Isaacs, Joshua Griffith and Joseph Reynolds for a trip to Arizona to trap on the Gila.[12] A massive Indian attack at the mouth of the San Pedro put an end to the trip, but all in the party kept their hair. The successful defense against overwhelming odds gave William Bent an impressive frontier reputation as the story enlarged in the retelling.

That December saw Charles Bent approaching Ceran St. Vrain to form a partnership.[13] Charles needed an experienced businessman to handle the dispersal of the goods brought from Missouri. Merchandise was plentiful, but

---

[12] *Missouri Intelligencer* (Columbia, Mo.), Oct. 6, 1832. From *Missouri Republican* of St. Louis.

[13] Lavender, *Bent's Fort,* 126. Letters from St. Vrain to Bernard Pratte.

money scarce in Santa Fe. With high duties, and the problems of making enough trips across to Missouri and back for a profit, the necessity for a Santa Fe office became clear. When several wagon trains arrived at about the same time, goods were sold at cut prices and the seller suffered losses. By waiting until the demand outgrew the temporary glut, a merchant could realize a better profit.

Partnership with Charles Bent may have been welcome to St. Vrain for it combined the capital and credit of both. Charles' success in speedily bringing trains across the Santa Fe Trail made a partnership with competitor St. Vrain logical. By joining forces they were soon able to build a strong economic and political power in New Mexico.

Following William Bent's adventure on the Gila in late 1830, it appears likely that he carried the business of the newly-formed Bent, St. Vrain & Co. back to the Arkansas River area. The 1829-30 Arkansas River trip had given promise of Indian trade possibilities, and the initial friendship with the Cheyennes was a foot in the door. One may surmise that the much-described meeting of the Bents (Charles, William, and the newly-arrived younger brothers George and Robert) with Yellow Wolf and his Cheyennes took place sometime during the year 1831 at the mouth of the Purgatoire near present-day Las Animas. Yellow Wolf at that time counselled them to build a trading fort in that area. As Big Timbers nearby was a favorite spot for the Cheyennes because food, shelter and fuel were available, an agreement was made that the Bents would have the Cheyenne trade if they located there. It would seem logical that the Big Timbers fort was built shortly thereafter.[14]

---

[14] A strong case may be presented for the Big Timbers Fort: according to Grinnell, George Bent states that two stockades were built – the first above Pueblo and the second near the mouth of the Purgatoire in 1828. Grinnell also states that he heard from Porcupine Bull that the agreement for a stockade at the mouth of the Purgatoire was made. Moreover, Gibson's diary in 1846 states, "Our camp is where Bent's Old Fort stood, 45 miles from the present one, and very few vestiges of it

In the meantime trader John Gantt entered the scene. With his partner Jefferson Blackwell, Gantt built a trade fort near the confluence of the Arkansas and Fountain rivers, which marks present-day Pueblo, Colorado. It is likely that it was erected about September of 1832. Named Fort Cass for President Jackson's new Secretary of War, the trade center competed with the Bents.[15] It appears that William Bent, sensing the need for eliminating competition with Gantt, built his Ft. William log trading post during the spring of 1833. It was located three miles east of Fort Cass, and like Gantt's, was a stockade type building. Gantt retaliated by hiring Mexican adobe-makers the next spring to build a more permanent adobe structure.

That summer of 1834, there was bad blood between Fort Cass and the Bents. Competition was fierce. Both Gantt and William Bent were trying to attract Indian trade and it was a fight which would eliminate one of them. It appears that some mules had been stolen from brother Charles Bent in Taos by Indians whom they believed were Snakes. On July 29, 1834, William Bent with a force of men attacked a trading party of Snakes at Fort Cass. Three were killed and scalped and two were wounded. Two women and thirty-seven horses were taken by Bent. Rather than fight, the men at Fort Cass, including John Gantt, stood by, warning Bent that the government would consider it an "improper action which would not meet the view of the government." William was quoted as saying, "Damn the government . . . I do it now anyhow." The fact that William saw Mexicans making adobes for a bigger fort may have spurred him on.

---

remain, scarcely enough to indicate its former size, though it was deserted only about twelve years ago." G. R. Gibson, *Journal of a Soldier under Kearny and Doniphan,* ed. by R. P. Bieber (Glendale, Calif., 1935), 163.

[15] Janet Lecompte, "Gantt's Fort and Bent's Picket Post," in *Colorado Magazine,* XLI, no. 2, Spring 1964. Mrs. Lecompte presents firm evidence of the two forts near the mouth of Fountain River. The reproduction of the Dodge Expedition map definitely establishes forts Cass, William, and Bent's in 1835. The account of William's attack on Fort Cass is included in this article.

Gantt's new adobe fort would have been completed by the fall of 1834, six miles below the mouth of the Fountain. William must have felt outclassed by Gantt's more permanent adobe fort. In a superb example of "oneupmanship," William began construction of a huge castle-like fort farther east (near present-day La Junta). Crews were brought from New Mexico to make adobes. Raw wool was apparently used as a binder for the powdery fine soil.[16] Two massive bastions at opposite corners of the structure gave protection against possible scaling of the walls.[17]

William's Big Timbers fort was abandoned in 1834 with the establishment of Fort William.[18]

While it is possible that William Bent may have begun building his famous adobe castle in 1834, it is probable that it was not complete until the summer of 1835. The government permit for trade at Fort William was issued in St. Louis on December 13, 1834. This was nearly a year after William Laidlaw wrote Pierre Chouteau on January 10, 1834, "Charles Bent has built a fort upon the Arkansas for the purpose of trade. . ." The license describes the fort near Fort Cass. Another, issued November 8, 1836, describes the location of Bent's adobe fort. One may surmise that William made peace with John Gantt in the end.

It should be noted that by the end of 1833 the price of beaver had skidded downward from $6 per pound to $3.50 in St. Louis. Gantt, who depended primarily on beaver, finally folded up in 1835 and hired out as a scout for Colonel Dodge. Bent, St. Vrain & Co. took over his fort and used it

---

[16] Recent Park Service excavations indicate that wool apparently was used as reported by Grinnell. [18] See note 14.

[17] Alexander Barclay, in a letter to his brother George in England, written March 10, 1840, states, "The fort is to undergo improvements and additions under my surveillance this summer and I shall endeavor to make it as defensible as possible. The Comanche tribe have threatened this last two years to destroy us and I shall be happy to have an opportunity to treat them warmly for their intentions. Two of the transverse corners are flanked with bastions. We have one six-pounder and two swivels so they may come and welcome." Barclay Papers, Bancroft Library.

as a minor trading post. For convenience, the name Fort William was given to Bent's new adobe fort.[19]

In the summer of 1835, Colonel Henry Dodge, with the help of John Gantt, assembled representatives of the Cheyenne, Arapaho, Gros Ventre, Comanche, Pawnee, Osage and Arikara tribes for a peace meeting at the fort. Medals bearing the president's picture were distributed amidst protestations by the Indians of peace and good will forevermore. William had returned from a trip to the North Canadian River deep in Comanche country in west Texas, and reported having seen about two thousand Comanches. But he also reported that they were not on the warpath.

Very little is recorded about William Bent's thoughts and manners, aims and actions. Tradition has William called "Little White Man" by the southern Cheyennes and "Roman Nose" by the Kiowas, Comanches, and Prairie Apaches. In later photographs the smallpox marks on his face are easily seen. A spread of the dreaded disease occured during the building of one of the forts. An oft-repeated story tells of William sending a Mexican herder named Francisco to find the Cheyennes and warn them to stay away during the course of the disease. The "stockade" was burned after this episode. This may have been either the fort at the Purgatoire or the Fort William stockade.[20]

The years from 1835 to 1840 saw a rapid influx of traders and emergence of trade forts. Beaver pelts had been largely replaced by the large market for buffalo hides and smoked buffalo tongue. Moreover, the Bents and others in the area traded extensively for New Mexican mules and horses. These were bought legally from Taos and Santa Fe owners or, as often, obtained from New Mexican or Indian without

---

[19] The Col. Dodge map of 1835 shows Fort William near the Fountain. The name transferrance had been made to the new fort by October, 1838. This is proven by a letter from Barclay from "Fort William" and definitely written from the adobe fort near present day La Junta.   [20] Grinnell, *op. cit.,* 6.

clear ownership title. Missouri's well-known mules sprang from California and Mexican heritage. As many as 1200 mules per wagon train made the long trip east. Horse stealing expeditions were common among both Indians and Mountain Men. Kit Carson bought a young Digger Indian boy and trained him.[21]

In the period of 1836 to 1838 the Bents saw the establishment of Fort Jackson, Fort Vasquez, and Fort Lupton on the South Platte, north of present-day Denver. To counter these, Bent, St. Vrain & Company founded a large, adobe, towered fort in the fall of 1837. It was called Fort Lookout. In time it came to bear the name Fort St. Vrain. Located on a bluff on the east edge of the Platte, Fort Lookout was a somewhat smaller version of the Arkansas company headquarters. Having tied down the trade with the Indians on the Arkansas, the Bents met head-on the competition from the powerful American Fur Company, now moving southward from Fort Laramie in the north.[22] Within several years, Fort Jackson was sold to the Bents and the other competitors had gone under. A portion of this success may have lain with the politic marriage of William Bent with Owl Woman, daughter of a Cheyenne leader, Gray Thunder. Owl Woman and William's first child, Mary, was born January 22, 1838.

This marriage alliance with the Cheyenne has been greatly emphasized by historians. Yet when one considers that William had lived in the area for some years, was a principal in a powerful trade empire stretching from Wyo-

---

[21] Charles Preuss, *Exploring with Fremont* (Norman, Okla., 1958), 134.

[22] There is considerable suspicion that a close alliance existed between the Bent, St. Vrain & Co., and the American Fur Company. Though not established, it is likely that there was an interchange of financing and a pooling of buying power. The American Fur Company at Fort Laramie appears to have been merciless with all competitors except the Bents. A territorial boundary north of Fort St. Vrain seems to have been established by mutual consent. Some historians, without verification, have the opinion that Bent, St. Vrain & Co. was controlled by Astor. This is unsubstantiated to date.

ming to Texas, from Missouri to Mexico, one may surmise
that neither the appeal of the New Mexican senoritas or
hoop-skirted damsels of St. Louis compared with the qualities of this Cheyenne maiden. Unlike many morally loose
Indian tribes, the Cheyennes had a rather strict code. William's case was not that of a lonely trapper wintering in an
Indian village, finding a short-term marriage of convenience.

Descriptions of William throughout his life lead one to
believe that he became an Indian in many aspects. Obviously he enjoyed living in tipis, eating Indian food, and
partaking in ceremonies. While perhaps his Indian marriage was "good business," there seems little doubt that he
enjoyed the freedom from the confining sophistication of his
early St. Louis background. Though St. Julian Medoc
wine from France was served at the fort's tables, William
ate beaver tail and dog stew with relish.[23]

Throughout the late 1830s the southern Cheyennes carried on warfare against neighboring Kiowas and Comanches to the southeast. William's close affiliations with the
Cheyennes had prevented trade development with these
other tribes. In the summer of 1840, near the huge adobe
castle, William called together a meeting of Prairie
Apaches, Arapahoes, Cheyennes and Comanches. Peace was
declared among the tribes and the Bents promised to reopen
trade, including the no-questions-asked purchase of Comanche surplus horses. Thus the Bent, St. Vrain & Co.
influence spread east and south, lessening the fort's two-year
fear of Comanche attack.

Troubles in New Mexico kept brother Charles and St.
Vrain in constant upset. First in importance was the threat

23 A St. Julian Medoc bottle was found intact by the National Park Service exca-
vation. Vintners of the day sold "pipes" (half hogsheads) of wine to establishments
such as Bent's Fort. With these came a limited number of empty bottles into which
wine was decanted for use. Because of the fragility of the blown glass bottles, they
were re-used time after time.

of the Texans. Several abortive "invasions" by small "armies" from Texas served only to enhance New Mexican Governor Armijo's prestige, while building a distrust and hatred of all foreigners or "Anglos" among the populace. Moreover, for a time there was a heavy threat of Texan raiding parties ambushing wagon trains entering New Mexico. Bent, St. Vrain & Co. stood the chance of losing not only lives and merchandise on the trail, but its very existence. The Mexican government became increasingly restive about the growing American influence to the north, symbolized by the massive and powerful Bent's Fort on the border.

The Bent, St. Vrain interests now had spread beyond Indian trading for beaver and buffalo robes and the supplying of merchandise to New Mexico. By the 1840s the firm controlled large areas of land in New Mexican territory. Land, horses, mules and sheep kept more and more New Mexican peons in the Bent, St. Vrain employ. Charles Bent's marital alliance with the prominent Jaramillo family further strengthened his grip on Taos and Santa Fe's social and economic life.[24]

Not everybody loved him. One critic, the first district prefect Juan Archuleta, wrote Governor Armijo that "the majority of the people in my district, tired of evils originated by Bent, clamor for vengeance against him." Charles also attracted lawsuits in great number, indicating that his business dealings left something to be desired. In February of 1843, Charles was found guilty in a lawsuit. He was held in jail until paying the fine and barely escaped an angry lynch mob.

Records of William during this period indicate only a few trips to Missouri. He spent most of his time in the field,

[24] Though Charles Bent's wife, Maria Ignacia Jaramillo, was of a prominent Taos family and was known publicly as Mrs. Bent [Lewis H. Garrard, *Wah-To-Yah and the Taos Trail* (Norman, Okla., 1927), 181], no official record of a marriage is known to exist.

shoring up the Indian trade network. From their trade fort on the Canadian River to the southeast, to the operation of Fort St. Vrain on the South Platte, Bent, St. Vrain & Co. required William's firm and apparently straight-forward and honest hand. Time after time he succeeded in settling differences between Indians, though his prime alliance was with the Cheyennes. He appears to have developed a deep understanding of Plains Indian psychology, and indeed a great affection for their way of life. Home was a pair of double log houses at Big Timbers.[25] Home also was an Indian tipi among the Cheyennes which he shared with his wife Owl Woman, her sister Yellow Woman, and his children.[26]

With the joining of Texas to the Union, pressures increased nationally to fulfill the "manifest destiny" of a coast-to-coast America. It is doubtful that William Bent felt much love for the government. The firm's experience had been less than happy with contracts made by the military in the field. Although a giant American flag is reported to have flown over the fort, William's patriotism from the standpoint of some 800 miles west of American civilization must have centered largely upon how much military support could be obtained for wagon train protection.

Having hosted a military reconnaissance group in 1845, and being aware of the increasing rumors of coming war, it was no surprise when Charles and Ceran brought back the news of the May 13, 1846, declaration of war against Mexico.

Toward the end of July the troops began arriving. By the end of the month the entire area swarmed with military and hoards of equipment. The fort had been appropriated

---

[25] M. H. Coffin, *Battle of Sand Creek* (Waco, Tex., 1965), 16.

[26] Garrard, *op. cit.,* 112. This interesting reference mentions Garrard finding William Bent in his lodge, "with his wives."

by General Kearny. Supplies were decimated. Living quarters were filled with officers and ill soldiers. William Bent was asked by Kearny to make a spying trip to New Mexico. Irritated at the low price offered for his services, he walked out. But after a day, he consented to a new offer and led a scouting party. Traveling in advance of the army, William and his party could find no evidence of substantial Mexican opposition. Kearny seized New Mexico. Evidence of Mexican Governor Armijo sending large sums of money to Missouri early that spring, plus the presumed pay-off by President Polk's secret agent Magoffin, lead one to a conclusion that New Mexico may have been sold out several months prior.[27] Armijo's second in command, Colonel Diego Archuleta, also was lured into surrender with the promise that all New Mexico west of the Rio Grande would be his to control. He was double-crossed.

Charles' running feud of many years with Taos Padre Martinez and his increasing unpopularity in Taos were intensified with his appointment as the first Territorial governor on September 22. William did not stay for the social celebrations and the farewell ball given for Kearny prior to his departure for California. He headed back to the fort to save the stock and guard the assets of the firm against military expropriation. After his scouting tour for Kearny, he was granted the honorary title of Colonel, which he retained the balance of his life. Now a supply base, his fort was piled

---

[27] A letter from Manuel Armijo to Samuel C. Owens, July 15, 1846, describes his sending of 6,000 "eagle dollars" and 19 ounces of gold to Mr. Harmony & Company in Missouri. Armijo states that this was in payment of monies owing and was being forwarded sooner than due (the following October), because of the political conditions. Even if taken at face value, it is remarkable that the governor of New Mexico, then at war with the States, would be sending large sums into enemy territory just prior to the invasion of his own country. With the subsequent folding of Armijo's resistance to Kearny's army, one might suspect that the Magoffin pay-off of Armijo may have been earlier than their August 31, 1846, meeting in Santa Fe. This and other letters of Armijo's are listed in the *Missouri Hist. Soc. Collections,* June 1928.

high with equipment and provisions belonging to the military. His business of Indian trade had vanished. He and Cheyenne chief Yellow Wolf seriously discussed the possibility of turning the nomadic Cheyennes into farmers. An era had ended.

William was in his lodge at Big Timbers in January when Louis Simmons arrived with news that Charles Bent had been killed in Taos. Onlooker Lewis Garrard later wrote, "We pitied William. His murdered brother, being much older than himself and George, was loved and respected as a father." Turning down an offer from his Cheyenne friends to carry vengeance to Taos, William assembled a small party of Mountain Men. Fear that the rebellion in New Mexico would spill over the border into an attack on the fort kept William there.

By the time William's men arrived in Taos, the shooting was over. Price had brought the U.S. military from Santa Fe, and in a fierce battle, put down the rebellion. It is noteworthy of William's character that in this highly emotional period he did not take vengeance upon the several groups of innocent Mexicans whom he encountered on the Arkansas immediately after Charles' death. Rather than attend the hanging of the rebel leaders in Taos, he stayed at the Arkansas, working on a massive irrigation ditch two miles long.

In July of 1847, Ceran St. Vrain offered the fort for sale to the government.[28] During and following the Mexican war, virtually all the Indian tribes had caught the war spirit, finding the white man easier to find and kill, and infinitely more profitable, than buffalo. Only William's influence over the southern Cheyennes kept them from the warpath. And his hold was tenuous.

---

[28] Letter from Ceran St. Vrain to Lt. Col. Mackay, Quartermaster's Office, St. Louis, July 21, 1847.

William's wife Owl Woman died giving birth to his fourth child, who was named Charles after his dead brother. Yellow Woman, her sister, then became his wife according to Cheyenne custom. She had, however, lived in the same lodge with him for many years.

Tragedy continued to haunt William. In the fall, his brother George died. He was buried outside the fort's walls where, six years earlier, in 1841, Robert had been buried when his death followed a Comanche attack.

As Indian attacks grew more frequent and vicious, the military in the field began in 1848 seriously to consider the earlier idea of establishing a network of forts to use as bases in subduing the Indians.[29] William tried without success to carry on trade at his adobe fort on the Canadian. Indian trade had simply become too dangerous, and the losses too high for the return. Cholera struck the southern Cheyennes in 1849. Half the tribe was wiped out.

Legend has it that William emptied the fort, set it afire and abandoned it. It is also told that he had offered the fort for $16,000 to the military and that their counter offer of $12,000 angered him. The facts are these: the fort was badly burned, but whether from its owner's hand or from Indian attack is unknown.[30] Date of its destruction is believed to be August 21, 1849. Though William's home was farther east at Big Timbers, there is reason for speculation that the business operations had been moved to Fort St. Vrain on the South Platte several years prior to this.[31]

---

[29] See note 28. St. Vrain in his letter stated that he "had heard it intimated that the U.S. government had taken into consideration the project of erecting forts . . . with the view to afford protection against hostile Indians."

[30] It seems unlikely that the fort was blown up. Gunpowder was too valuable a commodity in the West. Moreover, the two-feet-thick walls and large size of the fort would require a tremendous amount of black powder, even were it plentiful. Probably, Bent burned the wood areas (ceilings and supporting beams), and destroyed sufficient of the building to prevent its being effectively used by anyone else.

[31] "The Siege of Fort Atkinson," *Harper's,* October 1857, indicates that Bent moved his operations to the reactivated Fort St. Vrain.

Yellow Woman bore William his fifth child, Julia.

From the east came hoards of westward-bound gold seekers. Fort St. Vrain, being on the South Platte route to Fort Laramie, grew again in importance. William swapped the emigrants fresh oxen and horses, taking their travel-worn beasts off their hands at a minimal price. These animals were then fattened up and resold to more Oregon Trail emigrants.[32] Business relations with Ceran St. Vrain seem to have been terminated sometime after the summer of 1847. Although William and Ceran lived in the same area for years following, their relationship never appeared to be warmly close.

Over the years William had gained deep insight into the Indian nature. Time after time he prevented war: war between tribes and war between Indians and Americans.

In 1853 he constructed a large sandstone fort along the Arkansas, about thirty miles east of the abandoned adobe fort. Perhaps he planned to rebuild Indian trade, though the tribes were becoming increasingly restive. Buffalo herds had long since left the Arkansas, putting an end to the lucrative hide business. It is most likely that William scented dollars to be made from the westward movement to California's gold fields. Or he may have speculated on the government's growing policy of buying existing forts for protection of the military, civilian settlers, and westward migrants.

"Bent's New Fort" was smaller than William's former adobe castle. It was located on a high bluff overlooking the Arkansas. It soon became not only headquarters for the distribution of annuities for the Indians, but also a stopping point for the military. Troop supplies were maintained at the fort. William found his freighting business prospered, and more and more government supplies found their way into his storage rooms.

---

[32] Lavender, *Bent's Fort*, 319.

In the summer of 1856, William wrote from Westport that he wished the government to remove its goods as he intended to sell the fort.[33] Displeased with increasing friction between the military and the Cheyennes, William entered into a rental agreement with the government, left his fort, and returned to spend the winter of 1857-58 in the States. Because of his demonstrated ability to deal fairly and effectively with the Indians, William was appointed Indian Agent in April of 1859.[34] He was reluctant to take the position, for he had his caravans to oversee, business and personal obligations, and the fort to care for.

Thousands of whites were flocking to the Colorado gold fields. The Indians were on the warpath. William wrote, "A smothered passion for revenge agitates these Indians, perpetually fomented by the failure of food, the encircling encroachments of the white population, and the exasperating sense of decay and impending extinction with which they are surrounded. A desperate war of starvation and extinction is imminent and inevitable, unless prompt measure shall prevent it." He proposed a new treaty setting aside definite lands for the Indians, an agricultural effort, and the strengthening of the settled areas by establishment of government forts.[35]

In the summer of 1860, William negotiated a rental agreement for his fort to the government: sixty-five dollars was to be paid monthly.[36] Feeling that his job as agent was

---

[33] Letter dated August 25, 1856, William Bent from Westport (Quartermaster Files, Box 77, War Records Division, National Archives).

[34] A temporary commission was signed on April 27, 1859. A permanent nomination was confirmed by the Senate on March 2, 1860. National Archives. A letter from Bent to Robinson, Superintendent of Indian Affairs, indicates that the value of his business in the States "amounts to more than three times the amount of my salary."   [35] Letter from William Bent, Oct. 1859, to Washington.

[36] Letter from William Bent to the commanding officer at Fort Lyon, July 9, 1862. This letter states that on Sept. 9, 1860, Bent agreed with Lt. McIntyre to rent Bent's Fort for $65 per month. See Nolie Mumey, *Bent's Old and New Forts* (Denver, 1956), 179.

over, he resigned and recommended Albert G. Boone as his successor. Boone carried out the Indian treaty proposal, but failed to make a satisfactory or effective agreement.

Meanwhile, William enlarged his home at Big Timbers, building a huge stockade enclosing living quarters, warehouses and employees' rooms. It was well fortified against possible attack. Robert Bent helped his father with the construction. Mary Bent Moore, his newly married daughter, came west with her husband to join them. Sons George and Charles enlisted in the Confederate Army. But William remained loyal to the Union contracts for hauling army freight to Santa Fe and Fort Union. When the Confederates sought to enlist Indians to assist their New Mexico campaign, William Bent successfully urged them to stay neutral.

The government regularly paid its $65 monthly rental for the fort through August of 1861. Then no further payments were received, the government having built Fort Wise nearby. In 1864, William began pushing for old rents, urging the government to exercise its purchase option included in the original rental agreement. Meanwhile, the army set up a military reservation on the property. The quartermaster general replied to the back rent request with the statement that the whole area was on a reservation for Cheyennes and Arapahos set up in 1861, and that William's title "is only that of a trespasser who has taken possession of land without legal authority." [37]

William made several trips to Washington, D.C., in the ensuing years to pursue his claim, but it was never settled. It was claimed that he had been paid through August of 1862. The army clouded the facts, then wrapped them in red tape. Bent continued to haul freight.

---

[37] Letter from Secretary of the Interior, Caleb B. Smith, to E. M. Stanton, Secretary of War, Aug. 30, 1962.

In the summer of 1864, William tried to effect peace between Indian and white. A hot flame of terror had sprung up between the army and the Indian and violence was pouring over Colorado. Bent tried to slow it down. An escalation of retaliatory murder bypassed his efforts to make peace councils. On the eve of the Sand Creek massacre, at his Purgatoire house, William ate beaver tail prepared by his Indian cook.[38] His thoughts must have been with his children; George, Charles and Julia, already visiting at the ill-fated Cheyenne camp; and Robert, who had been conscripted by Chivington to lead his column to the village.

While Charles had earlier chosen the Indian way, it was not until after the massacre that George chose the redman's path as preferable. Robert Bent later testified at the inquiry, listing the grisly mutilations and murders he had witnessed against his mother's people. Both brothers joined with the Indians in striking back along the Platte. Charles gained a reputation as the worst desperado of the West by using his white appearance and western know-how to trick, deceive and murder.[39]

Kit Carson was called upon by congressmen to offer an answer to the increasing carnage. Kit admitted that William Bent wielded even more influence over the Indians than he. William stated, "If the matter were left to me, I guarantee with my life that in three months I could have all the Indians along the Arkansas at peace without the expense of war."[40]

He was given instructions to help call the Indians together in mid-October for peace talks at Bluff Creek. Kit and William found that only the peaceful Indians appeared. They sought, however, as part of the government's panel of

---

[38] Coffin, *op. cit.,* 16.

[39] Inman, *Old Santa Fe Trail,* 183-85.

[40] Testimony of William Bent, Aug. 1865, at Fort Lyon, before Congressmen Foster, Ross and Doolittle.

commissioners, to persuade other non-attending Indians by fair treatment of those assembled. The conference ended with the repetition of the same mistakes of former peace talks; nothing but reparations, increased annuity allotments and boundary talks. William and Kit could see from many years' perspective that what the Indians needed most was true help toward self-sufficiency. As one observer wrote, "Their fate as commissioners will be that they died of too large views." [41]

William's wife Yellow Woman had been killed that summer of 1865 by some Pawnee scouts for the army who were chasing a band of Cheyennes.

Two years later, still trying to settle his claim for rental of the fort, William traveled to Washington and spent the winter of 1867-68 in the East. In Westport during the spring of 1867 he married Adalina Harvey. A daughter of famed Missouri fur trader Alexander Harvey and a Blackfeet woman, Adalina came West with William in the summer. An unverified family story tells of William seeking revenge on a young Indian who paid court to William's wife in later years. Whether this wife was Adalina or Yellow Woman is unsaid. Adalina, however, seems to have disappeared in history after the return West that summer.

In May of 1869, William started a caravan eastward from Santa Fe. By the time he reached the Purgatoire ranch he was feverish with pneumonia. On May 19, four days short of his 60th birthday, he died. William was buried in the family plot by the ranch. Later, with daughter Mary beside him, he was reinterred at the Las Animas cemetery. His estate was estimated at between $150,000 and $200.00. [42]

It is noteworthy concerning William Bent's character that in photographs taken in the late 1860s he wore Indian

---

[41] Diary of Samuel Kingman, 1867, in *Kansas Historical Quarterly,* Nov. 1932.
[42] *Pueblo Chieftain* obituary.

moccasins.[43] For in spite of his wealth, St. Louis cultural origins, and ability to succeed in business, he doubtless found his moments of greatest happiness among the lodge-fires of the Cheyennes, his adopted people. His heart must have been heavy to see men of his own race destroy first the life-giving buffalo, and finally decimate, degrade and scatter the once noble Cheyenne people.

But the crushing wheel of progress was too heavy for even William Bent, with all his energy, influence, courage, fair play and heart, to impede.

---

[43] Photograph of William Bent and Little Raven at Fort Dodge, 1869, in Smithsonian Institution.

Charles Autobees

by JANET LECOMPTE
Colorado Springs, Colorado

For a man whose name became famous in the history of
Colorado, Charles Autobees' beginnings were unpropitious.
At least one of his parents was of mixed race, and Charles
inherited features that were far from handsome by Cau-
casian standards. His skin was dark, his mouth wide and
thin-lipped, his nose broad, his eyes small and close together.
But he was built with great authority – over six feet tall,
heavy-boned and powerful, of fine physique and commanding presence.   More important, he was endowed with courage, honesty and intelligence, and it was these qualities that
lifted him above his humble origins.

He was born in St. Louis in 1812, the son of Francois
Autobees (or Urtebise or Ortivis, or any number of other
variations resulting from generations of a family unable to
spell its own name). When Charles was three years old,
his French-Canadian (perhaps half-breed) father drowned
while logging in the St. Lawrence River. His mother, who
signed her name Sarah T. Tate, then married Bartholomew
Tobin, a St. Louis laborer.[1] By Tobin she had another son
in 1823 called Thomas, who was also to become a well-
known pioneer of Colorado.

Although Sarah T. Tate could sign her name, neither of
her sons ever learned to read or write. Their childhood,
judging by the meager records, was one of indigence. By
1827, Sarah Tate and Bartholomew Tobin were legally

---

[1] In 1821 he lived at 106 N. Church, corner E.   John A. Paxton, *The St. Louis
Directory and Register* (St. Louis, 1821).

separated, and the financial pressures on Sarah doubtless increased.[2] A pathetic little notation in the Chouteau papers shows that a Mr. Sire owed Sarah Tobin eight dollars in October, 1828, for "enshrouding and attending the Funeral of his wife."[3] About this time Charles, aged sixteen, began earning his own salary, almost all of which he sent to his mother and half-brother, Tom Tobin. As soon as Charley had acquired a wife and home in New Mexico, he sent for Tom, then fourteen, who came to live with him far from the choking poverty of the city.

Like many another St. Louis boy of the era, Charles Autobees went up the Missouri with a trapping brigade, inspired, perhaps, by other members of the family engaged in the fur trade. A Jean-Baptiste Urtubise (or Hurtubis) was a clerk in a British company trading on the Upper Mississippi in about 1816[4] and for the American Fur Company's Upper Missouri Outfit in the early 1830s.[5] Pierre Ortubise (Ortibise, Ortubize) was a half-breed Sioux interpreter and trader for the American Fur Company at Fort Clark and Fort Pierre throughout the 1830s, and was described as "a good young man; but he has one failing, he is fond of liquor."[6]

There are several stories about how Charley first entered the fur trade. One was that he tore down a Whig liberty

[2] St. Louis (Mo.) County Records, c3-359. Sarah T. Tate and Bartholomew Tobin, "by articles of agreement separated," sold to Phillip McGovaren for $100 a lot in Connor's addition, St. Louis. Sarah and Bartholomew both signed their names.

[3] Missouri Historical Society, St. Louis, Mo.

[4] William Clark Papers, III, p. 33, Kansas State Historical Society, Topeka, Kan. Unless quoted directly or otherwise footnoted, the material for this article is all drawn from Janet Lecompte's "Charles Autobees," in *Colorado Magazine,* XXIV, XXV, XXVI (July 1957 through July 1959).   [5] Chouteau papers.

[6] Fort Tecumseh Letter Book, p. 116, Chouteau Papers. There are many references to Pierre Ortubise in the Chouteau Papers, also in "Maximilian's Travels," R. G. Thwaites, ed., *Early Western Travels* (Cleveland, 1905), and in Annie H. Abel, *Chardon's Journal at Fort Clark, 1834-1839* (Pierre, S.D., 1932).

pole erected at Fourth and Chestnut streets in St. Louis and escaped punishment by leaving with some trappers to go up the Missouri. Another was that he left St. Louis in 1825 and spent seven years trapping at the headwaters of the Missouri and Columbia rivers and as far south as Arizona's Petrified Forest and Gila River, "during which time he never saw bread." Charley's son Tom said in 1907 that his father joined an American Fur Company brigade at St. Louis when he was sixteen (or in 1828) and went up the Missouri "with Jim Bridger, Kit Carson, Laforey, Beauvais, Bordeaux, Chas. Nadeau, Chat Dubray, old Charlefou, Tom Tobin, A. G. Boone, Carlos Beaubien, Joseph Barnoy (generally nicknamed Levanway) and others," – an imposing list of old-timers only a few of whom could have been on this particular expedition, but all of whom were associated with Autobees at one time or another.

Tom Autobees says his father made another trip up the Missouri in 1831 in a party of 35 American Fur Company trappers under a Captain Weiser (or a name that sounded like it). In the spring of 1832 the trappers had a fight with the Blackfeet Indians on Salmon River. During the battle "Levanway" (Joseph Livernois) was shot in the eye, and Pete Simmons, a Dutchman who always fought Indians with a pipe in his mouth, burst out laughing every time he saw an Indian fall. Charles Nadeau and Jim Beckwourth were also in this fight, but of the score of battles with the Blackfeet described in T. D. Bonner's *Life and Adventures of James P. Beckwourth,* it would be difficult to choose the ones Beckwourth shared with Charley Autobees, whom he does not mention.

If the battle described above by Tom Autobees is not the same as the 1835 fray dealt with later in this sketch, it might have been one described by John Work, leader of a Hudson's Bay Company brigade:

In the evening [of September 12, 1832] a Caiouse Indian, the Young
Chiefs brother came up with us accompanied by another Indian, he is
just arrived from the plains, he informs us of two great battles fought
with the Blackfeet by the Nezperces & F. Heads and again by these
joined by the Americans. The first battle was fought on Salmon river
a few days after we left it in the spring, the Blackfeet were very
strong, they fought two days & carried off half of the N.P. & F.H.
horses. . .[7]

The second battle referred to by John Work was, of course,
the memorable event of the rendezvous at Pierre's Hole in
July 1832. Charley Autobees was no doubt at the rendezvous
with most of the trappers then in the mountains, but his
presence is not recorded in contemporary accounts of the
famous battle.

After the battle on Salmon River, says Tom Autobees,
Captain Weiser and his brigade wintered in the country
between the Salmon and Bitterroot rivers with the Nez
Percés and Flatheads. Charley Autobees and Charles Nadeau both took Flathead squaws, and in due time Autobees'
squaw produced a little girl whom Nadeau christened
Eliza. Tom says his father remained on the headwaters of
the Missouri and Columbia rivers until he went to Taos,
New Mexico, in 1834. There is nothing in contemporary
accounts to refute what Tom says, except the date his father
went to Taos, which was not 1834 but 1836. There is, however, material in accounts of fur companies and their forts
that adds considerably to Tom's story.

Contemporary records of Charley up until December of
1834 are puzzling. From 1830 to 1834 he had an account
with the Upper Missouri Outfit of the American Fur Company. Through the four years Charley "Urtubise" was on
the American Fur Company books, he was credited with a
total of $180, only $15 of which was paid in cash direct to

---

[7] "Fur Brigade to the Bonaventura: John Work's California Expedition of 1832-33
for the Hudson's Bay Company," Alice Bay Maloney, ed., in *California Historical
Society Quarterly*, XXII, p. 198.

him. The remaining $165 (more than most engagés earned in a year) was paid in cash to his mother in St. Louis.[8] Autobees was not an engagé of Fontenelle & Drips; there is no notation of him drawing wages from the company or buying anything from its outfit in the mountains or its store in St. Louis. Perhaps Charley was a free trapper, or an engagé of another company who prudently chose to bank with the American Fur Company and bring enough of his furs to its representative in the mountains to keep his mother at St. Louis in funds.

In December 1834, the blurred image of Charley's trapping career comes into sharp focus in the account books of Fort Hall, the log post built by Nathaniel Wyeth on the Snake River near the mouth of the Portneuf. The post had been finished in August 1834, at which time Wyeth departed for the mouth of the Columbia to begin a salmon fishery. He left at Fort Hall eleven inexperienced men under the former Ashley and Sublette trapper, Robert Evans, who was instructed to "exercise as much *hospitality* as the state of your provisions will admit of." Wyeth's hospitality was not mere etiquette; he hoped to lure experienced trappers from four brigades wintering in the vicinity to desert their leaders and join his ranks.[9] Sixty miles up the Snake were James Bridger and sixty men of the Rocky Mountain Fur Company;[10] Thomas McKay and his Hudson's Bay Company trappers were downriver building Fort Boise as opposition to Wyeth's post;[11] Captain Bonneville and his men were at

---

[8] Ledger R, pp. 108, 257; Ledger U, p. 125; Ledger X, p. 229, Chouteau Papers. My thanks to Frances Stadler of the Missouri Historical Society for copying these items for me.

[9] Richard G. Beidleman, "Nathaniel Wyeth's Fort Hall," in *Oregon Historical Quarterly,* LXIII (Sept., 1957). Dr. Beidleman generously loaned me his microfilm copy of the Fort Hall account books, originals in the Oregon Historical Society library, from which and from Dr. Beidleman's article, Charles Autobees' life at Fort Hall has been pieced together.

[10] Osborne Russell, *Journal of a Trapper* (Boise, 1921), 15.

[11] "Farnham's Travels," R. G. Thwaites, ed., *Early Western Travels,* XXVIII, p. 321.

the northern end of Bear Lake; and the American Fur
Company had a winter camp just over the divide on Green
River,[12] having this year made an agreement with the Rocky
Mountain Fur Company to forego trapping west of the
Rockies.

From one of these gatherings of trappers came Charles
Autobees (or Ottabees as the storekeeper at Fort Hall
spelled the name). On Christmas Day, 1834, he made his
first purchase at the Fort Hall store, a "white blanket
Capeau" for which he paid $25, a rather high price for a
hooded cape. On the same day his old friend Charles Nadeau
(called "Neydo" in the ledgers) who had been at Fort Hall
since Wyeth hired him at the rendezvous the previous summer, paid $20 for a blue blanket capote. Nadeau bought a
half pint of alcohol as well, for all the men at Fort Hall
were engrossed in a Christmas celebration that had already
been going on for a day and was to continue for another two
or three – as the fixings for the celebration continued to be
labeled in the ledgers, "liquor for Christmas." During this
spree the store did a vigorous business in half pints of rum
and alcohol, pints of sugar to sweeten it, and articles bought
willy-nilly by semi-conscious patrons.

From accounts of this general dissipation we discover an
intriguing fact about Charles Autobees – he did not drink!
Now we see how Charley was able to send home so much
money to his mother, for the wild revels of the rendezvous,
which often stripped a trapper of all the credit he had built
up through the year, were not for him. He was at that time,
as he was always to be, sober and prudent, responsible and
independent. The books of Fort Hall show no gambling
debts charged to Charles Autobees, no frivolous purchases
other than that expensive white capote, a few bright handkerchiefs, a red cap, and quantities of tobacco. The rest of

---

[12] Washington Irving, *Adventures of Captain Bonneville* (Norman, Okla., 1961),
350, 356.

his purchases covered his needs – gingham, flannel, calico and twilled-cotton shirts; blankets; powder and balls; sugar, rice, coffee, flour, and when it was available, chocolate; brown soap and shaving soap. He also bought knives, dozens of them – butcher knives, dirks, Indian knives, duck knives, round-handled knives, red-handled knives, scalping knives – some for trade, some for himself. Charley liked a bargain, too. He invested in a damaged dressing comb, a damaged wrapper blanket, a damaged elk skin, a used dressing-case, and a reduced-price remnant of scarlet cloth, which probably went to his wife.

His wife accounted for many of Charley's purchases, for frugal as he may have been, he could not resist the temptation to dress her up as elaborately as other trappers' wives were dressed. Sometimes it is difficult to separate items in the ledgers bought for trade and those Charley meant for his woman, but probably the items in small amounts were for her personal use: half a yard of scarlet cloth, half a dozen glass or gilt buttons, a bunch of blue cut beads or white seed beads, a hank of linen thread, a cotton shawl, a pocket looking-glass, a dressed elk or deer skin, a paper of vermillion, and an assortment of coarse combs for her long hair. One fine ivory comb was very likely a gift for their baby, Eliza. Charley also spent money for squaw-work done by other women, which makes us wonder if his wife was really worth her salt. Once he bought a pair of moccasins for one dollar from Amable LaEcuyé's squaw, and on another occasion he paid the same lady four dollars for labor done on a surcingle.

Charles Autobees arrived at Fort Hall at Christmas, 1834, and by January first he was given a contract for one year as interpreter at a pretty good salary. He was to be paid $380 per annum, or $31.65 per month, less than the company paid its best hunter Davis Crow ($50), its chief clerk Abel Baker, Jr. ($41.67) or its partisan Joseph Gale

($33.33), but more than the rank and file of men including, for example, Charles Nadeau, hunter ($25), Robert Evans, storekeeper ($25), and Calvin Briggs, camp keeper ($15.88). Until April there was not much for Charley to do around the post. On January 17, 1835, some trappers who had deserted from Bridger's camp came to find work at Fort Hall. On March 25 some of them left under leadership of Joseph Gale to make the spring hunt, an adventure described in detail in the journal of Osborne Russell. After Gale's party left, preparations were made for Joseph Thing to lead another party of twelve men, including Charles Autobees and Charles Nadeau, to trade with Indians at "Racine Amère" and to establish a trading post on a branch of the Salmon River. Both Gale's and Thing's outfits were financed jointly by Wyeth and Thomas McKay, stepson and chief partisan of John McLoughlin, the Hudson's Bay Company factor on the Columbia. Autobees and Nadeau appear to have been the only Wyeth men besides Joseph Thing on the expedition, and neither one brought in any beaver. The rest of the party were Hudson's Bay Company trappers whom Thomas McKay had brought from Fort Vancouver – John Gray, John Favel, John Finley, Joseph LaRocque, Joseph Peneau, and Joseph (or Charles) Carpintier – and Flathead and Nez Percés trappers named Chimilikecha, Left-handed Gocia, Louis Mackaman, and Cateau Finley, who had arrived at Fort Hall in February. Thomas McKay was not a member of the "Racine Amère Outfit," as it was called in the books, but headed his own party which left in April to raise a cache of goods at Big Wood (Boisée) River and trade them to the Nez Percé and Pawnack (Bannock) Indians.[13]

Captain Thing's party left on April 4th or 5th and proceeded to the camp at "Racine Amère," or the beautiful

---

[13] Fort Hall account books.

valley of the Bitterroot river. After trading with the Flatheads, Thing and his men crossed the mountains and made
camp on a branch of Salmon River. They intended, according to Osborne Russell, to establish a trading post there,
but were thwarted by an attack of the Blackfeet Indians
which cost the total loss of their outfit except the men and
horses.[14] Besides Osborne Russell's brief notice, we have two
longer descriptions of this remarkable and little-known
battle on Salmon River, where a dozen or so white men and
their handful of Indian allies whipped a hundred (or even
five hundred) Blackfeet. The following account is Charles
Autobees' own, told to his son Tom many years later:

One night, when Eliza was three months old, Autobees
and Nadeau were on horse guard at the winter camp on
Salmon River, standing outside their lodges which their
squaws had erected close together. Suddenly Autobees heard
a sound like a stick hitting the taut skin-covering of the
lodge.

He asked Nadeau, "Did you throw a stick at the tent?"
"No," said Nadeau.

Alarmed, Autobees went into his lodge and built a fire;
the baby woke up and cried (as years later Charley remembered the details of this tense night). At dawn he sent out
his Indian brother-in-law to scout. The boy ran back crying
that he had seen the plain covered with Blackfeet, led by a
chief named Nick-oose. The fight began and raged all day.
Many Blackfeet were killed, including the chief, after
whose death the trappers plainly heard mourning cries of
"Nick-oose! Nick-oose!" from the Blackfoot camp.[15] The
whites killed many Blackfeet and considered themselves the
victors. Charles Autobees lost only his broad-brimmed hat

---

[14] Russell, *op. cit.*, 19.

[15] Perhaps Nick-oose was the Blackfoot chief whose name Maximilian rendered
in 1833 as "Ninoch-Kiaui," and who provided him with a Flathead vocabulary.
"Maximilian's Travels," Thwaites, *op. cit.*, XXIII, p. 88; XXIV, p. 227.

and two kegs of rum, stolen from his lodge while he was fighting.

This much Charley knew of the fight. During the 1840s, however, he learned more from a Frenchman, a stranger to him, who overheard Charley and Jim Beckwourth discussing the battle at one of the Arkansas valley trading posts. When Charley declared there were a hundred Indians in the fight, the stranger contradicted him, saying "No, not a hundred!" Charley became angry, but the stranger told him to hold on, keep cool, and then he proceeded to describe the battle accurately to show that he knew all about it. The gist of his story was that the Nick-oose band was only a fraction of the Blackfeet nearby, but that the others had gotten drunk on the rum stolen from Charley's lodge and were unable to fight.

The other account is that of Captain Thing, told to the naturalist Townsend several months after the fight. Because of its length and accessibility to the reader, it will not be reproduced here; it may be said, however, that it supports Charley's much later story surprisingly well.[16]

For the remainder of 1835, Charles Autobees stayed at Fort Hall, making regular purchases at the store, riding express to the Nez Percé village in August (for which he was paid $20 extra), and waiting for his contract to expire in January – for it was becoming increasingly obvious that Wyeth's venture was doomed. Losses sustained in the Salmon River fight and the spring hunt were not recovered in the fall hunt. From October on, according to Osborne Russell, the men at the fort hung about until Wyeth should arrive from the Columbia to discharge them. Their boredom was alleviated by a five-day alcoholic spree at the beginning of November, and by a visit of the Bannocks on December 14, when the men were issued arms and placed on guard

[16] "Townsend's Narrative," Thwaites, *op. cit.,* XXI, p. 327-8.

until the Indians showed themselves to be friendly. Wyeth arrived from the Columbia on December 21 with news that his salmon fishery was a failure; there was no other course but to pay off his men and go home.

Autobees' contract expired on January 1, 1836, and was not renewed, but he remained at Fort Hall for another three months. In January his account was credited with six dollars for a bale of dried meat he furnished a camp at "Cedars," apparently Captain Thing's camp on the Portneuf. On March 1, he was paid $100 for his services as horse guard during the winter. He made his last purchases at the Fort Hall store on March 6 – four shirts, 1½ pounds of tobacco, a lined blanket, a yard of scarlet cloth, half a yard of blue cloth, a dozen brass buttons, and a pocket looking-glass. At this time his account at the store was within a dollar of being balanced, but on March 16, his wife bought three yards of calico for $4.50, which was charged to Charley's account and never settled, perhaps because Charley was by this time on his way to New Mexico.

Tom Autobees indicates that Charley had no intention of remaining in New Mexico when he set out from the mountains. With other men, including Charles Nadeau (who had turned free trapper when his contract with Wyeth expired on June 24, 1835), Autobees went south through Utah to New Mexico. At Taos the trappers meant to buy goods and return to the mountains via Fort Laramie (then Fort William) on the North Platte. Nadeau and the others did just that, but Charley had all his horses stolen at Taos and was forced to remain there.

So goes the family legend, but of course if Charley had wanted to return to the mountains he would have done so. Even in the unlikely event that his old friends cruelly abandoned him in Taos, a few months' wages would have earned him the price of an outfit. Charley doubtless saw what his less astute companions were blind to – that the era of the beaver trapper was rapidly passing, and that the increasing traffic in buffalo robes demanded different skills and temperament of the men who would succeed at it. Besides, the instinct of the settler was always stronger than that of the wanderer in Charles Autobees, and, at age twenty-four, he decided to settle down in the beautiful valley of Taos.

He took a job with Simeon Turley, a Missourian who kept a flour mill and distillery on the Arroyo Hondo a few miles north of Taos. At Arroyo Hondo, Charley set up housekeeping with Serafina Avila, a widow two years his senior with three small children. Serafina bore Charley a son, Mariano, in 1837; another, José Tomás (Tom) in 1842. After the birth of their second son, Charles and Serafina were married by Padre Antonio José Martínez in the Taos Parish Church on November 28, 1842. Serafina shared Charley's life until her death nearly thirty years later. Her obituary gives us the only description we have of her: "She formed many acquaintances who respected her for her goodness of heart and many social qualities."[17]

Charles Autobees worked eleven years for Simeon Turley. They were increasingly good years for Turley. By 1847 he had a two-story distillery with one of the few plank floors in New Mexico; he had corrals filled with hogs, pastures filled with goats and sheep, barns filled with grain, mills filled with flour, and cellars filled with whiskey; and his rosy children (in George F. Ruxton's enraptured words) gamboled before his door. They must have been good years for Charles Autobees, too, for his employer had the reputation of being as generous as he was rich – "No one in the country paid so well, and fed so well, as Turley," said Ruxton.[18]

Charles Autobees' duties with Turley were closely con-

---

[17] [Pueblo] *Colorado Chieftain*, Nov. 23, 1871, p. 3, c. 3.

[18] George F. Ruxton, *Adventures in Mexico and the Rocky Mountains* (N.Y., 1848), 203.

nected with the fur trade, but a fur trade that had changed considerably since Charley's trapping days. Now the traffic was less in beaver skins than in buffalo robes, processed by Indians and sold to traders either at the Indian villages or at trading posts on the eastern and western slopes of the Rockies. Bent's Fort on the Arkansas near the mouth of the Purgatory was in operation by 1835; so was Fort Laramie on the North Platte. By 1837 four trading posts had been erected on the South Platte near the mouth of the Cache la Poudre, all within a few miles of one another, and all in bitter rivalry. On the western slope of the mountains there were others – Antoine Robidoux's two forts, Fort Uintah and Fort Uncompahgre, and Fort Crockett, the miserable little post run by Phillip Thompson and others on the Green River in Brown's Hole. Until 1841 or 1842 the bigger of these posts – Fort Laramie, Fort Vasquez on the South Platte, and Bent's Fort – had their supplies shipped out from St. Louis in wagons, and their supplies included whiskey, which the Indians valued above any other item of trade. The smaller posts appear to have gotten at least some of their whiskey in Taos, either from Turley or from his chief competitor, Rowland and Workman. As early as 1837, Charles Autobees led trains of mules packed with whiskey up the San Luis Valley, over the Sangre de Cristo Pass to the plains, and up to the South Platte forts. On March 1, 1838, Sarpy and Fraeb, proprietors of Fort Jackson, paid "Charles Ottabees" the sum of $13 from their outfit.[19] No accounts have come to light for the other posts; doubtless such records would show purchases of whiskey and flour from Simeon Turley's head salesman, Charles Autobees. (Phillip Thompson owed Turley $293 by April 1841, but whether Charley delivered the merchandise to Thompson at Fort Crockett is not known.)[20]

---

[19] Chouteau papers.
[20] Letter of Simeon Turley, Taos, April 18, 1841, and August 3, 1841. Turley papers, Missouri Historical Society, St. Louis.

In 1841 Simeon Turley complained that his business was bad, but it was the last year he could make that complaint, for he was about to come into a veritable monopoly of supplying Indian traders with liquor. By 1841 three companies ruled the fur trade in the west: The Hudson's Bay Company had all but taken over trans-montane trade, including Wyeth's old Fort Hall; Pratte, Chouteau & Co. (successors to the American Fur Company) operated almost unopposed on the North Platte and Missouri rivers; and Bent, St. Vrain & Co. had the South Platte, the Arkansas, and Canadian rivers almost all to itself. The two latter companies agreed to divide the territory east of the mountains between them. They also made an effort to stop the use of whiskey in the Indian trade, not only for humanitarian reasons, but also to eliminate what little opposition was left. A law prohibiting the sale (or gift) of liquor to the Indians had existed in one form or another since colonial times, but it had never been enforced in the Indian country to the south and west of the Missouri River. In 1842, at the demand of the big traders, a company of dragoons was stationed at Council Bluffs to search boats going up the Missouri. Other agents searched west-bound wagon trains, and a special agent was sent to inspect posts on the North Platte and Missouri. In a short time these measures, or the threat of them, sharply reduced the amount of liquor brought into the Indian country from the east.

Thus, from 1842 to 1847, Simeon Turley's distillery was the biggest source of liquor in the West, for his chief competitors, Rowland and Workman, had quit business and gone to California in 1841. As soon as it became known that the major trading companies had ceased using liquor, little traders began to buy their wares in Taos and Arroyo Hondo and vend them wherever a customer could be found. Communities of traders sprang up along the Arkansas, at Hardscrabble, Greenhorn and Adobe Creek. In 1842, at the mouth of the Fountain, the settlement and trading post called Pueblo was founded, and there Turley had a store and a man to run it. There also he kept a wagon. Now when Charles Autobees brought his liquor up from Taos, he deposited some of it at the Pueblo store for sale locally, then went north with the rest of it to Fort Lancaster on the South Platte or to traders' camps nearby. When he returned to Pueblo he loaded the furs he had traded onto Turley's wagon and took them directly east along the Arkansas to markets in Missouri. Turley thrived; Pueblo thrived. By 1844, the government agent on the North Platte and Missouri recognized that all the liquor in the Indian country was being brought in from New Mexico by a "reckless band of desperadoes" who "engaged in illicit and destructive trade with the Indians." [21]

Throughout this period we catch only brief glimpses of Charles Autobees which can no more than hint at his activities. He was at Fort Lancaster in the winter of 1841-42 and again in January, 1843, when he sold the proprietor 147 pounds of flour, a sack of corn, and 16 gallons of whiskey (at $4 per gallon), and received in exchange five cows, two steers and three calves. In April, 1843, Turley wrote his brother Jesse in Arrow Rock, Missouri, that he was sending his wagon east from Pueblo (or Robert Fisher's Fort on the Arkansas, as he calls it) with two hundred buffalo robes and some beaver. From Taos he was sending Charles Autobees with a wagon loaded with eighty buffalo robes, 71½ pounds of beaver, and six hundred dollars in silver. The wagon would return from Missouri with a new still, three large cocks for whiskey pipes and some goods – calicoes "of the most showie, lively colours" and bleached and unbleached

---

[21] Letter of Thos. H. Harvey, Oct. 8, 1844, *H. Doc. 2,* 28 Cong., 2 sess., (Ser. 463), p. 433.

domestics, evidence that Turley was expanding his business to include dress goods for either the Mexican or Indian trade.[22]

Charles Autobees was sent east again with Turley's wagon in the spring of 1845. He returned to New Mexico with a wagon load of goods which he introduced at the Santa Fe customs house on August 30, 1845.[23] Again in the spring of 1846 Autobees left for the United States by way of the Sangre de Cristo Pass. Since there was as yet no wagon road over this pass, he must have picked up Turley's wagon at Pueblo and gone east with it. By the time he was ready to return, probably in company with Jesse Turley, whose wagons left Independence, Missouri on May 9, the Mexican war had started and wagons bound for Santa Fe were kept at the rear of the United States troops bound for the conquest of New Mexico.

In the latter part of August, Kearny's Army of the West occupied Santa Fe and then went on to conquer California, leaving troops in New Mexico numbering several thousand, not including the hordes of teamsters, contractors and adventurers that swarmed about the soldiers. New Mexico became a boom-land where everything was in short supply, including the products of Simeon Turley's mill, distillery and farm. Turley prospered as never before – until January 20, 1847, when his whole operation collapsed in a smoking ruin after an attack by an armed mob of Taos Indians and Mexicans. Turley was murdered, along with all the men working that day at his mill; only John Albert and Tom Tobin managed to escape. While Turley's mill was under attack, Charles Autobees was on his way to Santa Fe with a mule train of whiskey. Later he had the bitter satisfaction

---

[22] Turley papers, Missouri Historical Society, St. Louis.
[23] Customs' receipt, Ritch papers, Henry E. Huntington Library, San Marino, Calif.

of joining the forces that put down the rebellion, of capturing the Indian leader, and of serving on the jury that tried
Turley's murderers.

So ended Charley's connection with the fur trade, but at
thirty-five his life was only half over, and his real accom-
plishment had hardly begun. For a few more years he continued to live in New Mexico, guiding troops sent out to
punish the increasingly hostile Indians, farming land
granted to him and his brother Tom by the late Mexican
governor, and trading with Indians in the Rio Grande and
Arkansas valleys. In 1853 he was sent by Ceran St. Vrain
to make a settlement on the huge Vigil and St. Vrain grant
in southeastern Colorado. He led his little group of settlers
to the mouth of the Huerfano River, twenty miles east of
present Pueblo, Colorado, and there he stayed, even when
other brave men were fleeing for their lives. He lived there
through Indian wars, drouths and floods, through invasions
of emigrants and the subsequent impositions of civilization
upon a free spirit. He did not move from the spot he first
chose to settle until death overtook him on June 17, 1882.

Warren Angus Ferris

by LYMAN C. PEDERSEN, JR.
Gray's Harbor College, Aberdeen, Washington

On August 13, 1842, the Mormon newspaper, *The Wasp,* carried an article entitled "Rocky Mountain Geysers." This was a reprint of the same article appearing in the *Western Literary Messenger,* of Buffalo, New York, on July 13, 1842. In neither instance was the author listed. The Mormon article, published at Nauvoo, Illinois, was found and preserved by N. P. Langford, Superintendent of Yellowstone Park. In the fall of 1900, Olin D. Wheeler, an eager student of Yellowstone Park history, through an unnamed informant, found the source of the *Wasp* article to be the *Western Literary Messenger.* In the same year a copy of *Life in the Rocky Mountains* was uncovered. Warren A. Ferris being the author, it was soon discovered that he also had written the article on geysers. Thus sixty-five years after he had left the mountains, the life of Warren Ferris, trader, trapper, explorer, writer, and cartographer, began to be unfolded.

Ferris was born of Quaker parentage at Glens Falls, New York, December 26, 1810. On both sides of his family were Revolutionary War veterans. At the beginning of the War of 1812 the Ferris family moved to Erie, Pennsylvania. Fighting in the War of 1812, Warren's father died on September 10, 1813, the same day as Perry's victory at Lake Erie. The widow and her two children moved the next year to Buffalo, New York, where she married Joshua Lovejoy and gave birth to four more children. Warren received a reputable education, being trained as a civil engineer. At the age of nineteen, Warren's wandering spirit was inflamed when he received a severe reprimand from his mother who discovered him smoking on a public street. Leaving his home, he wandered to St. Louis, arriving there in June, 1829. Of St. Louis he observed: "It was composed principally of French who are generally absolute strangers to the social virtues and remarkable for laziness and debauchery."[1]

It was about this time that Pierre Chouteau, Jr., of the Western Department of the American Fur Company was organizing and outfitting the first expedition of his firm to be sent to the Rocky Mountains in an effort to wrest control of the fur trade from the Rocky Mountain Fur Company. Ferris, seeing an opportunity for adventure, entered Chouteau's employ as a trader and trapper. With the departure of the trapping party from St. Louis on February 16, 1830, Ferris began his detailed diary which served as a basis for his *Life in the Rocky Mountains.*

Traveling with wagons and then with pack animals, the party went northwestward across Missouri and finally reached Belle Vue, the trading house of Lucien Fontenelle and Andrew Drips, established eight miles above the mouth of the Platte. Drips and Joseph Robidoux were the leaders for the expedition. After lingering for four weeks at Belle Vue, the party moved on to the trading house of John P. Cabanné, eight miles below the Council Bluffs.[2] Here a "Code of Laws" was issued "with penalties annexed, for the preservation of harmony and safety, in our passage through the immense plains."[3] The trappers continued to the Elkhorn River where a change was made in camp procedure, the careless and random camp giving way to a martial

---

[1] Warren Angus Ferris, *Life in the Rocky Mountains,* Paul C. Phillips, ed., (Denver, 1940), p. xxxviii. This is the basic source for the summary given here.

[2] According to Phillips, John P. Cabanné, a partner of Pratte, Chouteau and Company, built this post for the American Fur Company shortly after 1822. He was in charge until 1833 when he was succeeded by Pilcher, who moved the post to Bellevue.

[3] Ferris, *op. cit.,* 18.

appearance. Camps were formed in a square with one side, whenever possible, on the banks of a stream.

Continuing up the Platte River, Ferris passed Chimney Rock, or "Nose Mountain" and left a vivid description in his journal of the famous landmark. He also preserved an original story of the naming of Scott's Bluff. The party continued on, leaving the Platte and reaching the Sweetwater, so named, according to Ferris, because of the drowning of a mule loaded with sugar some years earlier. An evening was spent at Independence Rock, so named, explains Ferris, because an earlier party spent the Fourth of July in its shade. On June 20, Ferris and party crossed over South Pass and descended the Sandy.

After several more days of traveling, the trappers crossed the Green River in bull-hide canoes. After traveling twenty-five miles on Ham's Fork of the Green, several persons were dispatched in different directions in quest of a party of independent hunters and trappers. Although still a greenhorn, Ferris rapidly absorbed information about the West from the older trappers.

Passing through the present region of Kemmerer, Wyoming, the expedition reached the heavily grassed bottomlands of Bear River opposite the Utah-Idaho Bear Lake region. In the area of present Cokeville, Wyoming, the trappers tried to make contact with some "free men," or independent trappers, to ascertain the conditions of the present fur market. At this point Ferris correctly observed that the Bear River "rises in the Eut [Uintah] Mountains, flows northward about a hundred miles when it turns westward and after a further course of seventy-five miles, discharges itself into the Big Lake" [4] [Great Salt Lake].

Although but a youth, Ferris was chosen by leader Drips to accompany him, with three others, into Cache Valley in

---

[4] *Ibid.*, 42.

search of the free trappers. They reached the site of Logan, Utah. Ferris describes Cache Valley as one of the most beautiful in the West, and in full particulars relates the story of its naming.

Failing to find any free trappers, Ferris and his companions returned to their camp on the Bear, below present Cokeville. On August 16, by way of the Muddy, Ferris returned to Ham's Fork, where the party's goods were cached. Small parties were dispersed in quest of beaver, Ferris traveling with Fontenelle's group, which headed for the upper reaches of Black's Fork and Henry's Fork in the Uintah Mountains of Utah. After hearing that the free trappers were on the Yellowstone, Ferris returned with a party to trap the Bear River tributaries.

With the coming of late autumn, 1830, both the American Fur Company and the Rocky Mountain Fur Company men, together with large numbers of independent trappers and Indians, were encamped in the lush meadows of Cache Valley for the winter. The site was probably near present Hyrum, Utah. In a short time the American Fur Company men moved southward to Ogden's Hole [Huntsville, Utah] for several weeks.

In the latter part of December, Ferris crossed over to Great Salt Lake, near present Brigham City. Here Ferris discusses the proposed change of name to Lake Bonneville:

> An attempt has been recently made to change the name of this lake to Lake Bonnyville, [sic] from no other reason that I can learn, but to gratify the silly conceit of a Captain Bonnyville, [sic] whose adventures in this region at the head of a party, form the ground work of "Irving's Rocky Mountains." There is no more justice or propriety in calling the lake after that gentleman, than after any other one of the many persons who in the course of their fur hunting expeditions have passed in its vicinity. He neither discovered or explored it, nor has he done anything else to entitle him to the honor of giving it his name.[5]

[5] *Ibid.*, 87-8. J. Cecil Alter, "W. A. Ferris in Utah," in *Utah Historical Quarterly,* IX (April, 1941), 87-8.

March, 1831, found the company reassembled on the Bear River when word reached them that most of the tributaries of the Snake were already free from ice. A decision was made to move north, and on April 4, after making a cache, the trappers pressed their laborious way out of Cache Valley to the forks of the Portneuf.

Ferris' journal records J. H. Stevens' account of the expedition of Joseph Robidoux who had departed from Drips' party and had traveled northward, then down the Snake to the Portneuf and on to present American Falls, where the party was divided, one group trapping the Wind River while the other, including Stevens, went to the Malad, or perhaps Wood River. Jean Baptiste Charbonneau, son of Sacajawea, and a member of Stevens' party, was lost for a time but finally returned with several trappers belonging to a party of forty led by John Work, a clerk of the Hudson's Bay Company.[6] Ferris quotes Stevens as giving the reason for the name of the Malad River [La Riviere Maladi]: that beaver eaten from that stream induce "a singular fit, the symptoms of which are, stiffness of the neck, pains in the bones, and nervous contortions of the face."[7] In spite of this discouraging knowledge, Robidoux's hungry trappers indulged in a repast of fat beaver and according to Stevens without exception suffered severe consequences.

On the route north to the Portneuf, Ferris and the main party also met trappers from Work's brigade who advised them of the terrain. Having spent nine days traveling through heavy snow making the sixty miles from Cache Valley to the point where the Portneuf leaves the mountains, Drips and party were relieved to again reach dry ground. Within a day's travel down the Portneuf, the main camp of John Work was reached and bloodshed between

---

[6] For Work's account of this meeting, see T. C. Elliott, "Journal of John Work," *Oregon Historical Quarterly,* XIII (December, 1912), 368-70.

[7] Ferris, 65.

the two parties was narrowly averted. Work was convinced that Fontenelle had persuaded one of his men to desert and join the Americans; accordingly he leveled his gun at the breast of Fontenelle but was restrained from firing by a more calm comrade. The parting of the two companies was far from affable.

The journey was again pursued, passing the forks of the Snake, and on to Henry's Fork. They found game abundant, and took from forty to seventy beaver a day. A portion of the party was sent to "Burnt Hole" on the Madison, but returned with little success. From Henry's Fork the expedition passed westward to the head of Camas Creek where on May 28 two members of the party were killed by Blackfeet Indians. On Beaver Creek a large village consisting of fifty lodges of Flatheads, Nez Perces, and Pend d'Orielles came into the white camp. Ferris credits the Flatheads with having never killed or robbed a white man.[8]

The expedition remained on Beaver Creek until June 19, when Fontenelle and Drips with thirty men departed for St. Louis. Accompanied by twenty Flatheads, the leaders departed for Cache Valley, where under agreement they were to meet Rocky Mountain Fur Company men and travel east together. The remainder of the party set out for the Salmon River country. On June 28, Ferris reached Day's Defile and, ascending the stream flowing from it, passed the junction of Medicine Lodge Creek. Leaving the head of Day's Creek, the party crossed a narrow pass and entered the beautiful valley watered by the Lemhi River, or as they called it, the Little Salmon. Through a narrow defile the trappers entered the small valley watered by the Big Lost River, where they found great numbers of buffalo. Further travel west brought disappointing catches of beaver

---

[8] Paul Wellman, in his *The Indian Wars of the West*, (New York, 1947), 169, cites the Nez Perce boast that no member of the tribe had ever taken the life of a white man.

and so on July 24, 1831, the return journey was commenced.

By the middle of August, Day's Defile was again reached. From the headwaters of the East Fork of the Salmon, Ferris descended into Horse Prairie, and leaving that rolling plain on the last day of August, crossed the mountains to the northwest and descended into Big Hole. After a ten-day camp, the trappers crossed through Deer Lodge Pass and into Deer Lodge Valley.

On September 15, the company moved southward over Deer Lodge Pass and then southeastward over Pipestone Pass to the forks of the Jefferson and Big Hole Rivers. Frasier, the Iroquois hunter, was killed by marauding Indians on September 18, his body being found in the Jefferson. With the death of Frasier, the three Indian guides who had promised to lead the party to the three forks of the Missouri demanded their release. On September 24, Ferris reached the Philanthropy [Ruby] River and camped several miles from its mouth.

In the early days of October the expedition moved southward to a small stream that flows into the Jefferson below Beaverhead Rock. The stream was followed to its junction with the Jefferson. The trappers then continued up that river to the junction where Horse Prairie Creek and Red Rock Creek join to form the Beaverhead. On October 8, several men departed for the Trois Tetons to meet Drips, who was expected to return that fall with men, horses, and merchandise. Leaving Horse Prairie on October 11, they reached the east fork of the Salmon. After descending some distance they crossed into Big Hole Valley where, on October 29, they met the Rocky Mountain Fur Company men, returning from their hunt on the waters of the Missouri. Ferris gives an account of their earlier engagement with Indians on Grey's Creek.

Several days after the arrival of the R.M.F. men, the trappers sent to meet Drips returned, reporting that Drips had not arrived, but that Fraeb had fallen in with Fitzpatrick on the Platte at the head of thirty men with pack horses. Fraeb took the men and horses and was at the time on his way to the Big Hole Valley, while Fitzpatrick returned to St. Louis for more equipment and supplies. The latter had been delayed by his long trip, via Santa Fe.

While the trappers from both the American companies prepared to spend the winter of 1831-32 in the Big Hole, three A.F.C. men departed in a second effort to meet Drips, who was supposed to arrive that fall. On December 21, two men from Work's party of Hudson's Bay trappers arrived, stating that their main camp was two days' journey away and that they had been continually harassed by Blackfeet. On the 23rd of the month, Ferris and the A.F.C. trappers parted company with those of the R.M.F. and passed southward up the Salmon River to the western end of the Little Salmon River Valley.

On the 25th, Ferris and three companions returned down the Salmon River to reach the R.M.F. camp near Lemhi Pass and obtained some wanted goods. In several days a messenger arrived from Work's party, who at the time were camped with a large band of Pend d'Oreilles at Beaver Head. They were being hard pressed by the Blackfeet, who claimed that the white chief at the mouth of the Yellowstone River [McKenzie of the A.F.C.] had built a trading house at the mouth of the Marias [Fort Piegan] and had supplied the Blackfeet with guns and quantities of ammunition. They further stated that they were only awaiting the arrival of the Blood Indians from the north to wage a war of extermination against the whites. By February 4, 1832, Ferris was back at the main camp with a report of Indian activities and the latest news.

The winter was spent in trapping, moving generally to the vicinity of the Grand Tetons. From a wandering party of Bannocks they learned that a party of whites was at that time in Cache Valley. On March 4, the party crossed the frozen Blackfoot River and camped near its mouth. On the following day two men, John Gray and David Montgomery, departed for Cache Valley to ascertain if the white party there was Drips and company. Five days later hunters brought in the half-dead Gray, who had been found lying in the cedars near the Portneuf. He gave an account of their journey to Cache Valley, finding no traces of any white party, but many Indian signs. The pair of trappers were ambushed on their return trip, Montgomery being killed and Gray barely escaping with his life. The main camp was soon moved down the south fork of the Portneuf to the spot where Montgomery was killed. In honor of the unfortunate trapper, the pass from Cache Valley to the Portneuf was called Montgomery's Pass.

On the 20th the trappers reached Bear River in Cache Valley and three days later several hunters from W. H. Vanderburgh's company of fifty trappers arrived in camp. The latter had been outfitted from Fort Union at the mouth of the Yellowstone and had spent the winter in the southern end of Cache Valley. The fact that a party from Taos had already trapped the district that Ferris and his companions intended to hunt caused them to join Vanderburgh and proceed forty miles northward, up Bear River, to Sheep Rock, south of Soda Springs, Idaho. Ferris was not as enthusiastic about the springs as most early visitors, one such trapper even writing that the springs would become a "resort for thousands of the gay and fashionable world." [9] The zig-zag course of the river was followed for seventy-five miles, and then on April 13, the party traveled twelve miles to the east over rolling hills to Talma's Fork which flows southward into Bear River. Smith's fork was reached on the 14th,

[9] Osborne Russell, *Journal of a Trapper* (Boise, Ida., 1921), 9.

Ferris explaining that the stream was so called for the late "Jerediah" [Jedediah] Smith.[10] The 16th found the trappers a few miles above the mouth of the Muddy, where they saw an abundance of buffalo, geese, and ducks.

On April 24, 1832, Bear River was again crossed and on that day the Indian called Pascal, who had traveled to St. Louis with Fontenelle and Drips, arrived in camp with news that Drips with a party of forty-eight was then camped on the Muddy. The following day a glad reunion was held, and drinks in abundance, according to Ferris, were the order of the day. After a march of five days Ferris and three companions raised a cache of furs on Rush Creek and returned to the camp on Smith's Fork.

On May 8, the journey was pursued to Sheep Rock and thence continued northwestward through Gray's Hole, named for John Gray, who had accompanied David Montgomery to Cache Valley two months earlier. In a narrow canyon of Gray's Creek, Ferris met a party under Jim Bridger and wrote:

> Their encampment was decked with hundreds of beaver skins, now drying in the sun. These valuable skins are always stretched in willow hoops, varying from eighteen inches, to three feet in diameter, according to the size of the skins, and have a reddish appearance on the flesh side, which is exposed to the sun. Our camps are always dotted with these red circles in the trapping season, when the weather is fair. There were several hundred skins folded and tied up in packs, laying about their encampment, which bore good evidence to the industry of the trappers.[11]

On May 19, 1832, Ferris with two Indian companions departed camp to seek the Flatheads and induce them to come to the forks of the Snake for trade. The trip was successful and a party of hunters met Ferris on his return trip.

---

[10] Jedediah Smith was killed by Comanches on the Cimarron Desert of Southwestern Kansas in 1831.

[11] Ferris, 144.

On June 3, camp was reached and the spring hunt was declared to be over. Horses and men rested and prepared for the annual rendezvous to be held at Pierre's Hole, in eastern Idaho, where they expected to meet Fontenelle with supplies from St. Louis. A leisurely journey was pursued up Henry's Fork, halting at the East Fork several days to dry meat. While there Ferris recorded: "We killed hundreds daily [buffalo] during our stay on Henrie's fork." Upon reaching Pierre's Hole, Drips and company found the R.M.F. company encamped, awaiting the arrival of Fitzpatrick. Vanderburgh was expecting Etienne Provost [12] with provisions from Fort Union, while Drips daily expected Fontenelle with supplies from Council Bluffs. Thus, in the summer of 1832, the rivals were encamped in Pierre's Hole, a place, according to Ferris, "selected as a pleasant place for a general rendezvous." [13]

On July 3, word reached the camps that William Sublette, at the head of one hundred men, was on his way to Pierre's Hole. This company of fifty men, a party of twenty-two from Gantt's company, thirteen men from the Rio del Norte under Alexander Sinclair, and a dozen or so men under Nathaniel J. Wyeth, were all there. Fitzpatrick had left Sublette's company at the Red Hills and traveled on alone to make better time, but was attacked by Indians. Ferris records in full detail Fitzpatrick's perilous adventure and narrow escape from death.

The famous battle of Pierre's Hole, which occurred at this rendezvous, is described in the "Brief History" preceding the biographical sketches in this Series.

---

[12] Provost, previously operating from New Mexico, had joined the Astor enterprise.

[13] The R.M.F. company had named Pierre's Hole as the area for the rendezvous. Vanderburgh went there to get as much as possible of the fur trade while Fontenelle went east to obtain needed goods. According to Joe Meek, both Vanderburgh's and Drips' parties knew nothing of the country and recklessly declared their intention to follow their rivals wherever they went and outbid them for furs.

After the battle, trading was resumed, then the men departed for their trapping grounds. Since Provost and Fontenelle had made no appearance at the rendezvous, Drips and Vanderburgh concluded to move over on to the Green River, where they found Fontenelle.

On August 12, all arrangements having been completed, Fontenelle with thirty men departed for Fort Union with the year's catch of furs, while Vanderburgh and Drips at the head of about ten men, including Ferris, took a northwesterly direction toward the Salmon River country on the trail of Bridger and Fitzpatrick, hoping to be led to the best beaver country. On the 20th, with two companions, Ferris departed with orders to find the Flatheads and induce them to meet the company in Horse Prairie. Although failing to find the tribe, he explored the headwaters of the Missouri and the Columbia and from a great height surveyed the bottom lands bordering the Salmon and the Big Hole Rivers. Ferris reported that hunger struck both man and beast so severely that "ravens were seen picking at a bone, in the mouth of a wolf." [14] The main party was rejoined on the first of September.

On the trail of the Rocky Mountain men, the A.F.C. trappers reached Deer Lodge Valley in Montana and followed the Big Blackfoot which flows into Clark's Fork near present Milltown, Montana. Hell Gate Pass was reached and then the continental divide was crossed. After passing the Great Falls of the Missouri and Pipestone Creek, east of present Butte, Montana, a division was made on September 16. Drips continued to pursue Bridger and Fitzpatrick, while Vanderburgh, with Ferris in his company, departed to search out new fur country. The latter party was soon encamped on the banks of the Jefferson about thirty miles below Beaver Head. Early in October the Ruby was

---

[14] Ferris, 165.

ascended, the divide being crossed between the Ruby and the Madison.

The morning of October 12 found Vanderburgh's company underway in a northwesterly direction on the Madison River. On the 14th the remains of a buffalo freshly butchered was found on the trail. Vanderburgh decided that a party of seven should further investigate the incident, and accordingly a small group, including Ferris, set out. At a grove of trees about a mile below the Lower Canyon of the Madison, about 100 savages suddenly opened fire from their hiding place in the trees. Vanderburgh's horse was immediately shot from under him, "but," records Ferris, "with unexampled firmness, he stepped calmly from the lifeless animal, presented his gun at the advancing foe, and exclaimed 'boys don't run.' " [15] The thought of each trapper was to preserve his own life and each acted accordingly. R. C. Nelson looked back to witness Vanderburgh being cut down by a volley from the Indians. A Frenchman named Pilou was also killed and Ferris was wounded by a shot striking his left shoulder. Fear of further trouble in the camp, which was soon on the march, was quieted by the discovery of a camp of 150 lodges of Flatheads, Pend d'Oreilles, and other Indians before reaching Horse Prairie. At the prairie, Andrew Drips was found awaiting Vanderburgh's company. The caches were soon raised and, on October 24, Drips set out for the Snake River, where he intended to pass the winter. Ferris with two men also departed to engage in trade with the Indians.

Traveling fifteen miles through Horse Prairie, Ferris made camp at the "Gates," where a small party of Bonneville's men in search of game soon arrived. Several days later twenty-five men under Joseph R. Walker, also of Bonneville's party, arrived in camp. Before long the camp

---

[15] *Ibid.,* 177.

was further enlarged by the arrival of trappers from the
R.M.F. company. One day after their arrival the various
parties took their leave, Ferris traveling over the mountains
to the east fork of the Salmon, then to Bonneville's post
near present Salmon, Idaho, of which Ferris observed:

> This miserable establishment, consisted entirely of several log cabins,
> low, badly constructed, and admirably situated for besiegers only, who
> would be sheltered on every side, by timber, brush etc.[16]

Leaving Bonneville's "fort," Ferris joined Walker's company intending to travel with them as far as the mouth of
the Blackfoot, and then make his way to the forks of the
Snake and join Drips in his winter camp. Traveling south
and then southwest, Ferris overtook the R.M.F. company in
the Lemhi Valley. All of that party except Fitzpatrick and
one other man stayed there to spend the winter. The latter
two traveled with Ferris, intending to transact some business with Drips, whose camp was reached in mid-Decem-
ber, 1832. After completing his business, Fitzpatrick departed for the Salmon, and Ferris for the mouth of the
Blackfoot to pick up men and baggage left there. The 24th
of December brought Ferris to the camp of Joseph R.
Walker, and Christmas day was spent with that amiable
trapper.

The winter passed with little activity, but with the dis-
appearance of snow and ice toward the end of March, 1833,
the company, now grown to sizable numbers, was divided.
The Spaniard Manuel Alvarez, later prominent in the
Southwest trade, marched at the head of about forty men,
intending to trap along Henry's Fork, the Yellowstone, and
to eventually join the main party on the Green at the end
of the spring hunt.[17] Drips and the second division of the

---

[16] *Ibid.,* 184.

[17] It appears from Ferris' writing that Alvarez visited Yellowstone Park in 1827
and may have published the first account of it. See Ferris, *op. cit.,* 259, 261.

trappers, including Ferris, traveled for a short time up the Lewis River and called a halt to wait for warmer weather. With a turn in the weather, Drips and company moved south and by April 26 reached Gray's Hole, where they remained until May 3. Shortly after this date the venturers traveled up the Salt River Valley in quest of a new store of salt.

By May 19, the Lewis [Snake] River was reached and camp established a few hundred yards from the junction of the Salt River. Toward the end of the month the old battlefield of Pierre's Hole was revisited and then Jackson's Hole. June 6th brought the company to the Green, and on the following day Ferris and one companion rode to determine whether any of their long separated friends had by now arrived at Horse Creek on the Green River, the site of Bonneville's "Fort Nonsense," and the appointed place of rendezvous for 1833. At the rude fort was found Joseph R. Walker, John Gray, Benjamin O'Fallon, and a second Vanderburgh. The main camp soon reached the fort and, on June 25, Ferris with a small group departed to meet the St. Louis company, who were expected daily.[18] Immediately following the rendezvous of 1833, Ferris and Robert Newell, a trader for the R.M.F. company and later a pioneer of Oregon, departed at the head of a company to engage in the Flathead trade. The party passed over Gibbon's Pass, along the Lolo, and into Grass Valley to the junction of the Bitterroot with Clark's Fork of the Columbia. The trade was continued until they met Drips on November 2, the latter reporting a successful fall hunt. Ferris observed that trading houses had been established at the mouth of the Marias and also at the mouth of the Bighorn.[19]

After several days Ferris concluded to return to the Flat-

---

[18] William Sublette and Robert Campbell formed this company in 1832 to buy furs from and supply goods to the Rocky Mountain Fur Company.

[19] Fort Piegan was constructed at the mouth of the Marias in 1831 by James Kipp; and Fort Cass at the mouth of the Bighorn in 1832 by Samuel Tullock.

heads with Francis Pillet, one of the many H.B.F. company traders. Late in November the two arrived at the camp of the H.B.F. company clerk, Francis Ermatinger, the majority of whose party had departed for the Flathead or Saleesh Post. Ermatinger and Ferris traveled ahead through Little Cammas Prairie to overtake the British trappers. Ferris found the Hudson's Bay men much better supplied and clad than the Americans. He relished tasting some vegetables brought in from Fort Colville at Kettle Falls. Ferris watched with amazement as the British camp was broken up and the entire store of goods loaded upon light barges and canoes for the trip to Fort Colville. After the departure of Ermatinger and his trappers, Ferris decided to spend the winter with a trader and his family in the Salish Range. A small cabin was constructed, not from necessity, but because "we had nothing else to do." An enjoyable Christmas was spent with the trader, whom Ferris calls "Mr. Montour," [20] and he recorded:

> Our bill of fare consisted of buffalo tongues, dry buffalo meat, fresh venison, wheat flour cakes, buffalo marrow, (for butter,) sugar, coffee, and rum, with which we drank a variety of appropriate toasts, suited to the occasion, and our enlarged and elevated sentiments, respecting universal benevolence and prosperity, while our hearts were warmed, our prejudices banished, and our affections refined, by the enlivening contents of the flowing bowl.[21]

On April 13, Ferris left the Flathead post in a barge for Horse Prairie. Here Ermatinger again made his appearance. By April 23, Ferris and Montour were prepared with goods purchased from the H.B.F. company for their departure to the Flatheads. Near present Missoula, Montana, a crossing of the Arrowstone River was made. On the last day of the month, while Ermatinger and Ferris were engaged

---

[20] Probably David Montour, nephew of Nicholas Montour, who was with David Thompson on the Kootenai in 1811.
[21] Ferris, 238.

in the tedious ceremony of shaking hands with a large camp of Flatheads on the Bitterroot River, a large party of trappers arrived, among whom was Robert Newell, from whom Ferris learned that Drips had wintered at the forks of the Snake, where Henry's Fork and South Fork unite.

From the Indian camp on the Bitterroot, Ferris and Montour, with some Indians, departed for the south, reaching Big Hole on May 12. Toward the end of the month Ferris visited and described the wonders of Yellowstone Park.[22] By May 21, the party was again underway, crossing Henry's Fork and reaching the vicinity of Pierre's Hole. Coming to the plains of Green River, Ferris directed his course toward Fort Nonsense and learned from two Indians that Drips was encamped in the Wind River Mountains east of Green River. The trail thence was immediately pursued and Drips' camp was soon reached. After an exchange of news, Ferris learned that Fontenelle and others were trapping in the "Eutaw" country to the south.

Late in August Ferris and his companions neared the Uintah Basin of northeastern Utah, taking with them two Ute Indian women rescued from the Snakes by Joseph R. Walker, one of whom was the wife of the Ute Chieftain Commoraweap. A halt was made south of the Uintah Mountains, possibly on Brush or Ashley Creek. By September 3, Ferris had reached the vicinity of present Thistle, Utah, and on the 4th camped near the Sanpitch River, in the vicinity of present Mount Pleasant, or Ephraim, Utah. From the 4th to the 8th, Ferris traveled southward across Sanpete and Sevier Valleys to the vicinity of present Richfield, and then northward along the west side of the Sevier, which he calls the "Savarah." Salt beds were found near present Salina, Utah. Moving northward from the Sevier,

---

[22] A marker erected in Yellowstone Park gives Ferris credit for the best early description of the park.

Ferris camped "on a small stream that flows into the Eutah lake," presumably the Santaquin.

Little mention is made of Ferris' trip from Utah Lake eastward to the Green River in the Uintah Basin, the journal jumping to October 29, 1834, when Ferris describes the "Chanion of White River" located east of present Ouray, Utah. Camp was made presumably at the junction of the White and the Green Rivers, near the location of Kit Carson's winter camp of 1833-34. At this point either Ferris or his printer again deleted a great amount of travel narrative, and Ferris is suddenly found on the present Whiterock-Altonah bench lands in Ashley Valley. To make such a journey, their path surely would have led them past Fort Robidoux on the Whiterocks River, and yet no conclusive reference appears in the narrative.[23] Apparently traders from Taos arrived while Ferris was at Fort Kit Carson, about one mile south of present Ouray, Utah, for Ferris records: "During our stay on this river, one of the log huts was occupied by those trappers from Taos, who joined us last fall."[24] Presumably this forced Ferris into shifting his winter camp to the mouth of Ashley Gorge, above Dry Fork Junction, six or eight miles north of the present Vernal, Utah. The small party remained in winter quarters until the end of March, 1835. On the 30th of that month the party attempted to penetrate the chasm of Ashley Gorge but were soon deterred by the terrors of the tortuous canyon. Retreating, Ferris made his way over the Uintahs in a northwesterly direction, by way of the headwaters of Bear River and then far into the Snake River region. He continued eastward through South Pass, down the Sweetwater, the Platte, and finally the Missouri to St. Louis.

[23] Scholars disagree as to the founding date of Fort Robidoux, some suggesting 1832, others 1837. See Hafens' *Old Spanish Trail* (Glendale, 1954), 101-2.
[24] Ferris, 277.

After six years of adventure in the Rockies, Ferris arrived home never again to return to his favorite mountain haunts and cool mountain valleys, except in memory. He concluded his journal of his days as a trapper by writing:

> When the weather was warm and pleasant; the demands of nature satisfied, a reliance on the good qualities of my arms and ammunition, not misplaced; the confidence of bestriding and governing a truly noble steed, in the spirit of stirring excitement of the chase, gloriously bounding over the plains, in the panoply of speed and power, before which the swiftest and mightiest denizens of the forest and prairie must yield themselves victims; then – *then* I was really, rationally happy. Many times have I experienced the sensations, generated by either condition; but these scenes have now passed away, their delights and perils no longer thrill nor alarm, and I bid them farewell forever.[25]

After his return, Ferris began preparing his journal for publication, and in 1836 sent it to Carey, Lea and Blanchard, publishers in Philadelphia. They replied that they were unable to publish it at that time. At this refusal Ferris became indifferent and the journal remained untouched in the Ferris family for six years. Meanwhile Warren and his brother Charles apparently decided to join the Texas revolution. Traveling down the Ohio, Warren met a number of old friends from the mountains at Louisville. Taking a steamboat to New Orleans, the Ferris brothers continued on to Galveston. The war was over when they arrived and Charles returned to Buffalo, where in 1842 he assumed the editorship of the *Western Literary Messenger,* in which episodes from Warren's journal began to appear.

In December, 1837, Ferris was elected county surveyor, with a land office at Nacogdoches. He held this position until 1840, when he surveyed the area of the three forks of the Trinity, or present day Dallas, near which he settled and remained the rest of his life. In 1841 he married Melinda Cook from Paris, Illinois. After giving birth to two chil-

[25] *Ibid.,* 289-90.

dren, who both died in their youth, Melinda died in 1844. Ferris was married again in 1847, to Frances Moore of Palestine, Texas, who mothered twelve children, three of whom were still living in 1940. Not far from Dallas, Ferris built a farm at Reinhardt, Texas, on the east bank of White Rock Creek. To the end of his life the bullet wound in his left shoulder, received in a Blackfoot attack, caused him pain. Nevertheless, the mountains held a spell over him, and his prose articles and poems, only two of which survive, tell of this fascination. On February 8, 1873, at the age of sixty-three, Ferris passed quietly away at the farmhouse at Reinhardt.[26]

Along with his journal, the most important contribution of Warren Angus Ferris is his famous "Map of the Northwest Fur Country," drawn in 1836. It covers generally the territory from the 39th to the 48th parallel. From east to west it covers from the 109th meridian to the 116th. Covering the same fur-trade area, no other map of the early 19th century can compare with it in comprehensive accuracy. Ferris had no instruments to determine exact location, and a number of errors were made, such as making the Great Salt Lake longer from east to west than from north to south. The Great Salt Lake and Sevier Lake are too far north, while Flathead Lake is nearly three degrees too far south, and Yellowstone Lake is three degrees too far west. With exact latitude and longitude eliminated, the Ferris map is in excellent proportions and is a major contribution to the knowledge of the early West. Many of Ferris' place names persist on modern maps.

Besides the colorful and accurate descriptions of Bear Lake, Deer Lodge on Clark's Fork, Yellowstone Park, the sand hills of southern Idaho, Warm Springs Valley (Montana), Horse Prairie, Pierre's Hole, and Cache Valley

---

26 Phillips, *op. cit.*, preface, lxiv.

(Utah), various Indian tribes, and the life of a trapper, Ferris has preserved the original naming of such places as Chimney Rock, Scott's Bluff, the Sweetwater, and Independence Rock. He has also preserved excellent portraits of a long list of Mountain Men whom he knew personally, a list including Jim Bridger, Andrew Drips, Lucien Fontenelle, Thomas Fitzpatrick, Joseph R. Walker, Francis Ermatinger, William H. Vanderburgh, Robert Newell, Joseph Robidoux, John Work, and many others.

In all probability the importance of the life of Warren A. Ferris in the annals of western history will increase with the passage of years.

Manuel Alvarez

by HAROLD H. DUNHAM
University of Denver

Manuel Alvarez (1794-1856) was a distinguished individual of Spanish origin who merits more recognition than he has yet received for his participation in the development of western America. He was a cultured gentleman who became prominent in fur trapping and commercial and political fields, with his headquarters in Santa Fe, New Mexico. For several years he was associated with P. D. Papin and Company, and then with the American Fur Company in Rocky Mountain fur-gathering expeditions. His activities emphasize the interesting commercial relations between Santa Fe, St. Louis, the Missouri River, and the Green, Yellowstone-Snake River region. He is perhaps best known in three other lines of endeavor, namely: as a Santa Fe trader who maintained a large store in the New Mexican capital for nearly thirty years; as the United States Consul in Santa Fe for the period 1839 to 1846; and as an office-holder and prominent political leader in New Mexico during the 1850s.

Alvarez was born in 1794 (month and day presently unknown) in the village of Abelgas of the old kingdom of Leon, Spain.[1] No information has come to light on his life until he left his native land in 1818 for Spanish North America. For a time he resided in Mexico, including the period when its independence was established. A passport dated at Havana, Cuba, April 25, 1823, foreshadowed his voyage to New York. By the following year he had moved

---

[1] R. E. Twitchell, *The Spanish Archives of New Mexico* (Cedar Rapids, Ia., 1914), I, p. 339-40. Archive no. 1139.

to Missouri and there engaged in mercantile pursuits. On September 3, 1824, his name appeared, along with those of eleven other traders, on an official permit authorizing travel to Mexico.[2] Two of these traders were Isidore and Francis Robidoux, of the famous Robidoux family, and doubtless Alvarez accompanied the entire party of traders over the Santa Fe Trail to its western terminus.

Santa Fe must have appealed to the young Spaniard in several ways, not the least being its opportunities for trade and fur trapping. The Santa Fe trade, which had officially opened three years before, was increasing, and such well-known trappers as Sylvester and James Ohio Pattie, Ewing Young, Etienne Provost, and one or more of the Robidoux brothers were, by 1824, trapping or trading out of Santa Fe on the Green, the Gila, the Colorado and the Missouri Rivers.[3] Prospects for joining in such ventures, or continuing in the Santa Fe trade, may have caused Alvarez, on June 14, 1825, to petition the Governor of New Mexico for admission to Mexican citizenship. When there was delay in granting his request, he applied twice again in 1826, and ultimately he became recognized as a citizen of the new Republic.[4]

There is an apparent confusion of dates among the scanty records of Alvarez's early life in North America, for during

---

[2] *Ibid.*, I, pp. 341-42. All the traders bore French or Spanish names, and all were termed citizens of the U.S. For reference to Michel and Francis (or Francois) as familiar figures in the Yellowstone country and at Ft. Laramie, see: W. S. Wallace, *Antoine Robidoux, 1794-1860: A Biography of a Western Venturer* (Los Angeles, 1953), 9.

[3] *Ibid.*, 10; D. Morgan, *Jedediah Smith* (Indianapolis, 1953), 239.

[4] Twitchell, *op. cit.*, I, pp. 339-41. Gov. Baca endorsed the 1825 application, stating that Alvarez manifested a great zeal for the Catholic faith. The recognition of Alvarez's Mexican citizenship is noted in G. Miranda to M. Alvarez, Santa Fe, Apr. 23, 1840. Letter "B." Ms. Consular Despatches, Santa Fe, Mexico, vol. I, Aug. 28, 1830-Sept. 4, 1846. General Records of the Department of State, record group no. 59, The National Archives, Washington, D.C. Hereafter cited as Consular Despatches.

the summer of 1825, he was back in Missouri. On July 23, 1825 (only five weeks after he had signed his petition for Mexican citizenship at Santa Fe), he again received a U.S. permit, signed by William Clark, to travel to Mexico, and he reached New Mexico the following November.[5] The official records for this period also reveal that Alvarez used the name Manuel de Alvarez, that he spoke English, French and Spanish, that he identified his place of business as New Mexico, and that he intended to devote himself to agriculture. There is no available evidence to indicate that he did change then from merchandising to farming or stock raising, although a decade later, when applying for a land grant in New Mexico, he declared his intention to undertake sheep raising. This step will be mentioned again below. A description of Alvarez, drawn from his passports of 1823 and 1844, would indicate that he was five feet ten inches tall, possessed black hair and eyes, had regular features except for a rather prominent nose, wore no beard, and was considered light skinned.[6]

In the spring of 1827, Alvarez joined a party of seventeen men, which included Louis Robidoux, Thomas Boggs, Pablo Baillio, Samuel C. Lamme and Gervasio Nolán, that left Taos for Missouri.[7] By the latter part of July, he was ready to start back over the Trail, thus indicating that his relatively short stay in the States must have at least enabled

---

[5] Account of Foreigners who arrived in New Mexico. Ms. folder A, marked "Rich [Ritch] Collection," no. 97. B. M. Read Collection, New Mex. State Records Center and Archives, Santa Fe.

[6] The two passports do not agree on all points. The 1823 passport states that he was 5′2″ tall and that he had a regular nose. Furthermore, the 1844 U.S. passport describes his skin as dark; perhaps his outdoor life had produced this coloring by that time. In any case, this one is more complete and probably more accurate, except for this one item. Passport for M. Alvarez, signed by Sec. of State J. C. Calhoun at Wash., D.C., June 11, 1844. Ms. Alvarez Papers. B. M. Read Collection, New Mex. State Records Center. Hereafter cited as Alvarez Papers.

[7] List of foreigners arriving in and leaving Taos, N.M., Apr. 7, 1827. Ms. New Mexican Archives, New Mex. State Records Center.

him to purchase goods for his Santa Fe store.[8] As a matter of interest, the party, numbering thirty-two, with which Alvarez traveled the 770 miles (according to Alvarez's later calculations) back to Santa Fe, again included Boggs, Baillio, L. Robidoux, and Nolán, plus M. S. Cerre, Francois Guerin, and other prominent traders and trappers.

Sometime during the later 1820s, Alvarez decided to enter the Rocky Mountain fur trade; just when or how is not clear. Doubtless the possibilities became apparent through his contacts in Missouri, his companionship over the Santa Fe Trail, and his acquaintances using New Mexico as a base for trapping expeditions. Probably the first of these influences was the strongest, for he established business relations with P. D. Papin and Company, and by 1830 could be considered a Mountain Man.[9] This company had been formed during the winter of 1828-29, and consisted of eight partners, including, besides Papin, the two Cerrés, Chenie Fils, Henri Picotte, and D. Guion.[10] It was known as the French Company, and from bases along the Missouri and Teton Rivers, especially Fort Teton at the juncture of those two streams, it competed with the organizations controlled by the American Fur Company.

Alvarez had acquired a partner, J. Halcrow, in his fur trapping undertakings, and the two of them appear to have operated as free trappers in association with the Papin group by 1830. There seems to be small reason to doubt the person listed as "Alvaripe" in Jacob Halsey's journal at Ft. Tecumseh during May, 1830, was actually Manuel Alvarez.[11] On May 14, Halsey recorded that in the morning he rode from the fort down to Papin's house, on the south side of the

<hr/>

[8] R. G. Cleland, *This Reckless Breed of Men* (New York, 1950). Reproduction of traders' and trappers' permit, opposite p. 202.

[9] H. Picotte to M. Alvarez, Dec. 7, 1830. Ms. Alvarez Papers.

[10] H. M. Chittenden, *The American Fur Trade of the Far West* (Stanford, 1954), I, pp. 345-46.

[11] D. Robinson (ed.), "Records of Fort Tecumseh," *South Dakota Historical Collections,* IX (1918), 118.

Teton River.[12] Thus he fraternized with "our opponents" in the fur trade. Moreover, Messrs. Papin, Picotte, Winter, L. Cerre and Mr. Alvaripe (Alvarisse, written with the old style double "s"?) returned with Halsey to his fort in the evening, and there passed the night. Four days afterwards most of the same group again paid a visit to Fort Tecumseh, a place which the journal keeper a few months later described as the most disagreeable hole he "was ever at" in his life. Mosquitoes were very thick, but the fleas were in even "greater abundance." [13]

After the week or so of shared hospitalities, Alvarez, Picotte and others of the Papin company either ascended the Missouri River, where Alvarez and his partner separated from the others at the present Little Missouri River and traveled to the Yellowstone River, or the two partners said farewell to the French Company partners at Fort Teton, set out westward along the Teton River, and so pushed on to the Yellowstone.[14] In any case, on December 7, 1830, Picotte wrote from Fort Clark to Alvarez, at "Roche Jaune ou ses environs," a friendly letter expressing great concern at Alvarez's and Halcrow's long absence, without word of his success or welfare. The letter also reports the birth of a son to Halcrow, and claimed that his wife eagerly awaited his return on the Little Missouri (Teton?);[15] it

---

12 Papin's house was also called Fort Teton, the French post, and Cerre's establishment. *Ibid.*, 95 fn. Chittenden explains that the Teton River was called the Little Missouri to 1830, and then the Teton, finally ending up with the name Bad River. Chittenden, *op. cit.*, II, p. 767.

13 Robinson, *op. cit.*, 131.

14 Picotte refers to the separation as having occurred "au petit missouri," and he may have been referring to what was coming to be called the Teton River, or to the present Little Missouri much farther up the Big Muddy. H. Picotte to M. Alvarez, Dec. 7, 1830. Halsey, writing in Aug., 1830, used the name Teton River.

15 Alvarez was later reported to have married an Indian woman in the Rocky Mountains, in accordance with Indian custom. By her he had three sons, one of whom died early; the other two were taken to Spain, where Alvarez visited them in 1855. See deposition of Joseph Mercure, dated Jan. 4, 1861, before A. P. Wilbar, Ocate Grant files. Claim no. 1, reported as no. 143. Bureau of Land Management, Santa Fe, N.M.

laments the death of several friends killed by the Arickarees; it rejoices over the good season Picotte's outfit had experienced; it extends good wishes to Alvarez from "Lamie," Papin, Chenie and Paschal; and it informs Alvarez of the three-year agreement which the Papin Company had recently signed with Kenneth McKenzie, one of the Upper Missouri Outfit's ablest traders. In short, Papin and his associates had come under the control of the American Fur Company, and Picotte expressed the hope that Alvarez too could make a satisfactory arrangement with McKenzie.

The circumstances and route of Alvarez's return from the Yellowstone region are unknown, but during the following May (1831), he and his partner were back at Fort Teton, purchasing horses, mules, traps, powder, knives, cloth, needles, blankets, nails, kettles and other supplies and equipment, in the amount of $1,002.21, from P. D. Papin and Company.[16] Their supplies, though not the equipment, were secured at one hundred per cent advance on cost. Where Alvarez and Halcrow trapped in 1831 is a matter for speculation; yet the next year, 1832, they probably attended the rendezvous at Pierre's Hole in association with the American Fur Company brigade. By that time, Alvarez would certainly have become aware of the bitter rivalry then in progress between that company and the Rocky Mountain Fur Company. The former was represented by Henry Vanderburgh and Andrew Drips, with ninety men; and the latter by Thomas Fitzpatrick and William L. Sublette, with about one hundred men.[17]

Since he spent the winter of 1832-33 with Drips and his group, it also is probable that during the preceding fall Alvarez took part in the trailing of Fitzpatrick and Bridger

[16] Bill to Messrs. De Alvares & Halcrow, dated Teton River, May 21, 1831. Ms. Alvarez Papers.

[17] F. G. Young (ed.), *The Correspondence and Journals of Capt. Nathaniel J. Wyeth, 1831-1836* (Eugene, Ore., 1899), 159; and Chittenden, *op. cit.*, I, pp. 296-97.

into the regions north and northwest of present Yellowstone Park, to learn from the R.M.F. Company where the best beaver trapping could be found. Drips finally gave up the pursuit, separated from Vanderburgh, and led his own unit into the Three Forks, Salmon River, and upper Snake River area.[18] Because W. A. Ferris does not mention Alvarez as among the Vanderburgh detachment, it seems likely that Alvarez had not accompanied them at the time they encountered a Blackfoot ambush that led to the killing of Vanderburgh and one of his followers.[19]

The survivors of this attack joined Drips's winter camp on the upper Snake River at the close of December, 1832, and Alvarez most likely participated in the various forms of recreation that Ferris describes, while waiting for the coming of the spring hunt.[20] The latter reports that January 1, 1833, was spent in feasting, drinking and dancing, in keeping with the Canadian custom; and that other days, when the weather was fair, were devoted to riding, shooting, wrestling, and the like. Card playing served as entertainment when storms restricted outdoor activities. If one of Alvarez's later notebooks is any indication, he probably passed some of the time reading historical, philosophical or religious books. Drips's party moved camp three times during January, and in the following month visitors reached them both from the R.M.F. Company and Joseph R. Walker's outfit, attached to Captain B. L. E. Bonneville's enterprise.

Alvarez's standing in Drips's "numerous company" is indicated by the fact that when the snow and ice began to disappear, about March 23, 1833, he was placed in charge of about forty of the men to undertake a trapping expedition up Henry's Fork of the Snake River and eastward to

18 W. A. Ferris, *Life in the Rocky Mountains* (Denver, 1940), P. C. Phillips, ed., 159.

19 B. De Voto, *Across the Wide Missouri* (Boston, 1947), 88-89.

20 Ferris, *op. cit.*, 190-91.

the Yellowstone – familiar territory to Alvarez.[21] Renewed stormy weather pinned down his unit soon after they had left camp, until the latter part of April. At that time, however, more favorable conditions permitted the detachment to set out, and Alvarez led them to the Upper Yellowstone region. While undertaking this spring hunt, his party sojourned in what M. J. Mattes calls the Fire Hole Basin,[22] and beheld the awe-inspiring geysers, boiling pots and other natural phenomena of present Yellowstone Park.

Early in the summer of 1833, Alvarez headed for the Green River rendezvous, near Horse Creek and Bonneville's Fort Nonsense, to rejoin Drips and the rest of the A.F.C. units. The rendezvous that year proved to be one of the most significant ever held. Leaders of the most prominent and competing American fur companies forgot their rivalries for a time. E. W. Todd has observed that "The names of traders and trappers in this rendezvous constitute a veritable roster of men prominent in the [fur] trade." [23] The three July weeks of trading, celebrating, carousing, relaxing, and competing in various contests by the two hundred and fifty to three hundred white men, in addition to many Indians, need not be reviewed here.[24] At the conclusion of the holidays the A.F.C. representatives had collected fifty-one packs of beaver, weighing one hundred pounds each, as against fifty-five packs for the R.M.F. Company.[25] Bonneville's followers had acquired twenty-two and one half packs, and Dr. Benjamin Harris's, seven packs. Alvarez had made his mark among them all by having led an important detachment of the Astor group, and by reciting, and thus publicizing, the story of the spectacular displays of the geyser basin.

[21] *Ibid.*, 192-94.

[22] M. J. Mattes, "The Legend of Colter's Hell," *The Westerners Brand Book, 1947* (Denver, 1948), 94.

[23] W. Irving, *Adventures of Captain Bonneville* (E. W. Todd, ed., 1961), 145.

[24] De Voto, *op. cit.*, 97-102.   [25] Young's *Wyeth*, 69-70.

An indication of Alvarez's role is further attested by the fact that Lucien Fontenelle, the "Acting Agent of the American Fur Company" at "Green River Rendezvous," drew a note on William Laidlaw at Fort Pierre, for $1,325.98 payable to Alvarez "for services rendered." [26] After receiving this note, Alvarez may well have started out for a fresh hunt again with Drips, who headed for the upper Snake River and adjacent areas. In any case, he did reach Fort Pierre by fall and there receipted for the money due him (October 10, 1833).

Then, or in the following year, Alvarez seems to have retired from direct participation in fur trapping. He probably decided that the life of a Santa Fe trader was preferable to him, as an urbane and kind-mannered individual.[27]

For approximately the next quarter century of his life, which involved trade, travel and politics, Alvarez's records are much more complete than for the earlier period. They reveal that along side of the foregoing preoccupations, he did not completely abandon the fur trade. For instance, among his business papers there is a receipt dated at St. Louis, October 19, 1839, signed by an agent for Chouteau and McKenzie, for $1,313.25 worth of skins (including 253 beaver skins valued at $1,244.75, four otters, five muskrats, two mink, and one bear – damaged and worth $5.00).[28] In addition, Alvarez traded with Bent, St. Vrain and Company, and occasionally traveled with its chief partners between Bent's Fort on the Arkansas and Independence.[29]

---

[26] Ms. P. Chouteau-Maffitt Collection, Mo. Hist. Soc., St. Louis.

[27] See T. J. Farnham, "Travels in the Great Western Prairies," in R. G. Thwaites (ed.), *Early Western Travels, 1748-1846,* XXVIII, 82. Farnham describes Messrs. Walworth and Alvarez, whom he met near Pawnee Fork on the Arkansas, as: "Urbane and hospitable, they received us in the kindest manner. . ."

[28] Ms. Received from L. L. Waldo for the account of Manuel Alvarez, St. Louis, Oct. 19, 1839. Alvarez Papers.

[29] W. E. Connelley (ed.), "A Journal of the Santa Fe Trail," *Miss. Val. Hist. Review,* XII (June 1925), 87.

Some of his merchandise for the Santa Fe trade, such as all sorts of beads – purchased by the gross – seemed destined for Indian and trapper trade.[30]

How many trips Alvarez undertook across the plains as a Santa Fe trader after 1833 is difficult to state accurately. His Santa Fe store ledger records as its first entry, August 1, 1834, an account with Santiago Abreu, whose tragic death occurred three years later in a New Mexico uprising.[31] Within five months of this entry, Alvarez was back in St. Louis applying for U.S. citizenship.[32] Lansing Bloom found records of three major trips over the Trail in another of Alvarez's ledgers.[33] The first took place in 1838-39, and resulted in purchases chiefly at New York, Philadelphia, and St. Louis, to the total amount of $11,958.93. Incidentally, a bill for $15,176.21 dated at Independence, May 23, 1839, showing Alvarez's account with L. L. Waldo, was paid partly in peltries, but largely in gold dust – to the amount of $10,108.[34] Other records of his trade in this latter commodity reveal $4,934.52 sold in 1838, and $15,158.90 sold in 1843.[35]

Bloom mentions a second Trail crossing, as recorded in Alvarez's ledger, occurring in 1841-42. This round-trip over the prairies commenced at Santa Fe late in the fall, due to a delay in obtaining a passport from the New Mexican governor at the time of the Texas-Santa Fe expedition, and so Alvarez's caravan became caught in a severe snow storm

---

30 L. Bloom, "Ledgers of a Santa Fe Trader," *El Palacio,* XIV (May 1, 1923), 134.
31 *Ibid.*
32 On Dec. 16, 1834, Alvarez applied for citizenship papers at the Circuit Court in St. Louis, renouncing all allegiance to every foreign power, particularly Isabella, Queen of Spain, "whose subject" he claimed to be. M. Alvarez to Sec. Daniel Webster, Washington, D.C., Mar. 4, 1842. Consular Despatches.
33 Bloom, *op. cit.,* 133-34.
34 Ms. Alvarez Papers.
35 Ms. Receipt issued by the Treasurer of the U.S. Mint at Philadelphia to M. Alvarez, Aug. 25, 1843. Alvarez Papers.

near Council Grove.[36] In a few hours two members of the party and all of the forty-one horses and mules were frozen to death. The captain saved the remainder of his men by forcing them to keep in motion until the storm abated; many of them, however, became badly frozen. After recovering from this ordeal – that is, by early spring of 1842 – Alvarez, as American Consul in Santa Fe, reported in person on New Mexican developments to Secretary of State Daniel Webster at Washington.[37] Purchases of goods for the return to Santa Fe this time totalled $14,657.44.[38] Perhaps the larger amount of goods bought on this trip, as compared with the former one, arose from the fact that Alvarez and his partner, Domasco Lopez, not only stocked their store in Santa Fe, but also occasionally traveled to Chihuahua, Taos, and Abiquiu to sell or barter with individuals and firms.

A third journey to the States identified by Bloom, that for 1843-44, resulted in purchases of only $4,149.42 worth of merchandise.[39] There is more to this expediton, however, than is revealed by valuations in an inventory, as far as Alvarez was concerned. On this trip, not only did he stop at St. Louis, Chicago, Philadelphia, and New York, but he crossed the ocean to London, Paris, Bayonne (where he drew up a will) and perhaps to Spain to visit relatives, between August 10, 1843, and July 3, 1844.[40] By the latter date he had returned to Independence. Although of lesser

---

[36] R. E. Twitchell, *Leading Facts of New Mexican History* (Cedar Rapids, Ia., 1912), I, p. 126. Antoine Robidoux experienced the same storm and lost, in one night, one or two men and over 400 horses and mules.

[37] M. Alvarez to Daniel Webster, Wash., D.C., March 2, 1842. Ms. Consular Despatches. In this letter Alvarez itemizes losses and indignities he had suffered in Santa Fe and claimed $50,210 in indemnity, with interest until paid. Interest in Santa Fe was 18% per annum.

[38] Bloom, *op. cit.,* 134.   [39] *Ibid.*

[40] Various accounts included among the Alvarez Papers. Copy and translation of the Will of Manuel Alvarez made in Bayonne, France, before the Spanish Consul, Oct. 31, 1843. Ocaté Grant file, claim no. 1, reported as no. 143.

importance concerning these travels, it is worth noting that while Alvarez was touring Europe, he and Josiah Gregg corresponded. The latter, among other items, reported on the status of the Drawback Bill in Congress – a bill to permit tariff exemptions to Santa Fe traders who purchased imported goods – and on Gregg's forthcoming book, the *Commerce of the Prairies*.[41] Alvarez was greatly interested in the bill because he, as Consul, had urged its passage. Another connection which the latter maintained is disclosed by the money Chouteau and Company in St. Louis paid Alvarez for a draft on their New York office.[42]

The New Mexican Consul made other crossings of the prairies, one in 1845 and another in 1855, and connected with the latter was another ocean trip to Europe. These need not be detailed here. Rather, brief attention should be paid to his commercial activities in New Mexico and his duties as Consul. Bloom points out that Alvarez's clients in the northern Mexican Department included prominent New Mexican political leaders (three of them governors), several of the clergy, numerous army officers, many of the less well-to-do citizens (a teacher, a tailor, a laundress, an Indian of San Juan, etc.), and various American traders, trappers and merchants.[43] Among these Americans there appear: Louis and Francois Robidoux, Antoine Leroux, Simon Turley, Julian Workman, Christopher Carson, Thomas Rowlands, David Waldo, Josiah Gregg, Thomas Boggs, Charles Beaubien and others.

One of Alvarez's customers, although also a competitor, in the Santa Fe trade was the famous, or to some the infamous, Manuel Armijo, three times governor of New

---

[41] Josiah Gregg to M. Alvarez, Dec. 26, 1843, N.Y., addressed to Paris, France. Alvarez Papers.

[42] Ledger book HH of P. Chouteau and Co., 116. P. Chouteau-Maffitt Collection, Mo. Hist. Soc., St. Louis.

[43] Bloom, *op. cit.*, 134-35.

Mexico. The former reported in 1843 that Armijo was trying to corner the trade for himself,[44] and the latter accused
Alvarez in 1842 of being responsible for the loss of his
cargo, valued at between $18,000 and $20,000, when the
steamboat *Lebanon* sank en route from St. Louis to Independence.[45] Alvarez had come to realize that the Governor
disliked him; yet there had been a time, in 1837, when
Governor Armijo had approved Alvarez's petition for a
land grant of four leagues square on the eastern side of the
Sangre de Cristo Mountains, along the Ocaté River.[46] The
petitioner maintained that he desired to undertake stock
raising, particularly sheep. He hoped to improve the existing breed by introducing Merino type. Various factors,
including the threat of Texas "invasion," prevented Alvarez
from accomplishing his purpose, so his grant lapsed and in
1845 he requested a renewal of it. Governor Armijo approved the new application in December, 1845; yet the
grantee was again delayed in implementing his intentions.
Nevertheless, after the United States occupation of New
Mexico Alvarez applied for Congressional confirmation of
his land title, but was unsuccessful in obtaining it.[47]

Whatever changing personal status Alvarez experienced
with Armijo, it is significant that, for all but one of the seven
years (1839 to 1846) that the former served as the American
Consul at Santa Fe, Armijo was the Governor. Alvarez's
appointment as Consul involved at least two curious fea-

---

[44] M. Alvarez to the Secretary of State, dated Independence, Mo., July 1, 1843.
Consular Despatches.

[45] M. Alvarez to Daniel Webster, dated Santa Fe, Dec. 18, 1842. Consular
Despatches.

[46] Ocaté Land Grant File, claim no. 1, reported as claim no. 143.

[47] There is one indication that Alvarez may have pastured cattle on his grant in
1846. Ms. John Rowland to M. Alvarez, Feb. 28, 1846. Alvarez Papers. Strangely
enough, Alvarez, on May 29, 1845, considered purchasing Guadalupe Miranda's
land grant in order to raise stock. This claim became a part of the famous Maxwell
land grant which lay to the north of the Ocaté claim. Ms. M. Alvarez to Donaciano
Vigil, Vigil Collection, New Mex. State Records Center.

tures: first, he was not yet a United States citizen (though whether he was a Spanish or a Mexican one is a moot question), and second, he failed to obtain an *exequatur,* or official permit, from the Mexican government to serve as Consul. And yet that government permitted him to perform the duties of his office.[48]

Consul Alvarez was given no easy assignment. Not only was Governor Armijo in complete control of his Department and prone to abuse his power as governor, particularly in his treatment of U.S. Santa Fe traders, but the U.S. government was either unwilling or unable to respond to the representations of the Consul by causing the Mexican authorities to respect the rights of, or redress the wrongs committed against, U.S. citizens in New Mexico. Murders, robberies and other infringements on individual rights too frequently resulted in no punishment for the perpetrator, and official harassment of U.S. citizens was carried rather far. Numerous instances of both kinds were reported in the Consular Despatches that Alvarez filed with the U.S. Secretary of State, the New Mexican Secretary, and occasionally with the U.S. Minister in Mexico City. Protests against unwarranted official action by New Mexican officials burdened the Consul's mail (the letters of Charles Bent to Alvarez furnish many examples),[49] and he personally suffered several instances of attack or injustice himself.

Actually, Alvarez served as a medium for delivering U.S. trader protests to the New Mexican government prior to his consular appointment. Later, some of his most vigorous and justified requests for protection, and protests of abuses, arose from the Texas-Santa Fe Expedition of 1841.[50] Despite the

---

[48] M. Alvarez to Powhattan Ellis, Santa Fe, Dec. 12, 1840. Consular Despatches.

[49] Charles Bent Letters, B. M. Read Collection; New Mex. State Records Center. The letters have been printed in *The New Mex. Hist. Review,* XXIX, no. 3, ff.

[50] M. Alvarez to Daniel Webster, Washington, D.C., Feb. 2, 1842. Consular Despatches.

former type effort, he himself was physically assaulted by
Ensign Tomas Martin, a relative of the Governor's. Martin
was not even arrested for his attack, one which Alvarez
believed was designed to stimulate a general attack on U.S.
traders and their stores; instead, Martin was soon promoted
in rank. Alvarez, with the assistance of two others, failed
to secure the release of the U.S. citizen George Kendall and
a Mexican accompanying that Expedition, by means of a
sizeable monetary offer, from what was considered unjust
detention after they had been taken prisoner. Moreover,
Alvarez was denied a passport to leave for the United States,
until he threatened to depart without one, because the winter
season was fast approaching with its increased hazards for
Trail travel. Alvarez believed that, although his passport
was approved after this threat, it had purposely been delayed so as to cause him to risk the very misfortune he
encountered – namely, the severe snow storm mentioned
above.

The Consul's support for the passage of a Drawback
Bill,[51] and his efforts to prepare the way for the peaceful
entry of General S. W. Kearny's army into New Mexico,[52]
both bore fruit. And while his authority and the backing of
his government seemed to be enhanced by his appointment
as Consular Agent in 1846, in fact he did not receive notice
of the appointment until after General Kearny's entry into
Santa Fe; so he believed the need for the new title had
passed.[53]

Alvarez played a prominent part in the politics of New
Mexico during the transitional period from the establishment of a civil government by Gen. Kearny on September
22, 1846, to the inauguration of the Territorial government

[51] See his arguments in its behalf in: M. Alvarez to the Sec. of State, Independence, Mo., July 1, 1843. Consular Despatches.
[52] M. Alvarez to James Buchanan, Santa Fe, Sept. 4, 1846. Consular Despatches.
[53] *Ibid.*

under congressional authority, March 3, 1851. He served as
a delegate from Santa Fe to the House of the General As-
sembly that met on December 6, 1847.[54] During the ensuing
period – when the military in New Mexico dominated the
government and question of its role, of slavery, of the Texas
boundary and of Indian problems were uppermost, both in
local and national politics – Alvarez emerged as a leader in
the New Mexico statehood efforts. Encouraged by President
Zachary Taylor, many of the territorial residents pushed for
statehood, but there were two factions in New Mexico.
Those who favored continuance of territorial status had the
backing of the military, while those seeking to follow California's example came to be known as the "Alvarez fac-
tion."[55]

On May 15, 1850, there began a ten-day convention meeting in Santa Fe to draft a constitution, which was over-
whelmingly approved by the voters on the following June
20th.[56] At the same time, Henry Connelley, another Santa
Fe trader, was elected Governor, and Manuel Alvarez was
chosen Lt. Governor. Because Connelley was ill at the time
and in the States, the burdens of directing the administra-
tive efforts of what proved to be an abortive effort at statehood, fell to the Lt. Governor. He prepared an able address
to the "state" legislature; but he was blocked in his leadership by Col. John Munroe's refusal, as territorial governor,
to recognize the authority of that legislature and its officials
to operate, except for choosing and sending congressional
officials to Congress.[57] Alvarez ably defended, in lengthy
correspondence with Colonel Munroe, the right of the New
Mexican people to manage their own political affairs.

[54] H. H. Bancroft, *History of Arizona and New Mexico, 1540-1888* (San Francisco, 1889), 441.

[55] R. E. Twitchell, *The Military Occupation of New Mexico, 1846-1851* (Denver,
1909), 156-62.

[56] *Ibid.*, 180-82.   [57] *Ibid.*, 182-91.

Congressional refusal to accord statehood for New Mexico, and the passage of an act on September 9, 1850 authorizing a Territorial government for New Mexico, ended the effort for statehood at that time. Friends tried unsuccessfully to have Alvarez chosen Territorial Secretary,[58] but the new Governor, James S. Calhoun, designated him Brigadier General of the Central Division of the New Mexican Militia, August 20, 1851.[59] Seven months later, when the Governor planned a return to the States on important political business, he appointed Alvarez acting-Governor, only to withdraw the appointment three days later.[60] During the following January, a new Governor, William C. Lane, chose Alvarez to be Commissioner of Public Buildings in New Mexico; and a little over a year later, Congress authorized the expenditure of $50,000 for a capitol building in Santa Fe.[61]

Meanwhile, Alvarez continued his activities as a merchant, and maintained a widespread correspondence with leaders in New Mexico – ex-Governor Armijo, Padre Martinez, M. E. Pino, J. L. Collins, J. Houghton, Manuel Gallegos, D. Vigil, and many others – on political, business and personal matters. He tried unsuccessfully, as mentioned above, to secure recognition of his land claim, and he made his 1855 voyage to Spain. After his return from this trip he had only a little more than six months to live. He died in Santa Fe during July, 1856, after a strenuous and worthy life. Its full dimensions may be seen when a more complete study of it has been prepared.

[58] Twitchell, *Leading Facts of New Mexican History,* II, p. 283.

[59] Commission signed by Gov. J. S. Calhoun, Aug. 20, 1851. Alvarez Papers.

[60] Order signed by Gov. J. S. Calhoun, Mar. 30, 1852; revocation signed by David Whiting, Sec., Apr. 2, 1852. Alvarez Papers.

[61] Commission signed by Gov. Wm. C. Lane, Jan. 15, 1852; notice of congressional appropriation in J. L. Collins to M. Alvarez, at Washington, D.C., Apr. 7, 1854. Alvarez Papers.

Robert Campbell

by HARVEY L. CARTER
Colorado College, Colorado Springs

The birthplace of Robert Campbell has been established as Aughalane, in the Ulster Irish county of Tyrone. The date of his birth was February 12, 1804.[1] At the age of eighteen, he emigrated to the United States and joined his older brother, Hugh, at Milton, North Carolina, where he had been for some four years. Neither of the brothers remained in the little town on the Virginia border. Hugh removed to Philadelphia, where he prospered as a merchant. Robert went westward to St. Louis in the year 1824. Here a physician, Dr. Bernard G. Farrar, diagnosed his lung trouble as consumption and advised him to go to the Rocky Mountains.[2] Young Campbell took the doctor's advice, and joined a party of sixty trappers led by Jedediah S. Smith, who left St. Louis November 1, 1825. The party had been outfitted by General William H. Ashley, each man having two animals, one to ride and a pack mule or horse laden with goods.[3] Thus was begun one of the notable careers in the fur trade; by one of the first "lungers" to seek the benefits of the mountain atmosphere of the Far West.

Smith's party, which included Hiram Scott, Jim Beckwourth, Moses Harris, and Louis Vasquez, in addition to Campbell, was forced to winter among the Republican

[1] Dale L. Morgan and Eleanor Towles Harris, *The Rocky Mountain Journals of William Marshall Anderson: The West in 1834* (San Marino, 1967) contains a sketch of Robert Campbell, pp. 271-74. They give specific time and place of Campbell's birth, whereas W. J. Ghent, "Robert Campbell" in *Dictionary of American Biography* (New York, 1929), III, pp. 462-63, gives an approximation in both cases.

[2] *The Private Journal of Robert Campbell*, edited by George R. Brooks (reprinted from *The Bulletin of the Missouri Historical Society*, Oct. 1963 and Jan. 1964), 3.

[3] Dale L. Morgan, *The West of William H. Ashley* (Denver, 1964), 143. Morgan quotes from a reminiscent dictation made by Robert Campbell in 1870.

Pawnees, and suffered for lack of food because the buffalo had not come farther south than the Platte or farther east than Grand Island. Jedediah Smith recognized that Campbell had the education and the natural aptitude to make a good clerk. Campbell and Smith stayed in the lodge of Ish-ka-ta-pa, the Republican Pawnee chief. With the first indication of spring, the party went north to the Platte, where they were overtaken by General Ashley and his well equipped second expedition near Grand Island. Reaching Harris Fork, they met some of the Ashley trappers who had wintered in the mountains and proceeded on to the rendezvous in Cache Valley. At the close of the rendezvous, Ashley sold out to Smith, Jackson, and Sublette, the articles of agreement being signed in the presence of Robert Campbell, on July 18, 1826.[4]

When Jedediah Smith struck off on his southwestern expedition, Campbell accompanied Jackson and Sublette, who went on a hunt in the opposite direction. Campbell recalled that they "ascended the Snake River and tributaries near the Three Tetons and hunted along the forks of the Missouri, following the Gallatin, and trapped along across the headwaters of the Columbia" [i.e., the Clark's Fork or Hellgate].[5] They returned to Cache Valley for the winter and Campbell accompanied Jackson's spring hunt in 1827 on Green River.[6] At rendezvous time, the Blackfeet made an attack, which was driven off by William Sublette, while Campbell remained in charge of everything at the camp.[7]

In the fall of 1827, Campbell was entrusted with the leadership of a party going to the Flathead country. They were harrassed by the Blackfeet, who killed Pierre Tevan-

---

[4] *Ibid.*, 143, 145. Morgan reproduces the agreement referred to here on pp. 152-53.

[5] *Ibid.*, 161. This hunt is also described by Daniel T. Potts in his letter to his brother, Robert T. Potts, dated Sweet Lake [i.e. Bear Lake], July 8, 1827, wherein the first mention of Yellowstone Lake and the geysers of that area occurs. The letter is reproduced by Morgan, *ibid.*, 161-62.

[6] *Ibid.*, 166-67.   [7] *Ibid.*, 168.

itagon, the leader of the Iroquois hunters. Because of this, Campbell was unable to persuade his men to return to winter camp in Cache Valley. With only two companions, he made the trip himself and then set out to rejoin his party in the midst of a severe winter. Traveling by means of dog sleds and snowshoes, Campbell and two half-breed trappers reached the Hudson's Bay Company camp of Peter Skene Ogden on Snake River on February 16, 1828, where they remained for a week.[8] Campbell rejoined his men in the Flathead country after an arduous six weeks on snowshoes.[9] They made a successful spring hunt on the various streams of the rich beaver country between Clark's Fork and Bear Lake but on their arrival at the rendezvous in June 1828, they were attacked by Blackfeet. The cook, Louis Bolduc, was killed and Campbell was able to save his men and furs only by passing through the Blackfoot encirclement, accompanied by "a little Spaniard" and bringing up reinforcements from the rendezvous.[10]

After the rendezvous of 1828, Campbell went in a party of twelve headed by Jim Bridger to trap the Crow country of northeastern Wyoming. They wintered with Long Hair's band of Crows on Wind River, at the elbow where it becomes the Bighorn and, in the spring trapped again the Bighorn, Powder River, and Tongue River. Failing to meet Sublette coming up with supplies, they went to rendezvous on Wind River at the mouth of the Popo Agie.[11]

---

[8] See "Peter Skene Ogden's Journals, 1827-1828," edited by T. C. Elliott in *Oregon Historical Society Quarterly* (Dec. 1910), XI, pp. 374-75. Campbell told Ogden various pieces of news but the British trader was unable to get any information out of him as to where he intended to trap. Campbell's companions lost their beaver to the Britishers gambling at cards.

[9] Morgan and Harris, *op. cit.,* 272.

[10] Morgan, *op. cit.,* 186-87; 314-35. See also John Sunder, *Bill Sublette: Mountain Man* (Norman, 1959), 75. Campbell's party consisted of eighteen trappers and was attacked eighteen miles north of the Bear Lake rendezvous. Jim Beckwourth appropriated to himself Campbell's exploit of breaking out to get relief.

[11] J. Cecil Alter, *Jim Bridger* (Norman, 1962), 104-08; Morgan and Harris, *op. cit.,* 272; Sunder, *op. cit.,* 76.

Robert Campbell had now been four years in the mountains. He was twenty-four years old, and his health was now very good. He decided to return to St. Louis and set out with forty-five packs of beaver. Arriving in St. Louis in late August, the furs he brought down for the partners brought $22,476 and he received payment for his services amounting to $3,016.[12]

Smith, Jackson, and Sublette, having sold out, were now back in St. Louis making further business plans, and since Campbell had proved his worth and had money to invest, he was considered as a possible associate by a number of traders. However, he decided to pay a visit to Ireland at this point, and was out of the country from February 1830 to June 1831. By the time he returned to St. Louis, Jedediah Smith was dead. This removed the most probable of his potential partners from the scene. However, his relations with William Sublette had also been very close and he now joined with him in provisioning Fitzpatrick and his associates of the Rocky Mountain Fur Company. He had enough money left to provide for a small venture of his own and set out for the Rockies in May 1832, with ten pack horses laden with goods, in Sublette's train.[13]

The rendezvous was at Pierre's Hole and the famous battle which followed seems to have cemented the relations of Robert Campbell and William Sublette. Campbell has given us one of the best of the five known eye witness accounts of the fight.

Mr. S. and I, without being aware of the cause or nature of the approaching contest, felt convinced we were about entering on a perilous engagement, in which one, or both of us might fall.

We therefore briefly directed each other as to the disposition of our property; – or in other words, made our wills, appointing each other sole executor. . .

On reaching the party that gave the alarm, we found them debating on the propriety of attacking the enemy, who were strongly fortified in

12 Morgan and Harris, *op. cit.,* 272; Sunder, *op. cit.,* 80.
13 Morgan and Harris, *op. cit.,* 272-73.

a willow swamp about a mile distant. . . Their number was estimated at 250 warriors.

Our force consisted of from 40 to 50 whites – a few half breeds – and two small bands of friendly Indians of the *Peirced Nose* and *Flat Head* tribes. Mr. S. (brave as a lion) addressed a few words to the whites, telling them that the enemy was near, and that if at the commencement of the season we did not shew a bold front, our prospects in the mountains would be blasted. . . Addressing my old friends the Flat Heads, I told them of our determination to assail their enemies, in their strong hold, and that we knew we should have their assistance. Then raising the *war whoop,* Mr. S. and myself, with about twenty others dashed off at full speed toward the willows. . . On reaching the willows we fastened our horses in a thicket, a short distance above where the Black Feet were fortified. . . We approached according to the usage in Indian Warfare, on our hands and knees; and while in this attitude Mr. Sublette and I a little in advance, – a shot from behind the breastwork mortally wounded a brave fellow named St. Clair, who was within two feet of me. . .

We continued to keep up a steady fire, never rising higher than our knee to take aim, and never losing a shot by firing without an object. . . In the mean time another brave fellow, quickly, received a bullet in his head – gave one spring from where he stood leaning upon Mr. S. and me – and fell down a corpse. Either the same ball or, one fired at the same time, struck Mr. S. on the left arm, fracturing the bone, and passing out under the shoulder blade. He remarked that he was wounded, and continued the attack for a short time, but the loss of blood, and thirst which succeeded, obliged him to call on me for assistance.

By this time the Pierced Nose and Flat Head Indians began to join us, and the fire on the Fort became more formidable and deadly. I assisted Mr. S. from the scene to the creek, where I probed the wound, and dressed it as well as the means within reach adimtted of. We then made a litter and carried him back to the encampment, where I am happy to say he seems to be recovering. . .

In giving you these details of an encounter with savages, while the incidents are yet fresh on my memory, I fear I shall only add to your antipathy of the mode of life that *necessity* and *choice* have caused me to adopt. To confess the truth I am sick of it. In the course of a few days I hope to begin my return trip to St. Louis – from whence I may give some further account of "Mountain perils." [14]

[14] Letter of Robert Campbell, Lewis' Fork, July 18, 1832, to Hugh Campbell, Philadelphia, Pennsylvania, in *The Rocky Mountain Letters of Robert Campbell*

Disposing of his own goods, Campbell conducted his wounded friend and his party back to St. Louis, arriving October 3, 1832.[15] The firm of Sublette and Campbell was now formed for a period of three years from January 1, 1833, and, as the articles of agreement were twice renewed, the partnership lasted until 1842.[16] The new firm expanded its operations on an ambitious scale immediately. It is not clear whether it was actually hopeful of competing successfully with the American Fur Company or whether it was hoped only to be sufficiently irritating to that company to force them to pay handsomely to abate a nuisance, which was the eventual outcome of their operations.

First, the partners made a business trip to the east, traveling by steamboat up the Ohio, then by stage, and finally over the Baltimore and Ohio Railroad. They visited Philadelphia, New York, and Washington, made business arrangements, and renewed their political contact with Ashley. They spent Christmas with Campbell's brother, Hugh, in Philadelphia, and had a gay time. The trip embraced the month of December 1832, and the first two months of 1833.[17]

Next, Sublette launched a voyage up the Missouri for the purpose of establishing trading posts that would compete directly with the American Fur Company. At the same time, in the spring of 1833, Campbell led a supply train of forty-five men to the rendezvous on Green River, near the mouth of Horse Creek. He took with him Dr. Benjamin Harrison, Edmund Christy, Fitzpatrick's Arapaho Indian lad, Friday, and the Scottish sportsman, Sir William Drummond Stewart.[18] The first had his passage paid by his father, Gen-

---

(Printed for Frederick W. Beinecke, Christmas, 1951), pp. 8-11. A photocopy of this work was kindly provided me by Archibald Hanna, Curator of the Coe Collection, Yale University, New Haven, Connecticut. Campbell began his letter on July 18, before the battle, which interrupted his writing, and completed it on July 19, 1832.

[15] Sunder, *op. cit.*, 109-13. The party brought back 169 packs of beaver.

[16] *Ibid.*, 115-16.   [17] *Ibid.*, 116-22.

[18] Charles Larpenteur, *Forty Years a Fur Trader on the Upper Missouri*, edited by Milo M. Quaife (Chicago, 1933), 17-18.

eral William Henry Harrison, in the hope that the Rocky Mountain life would be a cure for alcoholism, but there is no evidence that the cure was effective. The last paid $500 for the privilege of traveling with the train and was making the first of several such trips.[19]

The party left Lexington, Missouri, on May 12, and arrived at the rendezvous at Green River on July 5, 1833. Campbell's goods had not been contracted in advance but falling in with Fraeb and Fitzpatrick on Laramie River, he was able to make a deal with them.[20] When the American Fur Company train under Lucien Fontenelle arrived on July 13, Campbell had already got a large share of the trade. Fontenelle reported that Campbell "made much of a boast" about his earlier arrival. He estimated that Campbell had been able to profit to the extent of about five packs of beaver. He also accused Campbell and Captain Bonneville of having "tried their best to injure the American Fur Co." and admitted that they had "in some manner succeeded as Campbell was no sooner in the country that [than] he spread the report through those who had beaver in hand that the agent of the company at St. Louis would protest any drafts given either by Mr. Drips or myself as he did some drawn by the late Mr. Vanderburgh last year."[21]

Campbell crossed the Tetons to Pierre's Hole to recover a cache of furs while the rendezvous was in progress. He left the rendezvous on July 24 and reaching the Bighorn on August 12, 1833, he constructed bull boats for a voyage down the river and the Yellowstone.[22]

[19] Mae Reed Porter and Odessa Davenport, *Scotsman in Buckskin* (New York, 1963), 27-28.

[20] Larpenteur, *op. cit.*, 17-26. Larpenteur's recollection was that they arrived on July 8. They had left St. Louis on April 14.

[21] Letter of Lucien Fontenelle, Rendezvous on Green River R.M., July 31, 1833, to Wm. Laidlaw, Esq., Fort Pierre; in the Drips Papers, Missouri Historical Society, St. Louis, Missouri.

[22] Larpenteur, *op. cit.*, 27-35, gives some interesting particulars of this journey until they reached the Bighorn. However, he was detached to serve under Louis Vasquez, who headed an overland party in charge of the mules and cattle.

Campbell himself wrote a terse summary of the trip by water on December 31, 1833, in closing out a daily journal that he had begun September 21, of that year, at the mouth of the Yellowstone.

In the Big Horn the skin boat in which I was sunk and I had like to have perished. Thrice I went under water and but for an all wise and all merciful God I should never have seen termination of this year. I got safe to shore and succeeded in recovering all but about 4 packs of Beaver and our arms. Besides I lost my saddle bags etc. I recovered again my boat and next day was joined by all the Crow Indians — and here again I must acknowledge my dependence on God who inclined those Indians to treat me kindly and return most of my beaver when they had us completely in their power. And I may here observe that those same Indians 17 days after at the instigation of the American Fur Co. robbed Mr. Fitzpatrick of all he had with him, but of themselves afterwards returned animals for nearly all they had taken.

I proceeded on down to this place where I arrived on the 30th of August and found Mr. Sublette who had got here the day previous. But to my mortification Mr. Sublette was taken sick and barely recovered when he left me on the 20th Sept for St. Louis with the return I had brought down. . .[23]

Campbell's stay at the mouth of the Yellowstone was not a happy one. He says, "I may date my trouble from my arrival here. I had to make a Fort build 10 Houses dig a well and make an Ice House. . ." In addition to Fort William, two other trading posts were constructed, one fifty miles up the Missouri and the other eight miles up the Yellowstone.[24]

Campbell remained at Fort William until late June 1834, when word reached him that Sublette had reached an agreement with the American Fur Company whereby a geo-

[23] *The Private Journal of Robert Campbell*, 34. Larpenteur puts the loss of beaver in the accident at two packs. Possibly Campbell's statement includes a further loss to the Crows, which was not restored. A letter of Campbell's dated Green River, Rocky Mountains, July 20, 1833, to his brother Hugh, in *The Rocky Mountain Letters of Robert Campbell*, pp. 12-13, indicates that he bore a diplomatic message from the Shoshones to the Crows on this journey. This may have accounted for the lenience of the Crows toward Campbell's party.

[24] *Ibid.*, 34-35; Larpenteur, *op. cit.*, 49-50, gives details of the construction of Fort William, which was finished by Christmas 1833.

graphical division of the fur country was made and Sublette and Campbell gave up their effort to compete on the upper Missouri. Campbell's journal extends only to the end of 1833 but it gives ample evidence of the trouble that the two companies caused each other. Considering the resources of the American Fur Company and the crafty ability of Kenneth McKenzie, in charge of their Fort Union, near which Campbell had built Fort William, it is remarkable that he was able to hold out as long as he did.

Glad to be relieved of his duties at Fort William, Campbell lost no time and arrived back in St. Louis on August 7, 1834. He paid a visit to his brother in Philadelphia early in 1835 but had returned to St. Louis by April 1, and set out for Fort Laramie on April 9, with only two companions.[25] His task was to effect the transfer of the fort and its supplies to Fontenelle, Fitzpatrick and Company to whom his partner had sold out. Two weeks was sufficient to accomplish this and he returned by boat on the Platte, a mode of travel that was seldom possible, with a cargo of buffalo robes.[26]

Campbell spent the winter of 1835-36 in Philadelphia, during which time he was not in very good health. Sublette and Campbell continued to supply trade goods to the trappers in the mountains to some extent for a few years but both were involved separately in other business concerns and the partnership was allowed to lapse in 1842.

Meanwhile, Campbell was married on February 25, 1841, to Virginia Kyle, of Raleigh, North Carolina. He had known her for some four years, having met her at the home of Hugh Campbell in Philadelphia. He was thirty-seven and she was nineteen at the time of their marriage. Hugh Campbell said in a letter to William Sublette that at the time of Robert's first attentions to her she had already been

---

[25] Sunder, *op. cit.*, 143-45. Fort Laramie, originally called Fort William, had been built by William Sublette in 1834.

[26] *Niles Weekly Register* (August 8, 1835) XLVIII, p. 406.

"four times courted and twice engaged." [27] Hugh and William opposed the marriage on the ground that she was too young and fond of admiration but Robert persisted and the marriage turned out well.[28]

Campbell accompanied his former partner and fellow consumptive, William Sublette, eastward on the trip on which he died in the summer of 1845.[29] Campbell himself was subject to frequent illness but he was of a steadier, less ambitious, less dynamic nature than Sublette and never drove himself so hard. On two occasions Campbell returned to the scene of his early labors in later years. In 1851, he attended the great gathering of Indians with whom Fitzpatrick concluded the Treaty of Fort Laramie and again, in 1870, he went out to Fort Laramie as a member of President Grant's Commission to treat with the Sioux under Chief Red Cloud.[30]

In 1846, with the advent of the Mexican War he helped raise, equip, and drill a regiment of which he was chosen commanding officer. Although this state militia regiment did not actually participate in the war, Campbell was often referred to by the title of colonel after this time.[31] His business affairs prospered steadily and during later years he was president of both the Bank of the State of Missouri and of the Merchants National Bank in St. Louis. He was also the

[27] *The Campbell House: A Romantic Survival of Early St. Louis and the Fur Trade,* 3.   [28] Sunder, *op. cit.,* 181.

[29] *Ibid.,* 228-29. They were, of course, heading in the wrong direction. Sublette's only chance for life lay in returning to the Rocky Mountains, but the days of business activity in the mountains had passed.

[30] LeRoy R. Hafen and Francis M. Young, *Fort Laramie and the Pageant of the West, 1834-1890* (Glendale, 1938), 191, 363. Campbell had won the bid to supply the Fort Laramie Treaty Council with goods but the goods did not arrive until three days after the treaty had been signed. Campbell himself had gone out with Indian Superintendent D. D. Mitchell as one of the commissioners. See Louise Barry, "Kansas before 1854: A Revised Annals," in *Kansas Historical Quarterly* (Summer, 1966), XXXII, pp. 254-55, 257-58.

[31] W. J. Ghent, "Robert Campbell" in *Dictionary of American Biography* (New York, 1929), III, p. 463.

owner of a dry goods store and of the Southern Hotel in St. Louis. As that city grew, his real estate holding increased in value and he became one of the wealthiest men of the city.[32] He never entirely abandoned the Indian trade, for he frequently fulfilled contracts to supply goods to Indians by steamboat up the Missouri in later years. One of the steamers bore the name "Robert Campbell." Likewise, he received at St. Louis consignments of furs from companies operating on the upper Missouri.[33] His real estate operations extended also to early Kansas City.[34]

Campbell died in St. Louis on October 16, 1879, after a bronchial ailment had sent him to Saratoga Springs in a vain search for health in the summer of that year.[35] His wife survived him by only three years.[36] Of thirteen children born to them only three sons survived for any length of time. The eldest, James A. Campbell, attended Yale, but his promising career was cut short by his early death in 1890. James left his estate to his brother Hugh in trust, with Yale University as the beneficiary at Hugh Campbell's death. Hugh and a younger brother lived on in the Campbell House in Lucas Place for many years, never marrying. Hugh died in 1931 and, in 1941, Yale decided to sell the house and its furnishings. Members of the William Clark Society raised the money to buy the furnishings and eventually, the St. Louis firm of Stix, Baer and Fuller contributed the money for the purchase of the house, which is now maintained in its original state as a museum.[37] It is a splendid relic of the mid-nineteenth century and a reminder of the great days of the

---

[32] *Ibid.*　　　　[33] Barry, *op. cit.,* XXX, p. 522; XXXII, p. 479; XXXIII, p. 206.
[34] *Ibid.,* XXIX, pp. 161-62.　　　　[35] Ghent, *op. cit.,* 463.
[36] *The Campbell House . . . ,* 3.
[37] *Ibid.,* 3, 5, 6. A full listing of the contents of the Campbell House is to be found in *Traditional Americana . . . belonging to the estate of the late Hugh Campbell . . . to be dispersed at Public Auction . . . February 24, 25, 26, 1941.* A copy of this interesting catalogue was kindly loaned to me by Professor John E. Sunder.

western fur trade which formed the foundation of Robert Campbell's prosperity.

Even as a young man, Robert Campbell was highly esteemed by his associates and by his employees for his kindness and fairness. Charles Larpenteur felt that he took a personal interest in him as an employee and remembered him for it with gratitude. His reputation for integrity among his fellow citizens in St. Louis was of the highest. He was a Presbyterian in religion and took his Bible reading seriously, as we learn from his journal. He was a Democrat in politics, a supporter of Senator Benton, and a hard money man. He was content to stay out of active politics, however, declining public office, and getting on well with those of the opposite party. He was rather above medium height, fair haired, and though warm, friendly, and above all, loyal to his friends, he was considered by some rather reserved and difficult to approach.

Campbell's story is one of steady success. One is tempted to describe it with three Horatio Alger titles – *Only an Irish Boy, Bound to Rise, By Sheer Pluck*. But though born in Ireland, he was a Scot; there was nothing inevitable about success in the fur trade; and though one cannot question his courage, surely thrift, sound judgment, and persistent application to business were his distinguishing characteristics. Above all, Campbell's reputation for financial integrity was unsurpassed. Anywhere on the frontier, among Indians or whites, his credit was considerably better than that of the government of the United States.[38]

---

[38] *The Rocky Mountain Letters of Robert Campbell*, p. 5. Obituaries of Campbell may be found in the *Missouri Republican* and in the *Daily Globe-Democrat*, October 17, 1879.

Index